THE GOLDEN MOUNTAIN

The Golden Mountain

Beyond the American Dream

Irene Kai

First Edition
Silver Light Publications ✢ Ashland, Oregon

The Golden Mountain
Beyond the American Dream
By Irene Kai

Published by:
Silver Light Publications
2305 C Ashland Street PMB#426
Ashland, Oregon 97520
thegoldenmountain.com
(541) 552-1363

Copyright © 2004 Irene Kai
First Edition
Printed in the United States of America

Publisher's Cataloging-in-Publication
(Provided by Quality Books, Inc.)

 Kai, Irene.
  The golden mountain / Irene Kai. – 1st ed.
  p. cm.
  LCCN 2003112826
  ISBN 09744890-0-X

  1. Kai, Irene. 2. Chinese American women–Biography.
  3. Chinese Americans–Biography. 4. Hong Kong (China)–
  Biography. . I. Title.

 E184.C5K25 2004   973'.04951'0092
         QBI03-200737

To David

my greatest love

—

To Lin and Casey

my pillars of strength

Acknowledgments

I am deeply grateful to Simon Warwick-Smith
for his guidance.
My sincere appreciation goes to Deborah Mokma,
Linda Gerschler and Lin Hendler.

TABLE OF CONTENTS

—

Family Tree

Leung Sing Tai – Wong Oi

|

Hong Kai – Chan Choi Kum   Hong Foo   Hong Quay   Quay Yeung

|

Tsim Yuen (James) – Mei Yuk (Margaret)   and James' nine siblings

|

Tsuen Tseen (Virginia)   Meew Ling (Teresa)   Oi Ling (Irene)   Lai Ling (Louise)

GREAT GRANDMOTHER

1877-1949
Toisan Province, China

1950-1965
Hong Kong

1 am sorry. It's another girl," the midwife said softly as she wrapped the newborn in a clean cloth. The mother turned her face to the wall. She bit hard on her lower lip to hold back her tears. The dancing shadow of her silhouette on the wall was cast from a single oil lamp on the table. The tiny flame struggled to stay lit as a cold wind blew in through the crevices of the worn windows. She shivered and pulled her tattered cotton jacket closer and stared at her feet.

If only they were bound, I would be able to keep you, Wong Oi thought. *I would not have to worry about feeding you for sixteen years and I would have a good dowry for you. You have come to this house at the wrong time.*

"Please summon my husband," she whispered as the midwife put the baby in a basket at the far end of the room, not daring to place the baby near her mother. The midwife ran from the room without making a sound.

Sing Tai came into the room and sat down on the bed next to his wife. Still facing the wall and without turning she said, "You know what to do."

He reached out to hold his wife's hand and held back his own tears. Silently, he got up and walked toward the basket where their newborn daughter slept. He picked her up and walked quickly outside. He had to get to the kitchen by way of a dirt path from the main house. He held the baby tightly in his arms. The cold night air woke her and she started to cry. Sing Tai's heart was burdened by what he had to do next and he stumbled on the path he knew so well. He reached the kitchen and frantically rummaged in the darkness for the bucket of ash next to the stove. With trembling hands, he poured half of the ash into a pan and lowered the wailing infant into it. He looked away as he poured the remaining ash over her, covering her completely. Within a few moments the crying stopped. He only heard his own heavy breathing. He picked up the lifeless body of his daughter and went outside to the garden to a spot under an old willow tree. He found the shovel and dug a small hole to accommodate the tiny body of his newborn girl. On his knees with cold bare hands, he lowered her into the freshly dug grave. He scooped dirt over her warm body. Next to her, her sister lay, born less than two years before. After Sing Tai smoothed the soil and covered the spot with dry grass, he let out a heavy sigh then collapsed, sobbing hysterically on the ground.

Wong Oi stood in front of her house in her faded blue cotton pants and jacket watching her six-year-old son Hong Kai run down to the field to forage for wild yams. It had become his job ever since the bandits and the revolutionaries began raiding the farms. Not one farmer in the village could afford to produce new crops and food was scarce. Stepping into the front yard, she breathed in the sweet air of baked earth and the fresh green sprouting everywhere in the late morning sun. The smell reminded her of childhood, when she was a young girl working beside her mother planting summer seedlings.

She dreamed that she sat in a well-manicured garden sipping jasmine tea prepared by a servant, but instead, her heart was heavy. She was pregnant again. The uncertainty of the fate of her unborn child was almost too much to bear. She walked into the kitchen and started a fire to cook the few handfuls of rice that had to spread between herself, her husband and their three growing boys. She hoped Hong Kai would be lucky enough to find a few yams to thicken the meal. If not, they would go hungry. It was an all too common occurrence these days. She stood in front of the hot stove, stirring the watery gruel, praying to the kitchen God to let her family get by just one more day.

A loud cry from the main house startled Wong Oi from her reverie.

"Hong Kai's mother! Come into the house quickly," Sing Tai called out. "I have important news!"

Wong Oi removed the pot of precious food from the hot stove and ran into the house, drying her hands on her apron.

Her husband's eyes danced with an excitement that she hadn't seen in a very long time. "What is it?" she asked cautiously.

"Yuen Fung has just come home from the Golden Mountain. He came back with a fortune and plans to buy a farm and build a big house." He reached out to hold his wife's hands and pulled her closer.

"I am happy for him, but what does that have to do with us?" She was surprised at his exuberance for someone else's good fortune. She had hoped for some news of food. Wong Oi pulled her hands from him and looked away.

"He is selling his citizenship papers! We can buy his papers and get a way out! I can take Hong Kai to America!" Sing Tai exclaimed, astonished at her lack of interest.

"And where are we getting the money to do that? Citizenship papers cost a fortune. You are dreaming in broad daylight!" Wong Oi rolled her eyes, sneering at her impractical husband.

Sing Tai stood up a little taller. "Yuen Fung is the father of our brother-in-law. I am sure he will let us pay him back after we earn enough money in the Golden Mountain," he reassured his wife.

Wong Oi looked out the window to the fields where her little son bent over the ground digging into the hard earth with a dull spade and then down at her own rough, bare feet.

"You must talk to him immediately!" she said, looking directly at her husband. For the first time in her life, she felt she had a chance to pursue her dreams.

"I haven't told you, but I am with child. If you have the opportunity to go to America, whether it is a boy or a girl, our child will be educated," she said firmly.

Sing Tai looked at his wife. Her back was straight and her feet were planted solidly on the ground. She was a woman accustomed to making decisions with an iron will.

"Even if it is a girl? Who has ever heard of educating a girl?" Sing Tai asked, raising his eyebrows incredulously.

"Money can only buy us things but an educated child brings status into our household. I want to be the mother of a person the villagers can look up to," Wong Oi said to her husband.

"Whatever you wish. I just want to get out of our situation and provide a better life for all of us. I will go to Yuen Fung's house tomorrow and see if I can arrange for our passage to America. His papers include one son. I will take Hong Kai with me. If this works out, we must make great offerings to our ancestors and thank them for their blessings." Sing Tai looked at the frayed sleeves of his faded black jacket and nodded appreciatively.

Wong Oi walked back to the kitchen with lightness in her steps. She put the pot of watery gruel back onto the stove.

She didn't care if she would not eat today; she was too hopeful to feel hungry.

"Mother, am I going on a big ship? Where is the Golden Mountain? Father told me that it takes weeks or months on a big ship to get there and we have to cross a big ocean." Hong Kai paused before continuing, "What is an ocean? What is it like to be at the Golden Mountain? Is the mountain really made of gold and we just pry the gold from the mountain and bring it home?" He rattled on to his mother as she packed his few pieces of clothing into a small cloth bag.

She envisioned her eldest son coming home one day a handsome "Guest of the Golden Mountain." He would bring a fortune back to the family, fulfilling his filial duty as the eldest son.

Hong Kai sat on the floor and held onto his mother's legs. "It is very far away just to get some gold," he whimpered, "I am scared."

"Stop your crying at once! Don't ask silly questions." Wong Oi stopped folding his clothes and looked at her son sternly, "You are the luckiest boy in this village. You get to go with your father to America. Most people pray all of their lives for a chance to go there. And you, my son, are leaving in a few days."

"I don't want to go. I want to stay here with you." He held onto her legs even tighter.

She reached down, held his hands looking into her young son's eyes and said, "You must learn to do what you are told. You have to take on the responsibility of being the eldest son. Our family relies on you and your father to come home with a better life. I will not hear of your nonsense. Stand up straight and show your backbone."

Hong Kai let go of his mother and stood up. He dried his eyes with the back of his hands and nodded. Wong Oi was pleased that she talked some sense into him. She tried to control her own excitement. She turned to face the window and envisioned a future life of luxury.

One morning, while she drank her cup of morning tea, a stranger called Wong Oi's name at the doorway.

"What is it? How do you know my name?" Wong Oi went outside feeling a bit uneasy. Not many strangers came by unless something was important.

"A letter from America. Are you Mrs. Lueng Sing Tai?" the stranger asked.

"Yes. May I have it please?" Wong Oi grabbed it and sent the deliverer away. She opened it carefully and found American dollars folded between two sheets of paper. She held them up and studied their design and color.

"So this is how American dollars look. I don't have to be envious of my cousin any longer," she murmured happily to herself.

She held the bills close to her nose, inhaled deeply and said, "Ah, the smell of the Golden Mountain sure is sweet." She put them carefully away into the inside pocket of her jacket. She needed to exchange the money and find the letter writer to read her letter. It was still early enough to make the morning market.

The market was busy. Wong Oi pushed through throngs of shoppers and hawkers as she tried to find the letter writer. The smell of live fish, chicken and raw meat was heavy, but the scent of cooked dumplings and sweet pastries made Wong Oi a bit hungry.

She walked by a stall with tempting teacakes. She normally tried to avoid looking at them but with the American dollars safely in her pocket, she felt she could afford to try one. There were baked ones with flaky crusts stuffed with savory meats or sweet coconut and crushed peanuts. Others were steamed and filled with mashed lotus seeds or red beans. There were so many varieties to choose from! Finally, she decided.

"I would like to have this one please," she said to the woman behind the stall, pointing to the one with soft steamed rice flour filled with a paste made from red dates. The woman handed the teacake to her in a piece of rice paper. Wong Oi took a bite and closed her eyes, savoring the sweet taste of the fragrant dates and the fine texture of the sticky rice flour.

She finally found the letter writer. He had on a plain gray Chinese jacket and wide pants and was sitting next to a small table laid out with a black inkpot, a brush leaning on a bamboo brush-rest and rice paper. For a small fee, he wrote and read letters. A chair was placed in front of the table for customers. Wong Oi sat down, showed him the letter and smiled.

"I would like you to read this to me. It is from my husband in America," she said proudly. The man nodded without showing any interest and started to read the letter.

Dear Hong Kai's mother, how are you and our children? Our daughter must be walking by now. Our journey to America was arduous. Hong Kai was sick most of the time on the ship. When we finally got here, we had a difficult time adjusting to the food. I still have much trouble learning the language. Hong Kai is smart and he has already learned enough to be enrolled in school. The only trouble with our son was that the children teased him about his long braid. He was miserable. The teacher asked me to cut it off the other day so the children would make less fun of him. I obliged, but Hong Kai cried for three days straight. He was worried that he now looks like a foreigner with his short hair and won't be able to face his friends and relatives when he comes home. I assured him that he will be the envy of the whole village but he doesn't believe me. What can you say to a seven-year-old boy?

Enclosed is some money. Treat yourself to something nice. I already have made a few payments to Yuen Fung. Our debt is going down. The laundry business is laborious but at least we make good money. Hong Kai is a good boy. He helps out after school. We work hard, but it will be worth it when we come home one day and have our relatives line up to get the roast pork that we will give out like Yuen Fung did. That image keeps me going when I get tired. You must be busy taking care of our children. We are all doing our share to have a better life. I will send you some more money next month.

Your husband.

Wong Oi paid the man and carefully folded the letter. She left the market and walked toward the main street of town to find the pharmacy that converted American dollars to local currency. It was the largest store in town. Different varieties of dried mushrooms, shrimp, oysters, scallops and sea vegetables in large straw baskets spilled out onto the street. She stepped inside the pharmacy and was distracted by a huge display of colorful candies. She thought of her children. She grabbed handfuls of candy out of different baskets and put them in a big bag. She was happy knowing how excited the children would be when they saw the amount of sweets she was bringing home. She popped a yellow one into her mouth and walked toward the clerk. After she converted the money and paid for the candies, she walked home quickly. She kept her hand over her pocket and avoided walking too close to anyone.

Monthly, Wong Oi received money from her husband. She often brought her children to town so they could shop with her. She treated them to toys, sweets and meals in the market that they never had dreamed of before. They were now the envy of all the other children in the village. Wong Oi enrolled her second son in the local school. She was determined that there should be at least one scholar in this family.

Wong Oi upgraded the furniture in their modest house, replacing the rickety table and stools with a set of lacquered table and chairs. All the children had their own beds. Each New Year, she made sure that there was something new, whether it was a set of pots and pans or a new set of bed linens. The entire family got new wardrobes. Wong Oi quickly grew accustomed to her more comfortable life style, but she anxiously waited for her husband's return so she could move into the grand house that he had promised to build for her.

Her second son became the scholar of the village and she also enrolled her daughter in school. Everyone nearby brought letters and documents for her son to read, so they wouldn't have to walk to the market and pay someone to do it. For her son's services, they showered her with compliments and small gifts. Wong Oi loved the attention.

Finally, the day Wong Oi so much looked forward to arrived. After ten years, her husband and her son were coming home. In preparation, Wong Oi cleaned and tidied the house. She dusted every surface and washed the floor. The bed linens were clean and she made sure the chairs were in perfect alignment with the table. As she wiped down the mirror, she caught her own reflection and wondered if she had aged well in the years that her husband had been gone. She pinched her cheeks to get a little color in them and looked again in the mirror. Satisfied, she smiled and quickly went back to cleaning.

Wong Oi had ordered two roast pigs from town earlier. One of the relatives was busy chopping them up so the meat could be divided among the guests, along with the fragrant soaps and candies Sing Tai had brought back from America.

Relatives filled the house and the courtyard was crowded with tables and chairs for the washing off the dust dinner, the traditional meal when someone returns from a faraway land.

In the midst of all the excitement was Hong Kai. He wore a navy blue western suit with a red bow tie. He stood tall and handsome. His short black hair was slicked back with a fragrant hair balm. Hong Kai stayed by his mother's side so she could hear all the compliments from the relatives.

"Look at him! What a handsome boy! I wonder who will be the lucky one to have a daughter become his bride." Wong Oi overheard her cousin from a neighboring village say to his friend.

"Lucky enough to have him as a son-in-law so the family could go to the Golden Mountain with him. I wish I had a daughter," the friend said and shook his head in disappointment. Wong Oi was very proud of her son. He had come home with an American education and a lot of money. With his good looks and status, she was not interested in matching him up with any of her relatives' daughters. She was sure he could now acquire a wife from a family of better standing.

Sing Tai had just finished building the house he had promised. It was much bigger and grander than Wong Oi had imagined. The brass knocker on the hefty front door gleamed brightly in the sun. Tiles covered the massive roof and the enclosed courtyard was stocked with the best variety of flowering trees and shrubs. She was happy that her husband knew what pleased her. She felt that he came home a rich man and he should show it, so they bought land for a big farm and opened a fine china store in the market place. For the first time in her life, Wong Oi had servants. Her favorite pastime was to sit in the garden among the jasmine and peonies under the shade of a willow tree, sipping a cup of fine jasmine tea while chatting with her friends and relatives. The life she had imagined years before had been realized.

Wong Oi felt it was time to find her son a suitable bride. She summoned the local matchmaker for the search, inviting her to the house for tea.

In the main hall, where Wong Oi usually formally received her guests, she gestured the matchmaker to sit on the ornate rosewood chair next to the tea stand that was placed between them. The matchmaker smiled broadly, showing off her newly acquired gold tooth, a symbol of a successful businesswoman.

"Ai Ya! Madam, do I have a good match for you! The daughter of Governor Chan from the Sai Kwok village is available." She took the teacup from the maid, dismissed her and turned to face Wong Oi. "Just imagine, the governor's daughter! The status that comes with such a catch and the size of the dowry will make anyone from this village drool with envy." She glanced around the room, surveying the size of the house and the quality of the furniture, calculating the fee she should ask for this match.

"You must consider this as the match of the century. Who has a chance to have a governor's daughter as her daughter-in-law?"

Wong Oi listened with great interest as the matchmaker's eyes settled on her.

"You know, the people from the government usually save their daughters for their peers who have titles. She is the only daughter with seven brothers, the moon surrounded by seven stars, the most precious pearl on her father's palm." She paused. Wong Oi sipped her tea slowly, savoring her every word. The matchmaker continued, "And besides, their household is known to produce male heirs, I have no doubt that she will bring you many grandsons."

Wong Oi couldn't believe her good luck. The governor's daughter as her daughter-in-law! She would be the envy of the village for a long time to come. The size of the dowry itself made Wong Oi salivate. She almost could not contain her excitement but quickly collected herself. She didn't want to show her eagerness. She was supposed to be a woman of status, not easily impressed by a mere mention of the governor as her possible future in-law.

The matchmaker saw through Wong Oi's placid expression and calmly added, "I will get her date and time of birth so you can consult the astrologer. I have no doubt that this match is made in heaven. With her status, I am sure that she is more than suitable for your son." She smiled, her gold tooth gleaming in the afternoon light as she waited for Wong Oi to respond.

"Yes, I would like to consult the astrologer. Then I will talk to my husband and see if he wants to negotiate this match," Wong Oi said casually, staying in good form.

"I will come back tomorrow with the information if the governor is not too busy to see me." The matchmaker got up quickly and walked toward the extensive garden that led to the front gate of the new house.

Red banners with the golden symbol of double happiness adorned the house. Banquet tables covered with crimson tablecloths were set up in the main house and in the garden. Lacquered chopsticks were placed elegantly next to each fine china setting on silver rests. Musicians and opera singers entertained the guests in the main hall. A dozen tea stands held plates of roasted watermelon seeds and candied fruits. The guests were bejeweled in their finest. This was the perfect time to show others their wealth. The dress Wong Oi wore for this important occasion had been made months in advance. Weddings and funerals were the most important events, as they defined a person's position in life. She had carefully chosen a deep blue silk brocade with the designs of pink plum blossoms and gold coins woven into the fabric. To go with her extravagant dress, Wong Oi had also put on a pair of her best jade and pure gold bracelets and matching necklace and earrings.

Outside the back gate, there was a long line of poor villagers waiting for the leftover food and the red envelopes of good luck money that the now wealthy family would hand out to them to honor this happy occasion. Most of the villagers had heard about the marriage of Hong Kai and the governor's daughter and were anxious to catch a glimpse of the bride's dowry. While Wong Oi was waiting with her guests for the bride to arrive, onlookers lined the main street leading to the house. Children waited eagerly at the far end of the village for the wedding procession to pass by. Wong Oi finally heard the faint sounds of music in the distance and the children shouting, "The bride is coming! The bride is coming!"

Musicians in red jackets led the procession and played traditional wedding music with trumpets, drums and cymbals. Twelve roast pigs with big red flowers in their ears were displayed on individual wooden trays. Each was carried on the shoulders of two men with wide red ribbons across their chests. They were followed by men carrying dozens and dozens of lacquered boxes filled with dumplings and teacakes. Then came the furniture. Finely carved rosewood and marble tables with matching chairs, tea stands, display cabinets and recliners were followed by bolts of silk and half a dozen carved cedar chests filled with the bride's belongings. Two men carried the red and gold wedding sedan, the bride within hidden by a curtain of red silk. The bride's personal maid walked in front. The villagers were clapping and shouting to each other, commenting on the opulent display of the dowry.

Firecrackers popped loudly as the wedding sedan reached the main gate of the house. The two men gently lowered it to the ground. The maid lifted the silk curtain and offered her hand to the bride and helped her step out of the sedan. The bride's head was covered with a large piece of red silk. She was not to be seen by anyone before the groom took his first look. Her maid carried the bride on her back into the house and to the wedding chamber where they would wait for the ceremony to begin. The children in the house followed them to the outside of the room and pushed at each other trying to get a glimpse of the bride through the window.

After the matchmaker meticulously prepared the ceremonial tea to ensure the full payment of her fee, she called Wong Oi and her husband into the main hall, where the musicians played the traditional wedding music. The proud parents sat down on a pair of rosewood chairs. Behind them hung a prominent golden symbol of double happiness. Wong Oi savored every moment of this event which would ensure her place at the upper echelon of the social circle. Hong Kai stood in front of his father, anxiously waiting for the ceremony to begin.

The matchmaker finally announced, "Our bride of the Leung family is here." Everyone turned toward the entrance of the hall. The bride's face was still shrouded by the red silk. With the matchmaker on one side of her and the maid on the other, they led her slowly in front of her new in-laws. She stood facing the groom with her head bowed. Hong Kai came forward and lifted the covering off her head. A loud murmur swept across the room as everyone marveled at the rare sight of her wedding regalia. They had never seen such wealth. She wore a phoenix crown, an elaborate traditional wedding headdress with filigreed peonies on the sides and a phoenix in the center, inlaid with bright blue kingfisher feathers and gold leaves. Hundreds of pearls were sewn onto the headdress with tiny gold springs between the peonies and the phoenix. They vibrated to the slightest movement of the bride. A large single pearl dropped from the bird's beak onto the girl's forehead. Her earrings, carved from fine jade and embellished with hanging pearls, symbolized good fortune. Her necklace brought gasps of admiration, the centerpiece being the size of her palm. It was a jade butterfly medallion encased in blue enamel studded with pearls and rubies. Her black silk wedding jacket was embroidered with several pairs of red, gold and silver dragons and phoenixes. The skirt was of the same design, but was made of red silk satin and with silver tassels swaying from the hem. On her feet were a pair of red slippers with multicolored flowers and butterflies, which the bride had embroidered herself. The matchmaker brought forward two cups of tea on a silver tray and announced, "The bride pours tea to Lo Yeah and On Yun!" The maid helped the bride get on her knees to bow three times to Sing Tai and his wife.

"Lo Yeah, drink tea from your new daughter-in-law!" The matchmaker handed the bride a cup of tea. She raised the teacup above her head to offer it to Sing Tai with her head still bowed low to show respect.

"On Yun, drink tea from your new daughter-in-law," the matchmaker said ceremoniously. The bride offered the tea to Wong Oi. Wong Oi accepted the tea, sipped it with great pleasure and put a big red envelope stuffed with money on the silver tray for the matchmaker. The maid helped the bride to stand up and face the groom. The new couple bowed three times to each other. The matchmaker lifted her hand, signaling the maid to lead the bride back into the wedding chamber so that Hong Kai's new wife could change into another outfit.

The guests sat at tables in the house and in the garden. Governor Chan and his wife sat with the groom's family at the head table in the main hall. Wong Oi sat next to her husband, a seat removed from the governor. She was now an equal with Governor Chan and his wife. Wong Oi basked in the open admiration from her friends and relatives. She had a permanent smile on her face.

Hong Kai went around with a small cup of liquor in his hand and called out to his guests, "Drink a few more cups and raise your chopsticks." The feast had begun. The servants rushed from table to table with big platters of glistening jet black sea cucumbers braised in shitake mushrooms nestled in a mound of mustard greens. While the guests ate, the matchmaker came around each table with the bride in a pink silk jacket and skirt with red and white peonies embroidered on them.

"To our most honored guests, please accept tea from our bride and thank you for coming." The matchmaker passed a tray full of teacups around the table. The guests looked up and openly gawked at the quantity of pure gold and jade rings, necklaces and bracelets piled on Hong Kai's new wife. It was customary for the bride to wear every gift of jewelry she received to show the wealth associated with her family. The guests took the tea and in turn, everyone put a red envelope filled with money on the tray for the new bride.

By the time the shark fin soup was served, Hong Kai had come around each table with his new wife now dressed in a pale blue silk ensemble embroidered with yellow and white chrysanthemums. They bowed to the guests and raised a small cup of liquor to ask them to drink and eat more. They were now greeting everyone officially as a couple.

The servants brought out urns of sweet lotus seeds in light syrup with small edible lilies floating on top. Most of the children were already asleep. It was time for the guests to leave. The bride and groom stood next to Wong Oi and Sing Tai at the entrance of the main hall to bid farewell to their guests. As Wong Oi said her goodbyes, the guests noticed that the bride had changed again. She wore a lavender silk dress with multi-colored butterflies cascading from her shoulders down to her ankles. Wong Oi was tired from the daylong excitement, but she glowed with pride. She had done well for herself.

"I want to take the next ship back to the Golden Mountain with my wife," Hong Kai said to his parents one evening after dinner.

"Why so soon? It hasn't been a month since you acquired your wife." Wong Oi set down her teacup, looked at her son and was surprised that he did not want to stay with her in China for a longer period of time.

"I want to make my own fortune. I have learned from father and now it is my turn," Hong Kai said, turning to his father for support.

"He is our oldest son and should go out to make a world of his own," Sing Tai agreed and sat back in his chair.

"I enjoy having the whole family together under one roof. I wish you would stay longer." Wong Oi looked away to show her displeasure.

"I am anxious to get started. I want to come back one day to China a rich man. Just like father." Hong Kai had his father's approval. He stood up, bid good night to his parents and left the room.

In two weeks, Hong Kai set sail to America with his new wife.

With her son and his wife having departed to the Golden Mountain, Wong Oi felt it was again time to increase her social status.

"It is time for you to get yourself a concubine," she said casually to her husband while they were having tea in the garden. "Anyone who is well established in the village has at least one concubine in his household. It is necessary for us to demonstrate our proper social standing."

Sing Tai sat up and looked at his wife. "I like to live my life simply. Things get complicated when you add another person into a household. Just look at Yuen Fung's family. He got himself two concubines and the house is in constant turmoil." He shook his head and continued, "The three women fight with each other over the smallest things. I don't know if it is a good thing to do."

Wong Oi spoke a little louder, "His wife just doesn't know how to control his household. I know how to run this house. I will send for the matchmaker to see if she has a good match for us."

"As you wish. But I don't think it is a very good idea," Sing Tai said lamely, as he sipped his tea. He knew it was useless to argue with her.

Despite her steely façade, Wong Oi was secretly torn. She did not like the idea of another woman coming into the house to share a bed with her own husband, but she felt that their status was more important than her private feelings. She knew how messy Yuen Fung's household was and determined to rule her house with an iron hand. The concubine should just be a maid. Occasionally, she would be allowed to share her husband's bed.

Within weeks, a wedding was planned.

Compared to Hong Kai's wedding, the house was subdued. Only a few tables covered with pink tablecloths were set up in the main hall. The places were set with bamboo chopsticks, not the sleek lacquered ones. Brown earthenware sat dully on the tables instead of the fine teal china. A pair of Wong Oi's trousers hung above the main entrance, with a red banner on top to show the dominance of the proper wife.

The matchmaker led the girl in a pale pink jacket and skirt to the outside of the house. The girl had her head bowed low. She looked tired and her shoes were covered in dust. The matchmaker gestured for her to kneel down. To enter the house, she was to crawl under the pair of pants on her hands and knees. The girl did exactly as she was told. Sing Tai and Wong Oi sat on matching rosewood chairs. Wong Oi fixed her eyes on the floor and only glanced at the girl out of the corners of her eyes.

Acknowledgement would be a sign of equality. Wong Oi held herself rigid and dignified. The matchmaker poured tea into the two cups and handed them to the girl to serve to Sing Tai and his wife. The girl, still on her knees with head bowed, raised each cup above her head without looking directly at either of them. Wong Oi tossed a red envelope with the match-maker's fee onto the tea tray. Not bothering to sip her tea, she stood up and began talking with relatives with her back turned to the girl. Without a proper dismissal, the girl did not dare to stand up. She turned her head and glanced in the direction of the matchmaker for help. The matchmaker gave her a stern look. She quickly lowered her head and remained on her knees until a servant summoned the girl to join her new husband and his wife for dinner. She got up and nearly fell after kneeling for so long. The servant reluctantly held her steady; a concubine was not someone she had to serve.

Coming from an extremely poor family, it was natural for the concubine to figure out ways to survive the difficult situation. She seized every opportunity to cater to Sing Tai. Even before he managed to put his rice bowl down after dinner, she would have his after dinner drink ready. She retreated into their room where she waited for him with warmed oils for his nightly mas-sages. She spoke softly and moved quietly, a direct contrast to Wong Oi. In the beginning, Sing Tai spent a few nights at a time with her, which was his duty. Then eventually, he only saw his wife on occasion. When Wong Oi openly complained about his absence, the concubine would smile knowingly at Wong Oi when no one else was looking.

Wong Oi was furious at this dirt-poor girl who had the audacity to steal her husband's affection. Every chance she had, Wong Oi would find fault with the concubine. She complained to her husband incessantly. At first, Sing Tai tried to remedy the situation. Gradually, he retreated into silence. When his wife complained, he looked away and said nothing.

Wong Oi found herself alone in bed, unable to sleep. She plotted revenge on the fox who stole her husband.

I will fix that whore. She will know who has the power in this house, she seethed with hatred. Wong Oi finally devised a suitable plan. She smiled to herself and slept soundly for the first time in months.

"Good morning, On Yun, here is your tea." The concubine bowed, serving Wong Oi her usual morning tea.

"Since you are with child and I don't like to take my meal with a crying infant, you will take your meals with the servants," Wong Oi continued, " also, the cook is too busy now with you in our household, you should help out in the kitchen. The maid is getting lazy. She doesn't do a good job washing my clothes anymore. I want you to wash my clothes from now on." She paused, "Oh and by the way, winter is coming soon. Take all of the blankets, shake them in the garden and air them out. While you are at it, sweep up the leaves off the pathways." Wong Oi's face showed no emotion, and the entire time she talked, her gaze was fixed on the teacup. She walked out of the room, her back to the girl, smiling.

One afternoon, the concubine served Wong Oi and her cousin their favorite jasmine tea in the garden and walked quietly back into the house to avoid further demands. Wong Oi finally was satisfied. She felt secure in her beloved spot, sitting on an over-sized rattan chair under the shade of the old willow tree. Jasmine, camellia and peonies bloomed in the garden around her. She particularly enjoyed the sweet scent of the jasmine as she sipped her tea.

"Did you hear about Aunt Sui Yee?" Bik Lan asked, putting down her teacup.

"Your aunt? What about her?" Wong Oi became alert. Gossip was her favorite pastime.

"The communists came to her village to punish the wealthy landowners. They put them on public trial claiming that they had accumulated their wealth by exploiting the poor. The Red Guards took Aunt Sui Yee's farm away!" She sat up and wiped her eyes with a handkerchief. "You know, she is a ninety year-old widow and has bound feet. You would think they'd have a little heart and leave her alone." She sighed and continued, "After they confiscated her farm, they came back just a few weeks later. They dragged her outside to the street in front of a large crowd and made her dance under the scorching sun, all because she had entertained guests on happy occasions with the opera in her magnificent garden." She paused to wipe her eyes again. "Not only did they call her an imperialist, but sparrow legs because she was so thin and frail! The crowd was throwing stones and spitting at her! When she was too tired to move, they caned her and made her continue dancing." Bik Lan began to sob. "She finally collapsed and died of exhaustion the following day," she said almost inaudibly.

Wong Oi listened in horror and wondered about her own fate. "I heard about the Red Guards. These insolent youths are roaming wild," she said with a shudder. She worked hard for what she had and without warning, all could be lost, including her own life. She felt perspiration on her hands. The tea suddenly tasted acrid.

"Do you think the communists are coming this way soon?" she asked Bik Lan, hoping for a few words of comfort.

"I am glad that I don't have any money. You never know when they are going to show up. Those Red Guards are ruthless. They turn against their own parents and teachers. There are just too many horror stories about them. For once in my life, I am glad that I am poor," her cousin said flatly and picked up her teacup and took a long sip. She found comfort in enjoying the fine tea and claiming no ownership to it.

Wong Oi got word that her son Hong Kai had finally returned from the Golden Mountain. He was staying in Hong Kong where there were better opportunities to invest and make better use of his fortune and had acquired two buildings in a good location. He came back with his wife and seven children. His oldest son, James was already a teenager and would soon be looking for a suitable wife.

"I heard the communists are closing in. I am going to contact Hong Kai and tell him that we need to shut everything down here and join him in Hong Kong. We must escape before they close the border," Sing Tai said to his wife during dinner, the only time they saw each other. He usually ate in silence as quickly as he could and left to avoid any unpleasantries. He concentrated on his food, avoiding eye contact with her. "Most of our relatives have already lost everything and some of them had been relocated to hard labor camps in Siberia. We don't have much time."

Wong Oi did not bother to look at him and nodded but was relieved that he finally had a solid plan to get away from the communists. Since the day she spoke to her cousin, she had worried about her own fate in China. Most of her relatives with any means had escaped to Hong Kong or had been transferred to labor camps.

Wong Oi was optimistic about her position in Hong Kong. Hong Kai was always willing to please her and he was her favorite son. She would have an ally and could wield more power against the concubine once they moved there. She glanced up at her husband as he shoveled food into his mouth. Anger began to well up in her throat. Most of his time was spent with the concubine and her young daughter. Wong Oi had tried to curtail this by ordering that the child and her mother take their meals with the servants and not to be included in any family activities. But even in this, they seemed to fare well because Sing Tai was always there for his daughter and the mother knew her place and did not fight for anything. The concubine had fully accepted her position. Wong Oi hated the fact that she was so compliant and that her husband remained drawn to her.

She is such a nail in my eye. I'll fix her when I get to Hong Kong. There I shall be the mother of the head of the household. She will know then that life is not pleasant for concubines, Wong Oi thought to herself as her husband left the table.

Tall buildings were packed together and hundreds of motorcars passed in front of their building in Hong Kong. Wong Oi choked on the foreign smell of the exhaust. When outside, she learned to cover her nose with a handkerchief. The constant rumble of the cars mixed with the incessant calls of the street venders selling their wares overwhelmed her. She found soot on everything she touched. Women wore dresses that showed their bare arms and legs. What was this world coming to? She found her new world distasteful and missed the leisurely pace and the friendliness of her village. Yet this was her life now. She sat in front of the building watching crowds of people with blank faces go by. Sometimes a whole day passed and not one person bothered to stop and ask how she was. They were always in a rush to get somewhere. They did not even glance in her direction. She felt invisible and lost.

Wong Oi had taken an apartment at the mezzanine level but Sing Tai and his concubine lived in a large room on the ground floor. The only comfort she had was at dinnertime. Every evening, she walked up to the fourth floor to have dinner with Hong Kai and his family. The seat next to her son was reserved for her. His wife sat on the other side of him. Sing Tai's seat was next to hers, one seat removed from their son's. The seating arrangement demonstrated that she was more honored than her husband. It pleased her that Hong Kai knew what made his mother happy. As soon as she arrived, the children greeted her. Hong Kai waited for his mother to sit and pick up her chopsticks before he picked up his own. No one was allowed to eat before Hong Kai picked up his chopsticks and the children were not to speak at the dinner table. Wong Oi liked this arrangement. Her son gave her the respect she deserved.

The concubine was not allowed on the fourth floor at all. Now that her daughter was grown, she cooked and ate by herself while a maid served the others with food prepared by a cook. She was not allowed to join the extended family or participate in any of the official gatherings, including banquets for family weddings and the birth of male children. Wong Oi's position as the matriarch of this family was secured.

One afternoon, Hong Kai came downstairs to talk to his mother, "I have great news! I have found a very suitable girl for my son James. She was born in America and is from a very wealthy family. I have negotiated her dowry and it will surpass my own wedding!" He was excited to tell his mother of his accomplishment, knowing that nothing would please her more than a boost of her status.

"My son, you have done well for yourself. I am looking forward to my grandson's wedding. When is the good date? I am anxious to pass out teacakes to all of our relatives on this happy occasion."

"They will deliver the dowry in less than a month. I am going to clear out everything in my flat and redecorate it with the fine rosewood and marble furniture coming from the bride's family. I hope I have enough room for all it," Hong Kai told his mother, happy to see the pride on her face.

The delivery of the dowry was slightly different than in China. Instead of having it delivered with the bride, her family sent it three days before the wedding. Led by a band of musicians dressed in red, the procession of the dowry was more than three-quarters of a city block long. It took half a day for the procession to march from the bride's house to Hong Kai's building. It was the talk of the town for months.

On her grandson's wedding day, Wong Oi got up early and went upstairs to make sure that her dress was well pressed by the maid and ready for her to wear. She had carefully picked a long dress of rich brown silk with images of bats woven into the fabric. Bats are a sign for good life. She put on her best jade and gold earrings with matching rings, inspected her new shoes and made sure they were well polished. She had not seen the bride and trusted Hong Kai to have picked a good match for his own son as she had done for him. She checked herself in the mirror when she was done getting dressed. She had the look of a successful woman. Pleased with herself, she proceeded to go up to the fourth floor to the wedding party.

The wedding began in the afternoon at city hall. The bride wore a white lace and satin gown with a long train, a veil, white lace gloves and a large bouquet of fern and white lilies. The groom had chosen a dark blue pinstriped suit with a bow tie and a matching lily on the wide lapel. A Justice of the Peace performed the marriage. This gathering was for the immediate family. Hong Kai had arranged the western style wedding because he wanted to show the world that both families were from the Golden Mountain. The traditional Chinese banquet with all the relatives and friends would be held in the evening.

Silk banners hung on the walls of the hall. The symbol of double happiness shone in gold cutouts on the bright banners.

They were gifts from Hong Kai's friends and relatives congratulating him on this happy occasion. In front of the largest one were two pairs of chairs for the in-laws to be seated to receive the bride.

Twelve square tables were set up on the side of the hall for the guests to play mahjong. Guests who wanted to play and catch up on gossip came early. By early afternoon they were already filled. Children ran around stuffing candied fruit and watermelon seeds into their mouths or sat playing card games. The bride waited in a small room at the end of the hall. Most of the guests had not seen her and she was not to be seen till the ceremony began.

In front of the red banner, Wong Oi and her husband sat in one pair of chairs and Hong Kai and his wife sat in the other. James stood in front of them. All of the guests gathered and waited for the matchmaker to present the bride to the family.

"Tai On Yun, please accept tea from the bride, your granddaughter-in-law." The matchmaker handed a cup of tea to the bride. On her knees, she raised the teacup above her head and offered it to her grandmother-in-law. Wong Oi took the teacup and sipped the tea with great pleasure. The acquisition of her daughter-in-law and granddaughter-in-law was the best she could have done. Sing Tai drank the tea as if it was an everyday occurrence.

"On Yun, please accept tea from the bride, your daughter-in-law." Hong Kai's wife accepted the tea and took a slow sip and stoically placed a big red envelope containing the matchmaker's fee on the tray. Hong Kai took the tea and drank it with pride. James stood next to his kneeling bride and watched without expression.

Wong Oi passed her time by sitting in front of the building watching crowds of faceless people walk by, waiting patiently for the time to go upstairs for dinner. Daily dinner with her family was what she lived for. It was one of her happiest times. She sat at the table as the matriarch, next to Hong Kai, the head of household. Everyone had to wait for her cue before they could start to eat. She was pleased to be in the company of his son and grandson, both of them had acquired suitable wives. Her life was what every woman would hope for. Everything was in order.

Shortly after the birth of James' first daughter, Hong Kai told his mother that he had decided to go back to America to expand his wealth. Business associates told him about the up and coming Chinatown in New York City. He instructed James to collect the rent from the buildings and send it to him in America. He left for New York with his wife and the rest of their children.

After her son left with his family, Wong Oi found herself completely neglected by her grandson. She was not invited to have dinner on the fourth floor anymore. James and his wife now occupied the entire flat. They kept the maid and the cook to serve just the two of them and hired a nanny for their daughter.

Wong Oi tried to have a word with James to correct the situation. She sat in front of the building and waited for her grandson to pass her as he went upstairs to his flat. She stopped him and said, "James, how are your wife and daughter? Aren't you having dinner at a regular time? I haven't been upstairs for weeks now."

James turned to look at his grandmother but continued to walk up the stairs, "You have to talk to Margaret about dinner. I usually eat with my colleagues at the police station when I get busy."

"I guess it is not easy to be the chief inspector..." before Wong Oi had a chance to finish her sentence, her grandson disappeared into the turn of the stairs. She felt it was inappropriate to approach her granddaughter-in-law who came from a wealthy family. Wong Oi knew that she lacked good training, and was not about to risk losing face by asking Margaret to invite her upstairs for dinner and have her refuse. She fumed every time she saw their cook come back from the market and go upstairs with the fancy food. She was used to being catered to by her son and now she had to fend for herself, as did the concubine. Now it was worse. The concubine cooked for herself and Sing Tai. They seemed very happy staying in their room on the ground floor. Wong Oi hated Margaret for her predicament. Margaret was supposed to be taught by her mother to respect and take care of her grandmother-in-law.

To pass the time, Wong Oi sat outside in front of the building, watching the flow of traffic and fanning herself with her favorite fan made of a palm leaf. For days at a time, she stayed in her apartment. She tried to avoid the satisfied glances and smiling face of the concubine and the pitying looks from her grandson's maid.

Several servants from the other tenants in the building took pity on Wong Oi due to her age and circumstance. They offered to get what she needed for her dinner when they went to the market. Wong Oi was grateful and became friendly with them. Most servants gossiped about their employers to each other and James' were no different. They started to tell her what went on in her grandson's flat. By now, James had two daughters, five years apart. Wong Oi learned that James almost never came home and that he had a mistress who had two children by him. His wife was always out with her friends. The nanny cared for her two daughters and the children rarely saw their parents. There was a rumor that James' wife was having an affair with one of her father-in-law's friends. Wong Oi was appalled at the vicious rumors. No woman in Margaret's position would risk being an outcast. Women lost their lives for having affairs in China. She questioned the authenticity of the stories from the servants.

On an unusually hot afternoon, Wong Oi sat in her usual spot in front of the building fanning herself and watching the passersby, hoping to see someone she knew to engage in conversation. She was shocked to see the wife of her son's friend run past her screaming and crying.

"Give me back my husband! Where is my husband? I want my husband back!" She found the gate leading to James' flat was locked. She sat on the steps and cried hysterically for hours. No one paid any attention to her. She finally walked past Wong Oi in exhaustion without casting a glance toward her.

Wong Oi was stunned and her face twisted with disgust. How could this be happening in her family? This public display of such a shameful act from her granddaughter-in-law was too much for her to bear. How could she face the servants now that everyone knew the rumor was true? She went back to her flat and was not seen for weeks.

To Wong Oi's relief, she got word that Hong Kai was coming back to Hong Kong. It had been five years. She waited for his arrival anxiously.

The minute Hong Kai set foot in the building, before he had a chance to go up to the fourth floor, Wong Oi pulled her son into her apartment up at the mezzanine, "I want to have a few words with you," she said in a hushed voice. Wong Oi gestured her son to sit down.

"I haven't been invited to have my dinner upstairs since you left. These young people have no respect," she said while taking a seat next to her son. "But it is trivial compared to the fact that your daughter-in-law is having an affair with your friend." She looked at him and raised her voice, "How can I face the world with this shame? I found out that your son rarely comes home. He has a mistress with male children and they are the same age as your granddaughters. I want you to have your son's mistress come home as his concubine. Legitimize his children and your son will become a man with more status by having a concubine in the house." Wong Oi sat up and stared at her son, "Maybe then people will hold their tongues and I would have legs to stand on. I want this done right away."

"I have to see what is going on and talk to James about this. I will take care of it," Hong Kai said quietly and left his mother's apartment.

In the evening, one of Wong Oi's great granddaughters came to invite her to have dinner upstairs with the family. She sat next to her son, as usual. That evening, they had dinner as if Hong Kai had never left. Once again Wong Oi resumed her position as the mother of the head of the household.

One day during dinner, Wong Oi decided to bring up the issue. James' wife, Margaret, was now pregnant with their third child. Wong Oi had waited for Hong Kai to say something about the matter for months but her son was silent.

"It is a known fact that James has male children with another woman outside of our household. I want him to bring them home and legitimize them. Their mother should be an official concubine living under our roof especially because he has only daughters with his wife," Wong Oi said with authority.

Margaret slammed her chopsticks down and said, "I will not have a whore living in my house! And how do you know the child I am carrying is not a boy?"

Wong Oi was startled and almost choked on her rice. She was shocked that her granddaughter-in-law had the audacity to display such insolent behavior, but she was willing to give her a little advantage since Margaret came from a lineage of wealth.

"You should hold your tongue and know your place. I am willing to wait and see if you are going to produce a male child. We should make the decision after your child is born," Wong Oi said firmly. If James brought home his mistress as his concubine, she would boost her status as the grandmother of a successful man. The people would not be so blatant as to openly gossip about Margaret's affair.

Wong Oi was glad when Margaret gave birth to a third female child. This meant Wong Oi had the right to press the issue of bringing James' mistress home as his concubine. She had waited for Hong Kai to bring up the subject but a month passed and there was still no word from him.

During dinner, Wong Oi looked directly to her son and said, "James should bring home his concubine since he has no male child from his wife. We are going to have a happy household now that our lineage will continue."

Margaret slammed her bowl on the table and yelled, "I forbid the stinking whore to come into my house. Did your husband get his concubine because you had no male child of your own?" She stood up with her hands on her hips and stared directly at Wong Oi, "Look at how he lives his life now. He doesn't even come up to have dinner with you anymore. He is glued to his concubine. I will have no sleazy slut sleeping with my husband in the same house."

Wong Oi's face grew ashen. How dare Margaret, the lowly granddaughter-in-law, refer to her situation? She looked to Hong Kai to rectify the situation. She expected him to have control over the spouse of his own child. After all, he usually tried his best to please her. To her amazement, Hong Kai looked down at his bowl and said nothing.

Margaret stared at Wong Oi triumphantly, slowly pulled in her chair and sat down. She began to eat the rest of her dinner cheerfully.

Wong Oi was baffled by her son's sheepish behavior but observed that Margaret used to take the seat on the other side of the table with her children and that James was never around. The seat of Hong Kai's wife remained empty when he first came home. Margaret now sat next to him at the dinner table. It had been that way for quite some time. She recalled the way they looked at each other. It was not the way a father should look at his son's wife. She didn't want to acknowledge her suspicion but now that her son had chosen Margaret over his own mother, Wong Oi felt certain her son was having an affair with his daughter-in-law.

Wong Oi felt the bitterness sting in her eyes. She resigned herself to the fact that James was not going to bring his mistress home. She rationalized that it was better to keep the dirt in the house than having Margaret roaming wild with other men to create more gossip. She lowered her eyes and shot a piercing glance at Margaret just to let her know she knew what went on. Margaret continued eating her dinner glaring back at Wong Oi and smiling defiantly.

It did not sit well with Wong Oi to have another woman gain her son's loyalty. She had always come before everyone, even her son's wife. She hated Margaret for this, just as much as she hated the concubine. She stopped talking to Margaret and would not even glance in her direction. In her eyes, Margaret had ceased to exist. Meanwhile, Margaret instructed her children never to speak to their great grandmother and never to accept anything from her. Hong Kai kept his distance from his mother and only saw her at dinner.

Every evening, Wong Oi went upstairs for dinner. She would not give up the position of matriarch. By rank, she came before Margaret and in front of company Margaret still had to bow to her. During dinner, Wong Oi ate her food in silence. The children did not dare to look in her direction fearing they would get in trouble with their mother. Hong Kai also ate in silence. She watched as Margaret ate with ease and comfort. Hong Kai acted as if nothing had happened.

Wong Oi saw her great grandchildren only during dinner and Margaret was always there to make sure they did not speak to her. They also were not allowed to visit her at her apartment.

But Margaret's third child was different from the rest of them. Despite her mother's warnings, she often went to her great grandmother's apartment to visit. She was physically strong and an expressive little girl. She laughed and cried easily. Wong Oi took a liking to her and felt she needed her guidance.

One afternoon, her great granddaughter played on Wong Oi's bed pretending it was a stage. She pinned paper flowers in her hair and sang a few phrases from a Chinese opera.

"Oi Ling," Wong Oi said, "You should have been a boy. You must have run too fast before you were born and forgot your penis." She watched her animated great granddaughter and smiled.

"I should be a boy? I'll be your great grandson. I am strong, see!" Her great granddaughter flexed her arms. "I have strong arms and can carry all of the things you want to bring to your relatives!" She flashed her great grandmother a big smile.

"You have a strong body and a strong spirit, the worst things for a girl. Be a good girl and learn to smile without showing your teeth," Wong Oi said and gave her a disapproving look.

"If you don't learn how to hide your emotions you will have a hard life. No man wants a wife who displays her feelings and always shows what she is thinking." She would try her best to teach the girl to contain her emotions.

"Like this?" the little girl mumbled to her great grandmother in amusement, her face all scrunched up as she suppressed her laughter and squinted with her mouth closed.

Wong Oi let out a long sigh and said, "You'll just have to learn the hard way."

Sing Tai had not gone upstairs for dinner since the confrontation with his wife and Margaret. He avoided the unpleasantness of the family feud by staying with his concubine in their room. He only went upstairs for important occasions.

One evening, as Hong Kai and the family finished their meal and the maid was collecting the rice bowls, the concubine rushed into the flat. Breathless, she held onto the doorjamb to support herself ranting incoherently. She had never set foot in this flat, not since they first came from China. Hong Kai quickly ran to her, held her arms to steady her, and asked what was wrong.

She was trembling, with closed eyes she said, "Lo Yeah is not breathing. I gave him some light broth a few minutes ago. Then he just stopped breathing!" She started to cry and held onto Hong Kai. He sat her down and ran down the stairs followed by the rest of the household.

Wong Oi pushed through everyone to get into the room her husband shared with his concubine. This was the first time she had seen the interior of their room. A lace curtain covered a large window at the far side of the wall, diffusing the light from the courtyard outside. In front of the window stood a small table with a light green vase of fresh coral gladiolas. Two simple chairs were placed on each side of the table. One could sense the calmness and simplicity of the occupants. On the other side of the room, her husband lay peacefully in the bed he shared with his concubine. Wong Oi walked over to the bed and took a closer look at her husband. His eyes were closed and his lips were slightly parted. She remembered the tender look in his eyes when he excitedly told her about his voyage to America. It seemed that was many lifetimes ago. She looked around the room and saw that he had lived his later years in contentment with his concubine. A wave of hatred overcame her and tears rolled down her cheeks.

Hong Kai went over to his mother, took her by the arms and escorted her back to her apartment.

"I will make sure father has a proper funeral," he said to his mother solemnly.

"I am sure you know what to do. You are a good son," Wong Oi replied quietly. Weddings and funerals were the gauge of one's social standing. Wong Oi was pleased that her son still wished to oblige her.

On the day of the funeral, Wong Oi went upstairs to join everyone for breakfast. Funeral robes for the entire family were prepared and laid out by relatives. White cotton and raw linen were for Wong Oi and Hong Kai, blue cotton for the grandchildren, and blue cotton with a red dot on the headband for the great grandchildren.

For the first time, the concubine was allowed to join the family at an official gathering as her presence at the procession would signify the family's wealth. This was the only time Wong Oi tolerated being in the same room with her. She wouldn't look at the concubine directly, still withholding recognition of her existence.

They dressed with the help from friends and relatives. The last items to be put on were white cotton hoods for the women. The entire family followed Hong Kai downstairs where the musicians and hearse waited in front of the building. Garlands of fresh white flowers and ferns draped the sides of the hearse. A small table was placed in front of it with incense and candles. Above the windshield of the hearse, a photograph of Sing Tai was displayed. Wong Oi stepped forward, helped by a relative, and knelt in front of the table. The musicians played traditional funeral music and the family knelt down behind her by their ranks. Wong Oi started to wail and chant. The concubine knelt silently behind her. A large crowd gathered to gawk at the elaborate funeral. Displayed on the sidewalk were dozens of buildings, cars, servants, domestic animals and food, all made of shaved bamboo and tissue paper, with baskets of folded gold and silver paper resembling ancient Chinese gold and silver bullion. They would be burned for Sing Tai's after-life.

The procession began with twelve-foot high plaques decorated with fresh flowers and green leaves which framed the names of Sing Tai and the person who had sent the plaques to the family. A pair of five-foot blue and white dragons were below the names, representing the creatures from heaven. The funeral band in white hats and uniforms marched between thirty-two plaques, which were propped up on three-wheeled cycles and peddled by hired men. The numbers of the plaques stood for friends and relatives who could afford such extravagance. Following the band and hearse, two people carried a pair of large lanterns with Sing Tai's age written on them in red. Hong Kai had on a sheer white cotton hat traditionally worn only by the eldest son. He held a lantern on a long stick made of white tissue paper trailed by a long garland of white flowers. This lantern was to light the way for his father to find his way to heaven. Hong Kai then led the family by their ranks behind the hearse to make the long journey to the burial ground. The funeral robes distinguished the generations of the descendants. By these standards, Sing Tai was a wealthy man and had had a good long life.

It was customary for the family of the deceased to invite everyone who was at the funeral to dinner. Hong Kai had rented a banquet hall and ordered a meal fit for a fine wedding.

The hall was decorated with silk banners in somber colors on which expressions of sorrow were written. Hong Kai sat next to his mother to receive the guests. The concubine sat on her other side by rank. Wong Oi was proud of her son for providing such a fine display of her position in the world.

After all of the guests had left, Hong Kai escorted his mother back to her apartment. Before he had a chance to say good night to her she asked him to sit down.

"Tell the stinking concubine to pack and go live with her married daughter. I don't want to see her face for another minute. She must leave tomorrow," she ordered, without looking at him.

Hong Kai slightly bowed his head as a filial son should and said, "I will do as you say. She will be gone tomorrow."

Wong Oi was pleased with his answer. She finally could dispose of the concubine.

Hong Kai was attentive to his mother, and now that the concubine was gone, everyone became more relaxed at the dinner table.

As the maid served the bowls of rice in front of each person, Hong Kai waited for his mother to pick up her chopsticks. Once they had started to eat, he turned to his mother and said, "I have to go back to New York to attend to my business. Margaret requested that I bring her oldest daughter with me to get an American education. She is already fifteen and my wife will see to it that she is taken care of." He paused, looked at Margaret and smiled. "I shall leave in a few weeks with my granddaughter and will return within a month."

Wong Oi nodded, not really caring what went on between the two of them as long as her son would come back to assure her position in the family. Margaret smiled at her daughter, who sat across the table. For once, the children ate their dinner at ease and did not have to be afraid of getting into trouble with their mother.

Wong Oi took her favorite great granddaughter, Oi Ling, to the market to buy a few gifts for her cousin, Bik Lan, who had just escaped to Hong Kong from her old village in China. The afternoon market session was busier than the morning one. The sidewalks were lined with hawkers with their wares and shoppers carrying straw baskets for their purchases. Tubs of live fish, baskets of produce, eggs, all kinds of tofu and cooked food were everywhere. Sides of pork and beef hung on huge iron hooks. The butchers cut pieces from the hanging carcasses to their customers' orders. The ground was wet and filthy, littered with discarded produce and waste from the livestock.

They walked among the stalls that sold live poultry which were packed in huge bamboo baskets. Ducks, geese and chickens squawked loudly. Wong Oi closely inspected the chickens and asked the vendor to show her a specific one. Wong Oi felt the breastbone and told the woman that she didn't want it because it was too skinny. Also the eyes were not very bright, which meant that the chicken was not raised in optimum conditions. After several tries, they found a chicken that was satisfactory. Oi Ling carried the chicken in one hand and the basket of fruit and cakes in the other. She walked proudly next to her great grandmother to Bik Lan's building located just a few blocks away.

As they walked, Wong Oi said to her great granddaughter thoughtfully, "It's better to travel for a month than to study books for three years. Make sure you learn from your experiences instead of just relying on your books."

Oi Ling was busy trying to hold onto the chicken which had been fighting and squabbling ever since they left the market. "What?" she said to her great grandmother absentmindedly, still trying to get the chicken to cooperate.

"When an elder speaks, you better pay full attention. When you walk out of our house, you represent our family. How you act reflects the teachings of our household. You are responsible for carrying our family's honor," Wong Oi said firmly, looking at her great granddaughter.

Oi Ling nodded and whispered, "Yes, great grandmother. I promise to be a good girl."

Hong Kai came back from New York in less than a month. Everyone seemed relaxed at dinner. The adults actually chatted and the children felt less hesitant to serve themselves seconds of their favorite dishes. An undercurrent of rivalry continued between Wong Oi and Margaret and they still did not speak to each other unless it was of the utmost necessity. Wong Oi tolerated Margaret's behavior because of her son's preference for her. With the concubine gone, she was much more at peace and she had come to accept her own fate.

One evening, two years later, when Wong Oi went upstairs for dinner, only the nanny and the maid were with the children. They told her that Margaret had taken Hong Kai to the hospital that morning, after he had vomited a large amount of blood. He was known to have a bleeding ulcer but had refused to get treatment because he did not trust doctors.

Wong Oi spent her days praying to Quen Yum, the Goddess of Mercy, for her son's speedy recovery. Five days passed and Hong Kai still did not come home. That afternoon, one of Margaret's cousins finally came to see Wong Oi at her apartment.

She stared at the floor and spoke almost inaudibly, "I am so sorry to bring you the bad news. Your son passed away this morning in the hospital."

Wong Oi held onto a small table to steady herself. She felt as if the wind had been kicked out of her. Her legs failed to support her and she collapsed onto a chair. Tears streamed down her face. The death of her eldest son was her own death sentence. She now had to rely on the kindness of her daughter-in-law to grant her position in the family. Wong Oi could not contemplate being under the mercy of another woman. Her grandson James had come home to stay almost a year before, but he looked ill. She had not seen him at dinner and dared not hold out hope that he would emerge and speak up for her. For the first time in her life, she had to be compliant to other women in the household. This diminishment of her being was too much for her to bear.

Hong Kai's wife, Choi Kum, accompanied by two of her daughters, came back to Hong Kong to arrange for the funeral. They planned to stay for two months to get things settled, and at Margaret's request, they would take her second daughter back to New York to get an American education.

After her daughter-in-law came back from America, Wong Oi was never invited upstairs for dinner. She only saw Choi Kum once before her son's funeral. The coldness of her daughter-in-law puzzled her but Wong Oi would not question her son's widow, preferring to stay in good form. She was resigned to stay in her apartment. Her position as the matriarch had vanished with the death of her favorite son. Her only hope was that the women in her household would treat her as the grandmother of James who was next in line to be the head of household.

Less than a month after Hong Kai's funeral, one of her granddaughters knocked on Wong Oi's door.

"Grandmother, mother wants me to tell you that my brother James died in the hospital this morning," she said before Wong Oi had a chance to open the door completely.

"James? Not James!" Wong Oi held onto the door and tried to comprehend what she had just heard.

Her granddaughter lowered her head and repeated what she had just said in a whisper, "James, my brother, has just died this morning." She paused and went on, "He has not been well since he came home a year ago. Mother said it was just a matter of time."

Wong Oi was stunned. She stared out into the courtyard and tried to make sense of the news. Slowly, she turned around and sat on a chair without noticing her granddaughter's departure.

All hope was lost. Wong Oi now was truly a nobody. Without her son and grandson she had lost her rank and had become a woman who would depend on the generosity of the other women in her household. There were no tears. She sat in the chair not knowing how much time had elapsed.

Choi Kum left Hong Kong with her two daughters, taking with her Margaret's second daughter. After their departure, no one bothered to visit Wong Oi. She would not even entertain the idea of going upstairs for dinner to subject herself to Margaret's derisive behavior. She resigned herself to her existence, taking her usual seat in front of the building. She sat and watched the blank faces file past her and spoke only when an occasional tenant walked by and said a cordial hello to her. Since the servants had gossiped about Margaret's affair, she would not associate herself with them. She spent much of her time reminiscing about her life in China. She recalled the wonderful days spent gossiping with friends and relatives, sitting in her favorite oversized rattan chair under the old willow tree, sipping a fine cup of tea served by the concubine. She could almost smell the sweet scent of the jasmine.

Wong Oi rarely saw her favorite great granddaughter. She only came around when called for.

"Oi Ling, I want you to buy a small piece of pork for me at the market and four ounces of peanut oil." Wong Oi handed her great granddaughter the empty oil bottle.

"I'll go get them right away. But I have to hurry, I need to cook dinner for us, too," Oi Ling replied without looking at her great grandmother.

"When did your mother get rid of the maid and the cook?" Wong Oi knew very well that Margaret had fired them long ago. She had not seen them pass by her seat in front of the building for months.

"I don't know. It is mother's business," Oi Ling said nervously. Wong Oi did not press for more answers because she knew her great granddaughter would never divulge her mother's business to anyone, like a good daughter. She was proud of her for protecting the honor of the family and keeping her mouth shut.

"Go on then, bring me my things from the market and you can go and get on with your own chores." Wong Oi saw the relief on her great granddaughter's face. Oi Ling left quickly.

Wong Oi sat in front of the building fanning herself, ruminating on the fact that Margaret had not passed by her for weeks. This had been the only occasion she saw her grand-daughter-in-law.

"Dirty whore!" Wong Oi would mutter as she walked by, just loud enough for Margaret to hear. Margaret would walk past her grandmother-in-law, without casting a glance at her. Wong Oi knew that Margaret must be having another affair. It disgusted her that she would put the family name in jeopardy.

Everyone seemed to be busy getting on with their lives. Wong Oi had to resort to getting her own food at the market when her great granddaughter was not available. She had to cross a major thoroughfare with cars coming from both directions to reach the market. Luckily, there was an island at the center divider with a policeman directing traffic on his platform. She usually was careful to watch for his direction before she attempted to cross the street as she wasn't walking as fast as she used to.

One morning, Wong Oi realized that she was late to the market. The morning session was about to close. She walked hurriedly to the edge of the sidewalk feeling her pocket to make sure she had money to pay for her purchase. She noticed the cars stopped in front of her. Without looking at the traffic policeman she proceeded to cross the street. A car turned from a side street. The driver did not see Wong Oi. The man slammed on the brakes when he saw her, but it was too late. The car hit Wong Oi and she fell on the asphalt. The policeman jumped down from his platform and rushed to the scene.

"Ah pau, are you hurt? Please let me help you," the policeman said to Wong Oi while she struggled to sit up.

"I am all right. I think I hurt my shoulder." She grimaced and said, "I didn't see the car turning. Please inform my family. They live at number six, on the fourth floor." Wong Oi gestured to the building behind her.

"Can you walk? Let me take you home." The policeman helped her to stand up.

"Yes. That's a good idea." Wong Oi got up and walked slowly with the policeman's help.

"I'll go upstairs to notify your family so they can get you some help," the policeman said to Wong Oi after he sat her down in her apartment.

After the policeman left, Wong Oi waited patiently for someone to show up from upstairs. Her shoulder throbbed with pain.

"Great grandmother, are you in great pain?" Oi Ling asked breathlessly after running down from the fourth floor. "A policeman came to the door and told me that you were hit by a car and hurt your shoulder. I called mother as soon as he left but it took me a while to get a hold of her. She told me to take you to see a bonesetter." Wong Oi was relieved that her great granddaughter had come to her rescue.

"I'll get a taxi. Mother left me some money and instructed me to do so," Oi Ling said while helping her great grandmother to get up from the reclining chair.

They went to see the bonesetter and were told to return to him every other day for three weeks. During that time, he put an herbal poultice on Wong Oi's shoulder. He prescribed a mixture of fresh herbs, six mountain snails and a dozen mountain cockroaches. Those would be put into four bowls of water and then boiled down to one bowl for Wong Oi's consumption. It should aid her bones to set perfectly. In a month's time, Wong Oi's shoulder was completely healed.

"When did you come back?" Wong Oi was shocked to see one of Choi Kum's daughters from New York walk by her place in front of the building.

"Mother decided to come back to take care of her business. My sister and I came back with her. Margaret has made a mess of things. She lost a hefty sum of money and incurred a large debt from Mother's friends. It is our money she played with," she said with disgust, "And by the way, a rumor reached us in New York that she is having a flaming affair with a stupid herbalist. Is that true?"

Only now did her granddaughter show an interest in talking to her.

"You'll have to ask Margaret yourself. I haven't spoken to her since you left four years ago." Wong Oi did not want to involve herself in the dirty business of cleaning up the mess that Margaret had made. Whatever the outcome was, she just wanted to secure her apartment in her son's building. Her plan was to stay out of the way of whoever had the power of making major decisions.

"I am sure you have some idea of what goes on. You live in the same building and you have eyes to see," her granddaughter pressed.

"It is your mother's business, you better leave it to your mother to take care of it. You should learn to know your place. It's best for the children to stay out of it," Wong Oi replied, and looked away to dismiss her.

"Old fart!" Her granddaughter muttered and stomped away.

Wong Oi could not believe she would dare talk to her in such an insulting way. She wondered if all American raised children were ignorant of Chinese protocols. She'd had enough of Margaret's insolent behavior and now she had to deal with her own grandchildren. She shook her head and let out a long sigh.

For the next two months, she watched the occupants of the fourth floor come and go. They were busy buying things and hiring men to make up crates to ship them to America. No one bothered to inform her what was going on. Then the activities ceased. Oi Ling came by one afternoon, bright eyed and smiling. Wong Oi had not seen her this excited for years.

"Great grandmother, I am going to America with Mother!" she announced to Wong Oi cheerfully.

"You are what?" Wong Oi became dizzy. She made her great granddaughter repeat what she had just said to help her comprehend what had been spoken.

"I am going to America!" Oi Ling said with her eyes dancing.

Wong Oi held her breath and trembled. Her last link to the world was being taken away from her. She looked away as tears welled up in her eyes.

"Great grandmother, are you all right? You are not happy for me?" Oi Ling asked, looking at her great grandmother intently. "I thought everyone's dream was to go to the Golden Mountain and make a better life for themselves."

"Of course I am happy for you. You are right... young people like yourself should be happy to have a chance to go to the Golden Mountain. I remember how happy I was when your grandfather was able to go with your great grandfather," Wong Oi replied with great effort.

"We are leaving in less than a month. Mother and I are so busy packing. We have to choose what to take and what to leave behind. If you need me to get anything for you before I go just call me. I will make time for you even when mother is being demanding. You know how she is. I don't understand why she is so mean to you at times." For the first time, her great granddaughter expressed knowledge of the friction between her mother and Wong Oi.

"You are a good girl. Just remember what I have taught you and don't become too Americanized like your aunts. Always know your place, do what you are told, and keep the honor of this family." These were the last words she ever spoke to her great granddaughter.

Wong Oi no longer bothered to get out of bed. Her great granddaughter had left with her mother only a few days before and the world had become very strange to her. Nothing seemed familiar. Wong Oi was left in the box of her apartment surrounded by strangers. They had left her with nothing and completely alone. She closed her eyes, and drifted in and out of sleep.

"Oi Ling, I am glad you have come to have lunch with me. I have made some sweet noodles with rice wine for us." Wong Oi was happy to see her great granddaughter. "Sit on your stool. I am going to show you how to knot a button from a strip of cloth."

She opened her eyes and found the apartment empty.

Wong Oi got up, walked over to the window that looked out into the courtyard and shouted, "Oi Ling! Come downstairs! I have a question to ask you." She stopped for a moment and caught herself.

"She isn't here anymore," Wong Oi muttered to herself and sat down on her reclining chair. She stared into her tiny kitchen thinking that if she wished hard enough her great granddaughter might materialize.

Wong Oi had not been out of bed for the entire day. She felt exhausted and remembered that she hadn't eaten since dinner the previous day. She got up and walked over to the kitchen to see if she had anything to cook with. After taking a few steps, she suddenly felt weak. She tried to steady herself by holding onto a small table but she slipped and fell to the floor. A sharp pain shot from her back to her legs. Blackness overcame her and she let herself go. Lying on the cold tile floor, Wong Oi went in and out of consciousness. Hours passed. She finally realized that she could not stay like this much longer. Her pain was becoming unbearable. She crawled toward the front door of her apartment, called out for help and fainted again.

When she became conscious, Wong Oi found herself in her own bed. A tenant had heard her and summoned others to help. They called for a doctor and were told that her hip was broken. The tenants tried to contact any nearby relative to come take care of her. Wong Oi felt relaxed in spite of her pain. She hoped someone might come back from America and looked forward to seeing who would show up.

"On Yun, I am here to help you."

Wong Oi heard a familiar voice and opened her eyes eagerly to see who had come to her rescue. Her lips curled in disgust and she quickly turned to face the wall without saying a word. She loathed seeing her husband's concubine standing in front of her bed.

"They told me that you have broken your hip a few hours ago. I came right away. One of the tenants is sending telegrams to your son in Boston and your daughter-in-law in New York to inform them about your condition," the concubine said patiently.

Wong Oi did not respond. She kept her face to the wall, still refusing to acknowledge the concubine's existence.

The concubine turned away and started to clean. When she was done, she went to the market for supplies to cook for Wong Oi and then to the pharmacy to get her medicine.

"On Yun, here is your medicine and I cooked some rice noodles in chicken broth for you. It is better to eat it while it's warm." The concubine put the food and the medicine on a small table beside Wong Oi's bed. Wong Oi did not turn around.

The concubine stepped back a few paces and said, "I will come back tomorrow to take care of your needs. Since you cannot get out of bed, your linen needs to be changed often so expect me early in the morning." She walked out of the apartment and closed the door quietly behind her.

As soon as Wong Oi was sure the concubine was gone she struggled to sit up in bed. The pain was so severe that she perspired from the slightest effort. She quickly took the medicine hoping it would ease the pain and realized it had been days since she had eaten. She picked up the bowl of soup and ate ravenously.

The concubine came to Wong Oi's apartment early the next morning. She found the empty bowl on the small table and remembered the routine they had established in China. She served Wong Oi tea by putting the teacup down next to her, bowing slightly and immediately leaving the room. Later, she came back to collect the empty cup without Wong Oi even casting a glance at her. She now collected the empty bowl and started cooking more food for Wong Oi, cleaned the apartment and then washed the soiled bed linen.

A week later, the letters from America finally came, one from Wong Oi's only remaining son, living in Boston and another one from Choi Kum. The concubine found a tenant to read the letters to Wong Oi. She sat up with great anticipation that one of them would send someone back to Hong Kong to care for her. Both letters came with American dollars folded in between the papers. They said that they were too busy with their businesses in America, could not find time to come visit her and wished Wong Oi would get better soon. Wong Oi was dazed. Her hope that someone would come back to take care of her vanished. She closed her eyes. She did not notice the concubine leaving the apartment. On the table, next to her medicine, the concubine left a bowl of rice with fish and chopped vegetables.

Wong Oi knew it was her fate to die the most horrible death, without her eldest son by her side, or anyone else from her bloodline.

The next morning, the concubine came and found the rice and medicine untouched. She coaxed Wong Oi to eat or at least to take the medicine. Wong Oi faced the wall and did not respond. The concubine finally resigned herself to cleaning the apartment and Wong Oi's dirty linens. Before she left, she put a bowl of freshly made soup and more medicine on the table.

The concubine came every day to find the food and medicine untouched. One morning, she found Wong Oi still facing the wall. The concubine tried to move her to change the bed linen. Wong Oi had waited for her body to cease functioning and slipped quietly away.

GRANDMOTHER

1896–1915
Toisan Province, China

—

1916–1935
Boston, Massachusetts, USA

—

1936–1942
Hong Kong

—

1943–1974
New York City, New York, USA

Congratulations! Lo Yeah, good luck is upon this household. As you have wished, it is a beautiful and healthy girl," the midwife announced breathlessly running from the bedchamber through the garden and into the study where Governor Chan paced the floor waiting for the birth of his eighth child.

When he heard the news, he smiled, stroking his thin beard. He pondered the beauty of the room, the intricately carved shelves filled with volumes of great literature, the antique vases and ivory carvings perfectly placed around the room, fine paintings and calligraphy hanging on silk-lined walls.

In a corner next to the window looking out into the immaculate garden, stood his prized possession – a four-foot tall Ming Dynasty porcelain vase holding a branch of plum blossoms. The vase decorated with a rare crimson glaze was in such perfect proportion, it was said that the temperature of the water it held would remain cool enough in summer to keep tofu fresh for a month, and in winter it was warm enough for plum blossoms to mature into fruit.

At this moment, everything seemed lustrous.

He already had seven sons and had hoped for the opportunity to raise a daughter. He would treasure her and teach her to be a woman of the new age. She would be educated and her feet would not be bound. She would be of the first generation of the liberated women. He was a progressive man of great insight with an ambition to bring change to the world. He knew change must come from within, starting from the family and then spreading to the community and beyond.

He followed the midwife to the bedchamber, where his wife waited in bed with their infant daughter wrapped in a red silk bunting.

"Come meet your daughter. My dear husband, I am grateful to have brought a precious gift to our family." She shifted her weight to allow room for her husband to sit on the bed.

"Don't bother to move, my dear wife. Please do not exert yourself. Allow me to get acquainted with my daughter." He put his hand on her shoulder and turned to look at the infant lying contently next to her mother. He picked up his daughter and looked deeply into her eyes and said, "My dear daughter, welcome to our household. Your name is Choi Kum and you will reside in my heart."

He looked to his wife tenderly and said, "You have brought great joy to this family. Please rest peacefully and I will take care of the great offerings to our ancestors to thank them for our good fortune."

A month later, Governor Chan invited over two hundred friends and relatives for a casual dinner to celebrate the birth of his daughter. Traditionally, families only offered banquets to friends and relatives for the male children when they reached their first month of life. The guests were shocked to find that the "casual dinner" involved catering from all the fine chefs of the village. The dinner took almost three days to prepare. It was unheard of to pay so much attention to the birth of a female child.

Governor Chan's wife was delighted to have a daughter to accompany her on visits to relatives. In the past, her sons got bored quickly while she gossiped with family and demanded to go home after a short while. Choi Kum loved to go with her mother so she could play with her cousins. She appreciated the change of scenery and having female playmates. But she was different from them. Choi Kum ran in and out of the rooms and into the garden where she enjoyed the fragrances of the flowers and the designs of gardens other than her own. Her female cousins generally stayed in their rooms. If they wanted to go out to the garden, they were carried by their servants. Their feet had been bound since they turned four. It was much too painful to stand on the three inch golden lilies.

"I am glad I don't have to do that." Choi Kum winced, watching the maid unravel her cousin's binding cloth to clean her feet and soak them in an herbal solution to reduce the pain. Her toes, except for the big toes were turned under the soles of her feet and her heels were forced towards the insteps so they would be aligned with the ankles. Her heels almost touched the toes.

"You should wish you have feet like mine. Your mother made a big mistake by not having your feet bound." Yim Fong shot a fierce glance at her cousin while her maid gently massaged her feet. "Nobody with any status at all would want a wife who has big feet. Only peasants who need to work don't bind their feet.

My mother told me if I can suffer the pain till my feet stop growing, I will be rewarded by marrying a husband who has higher status." She rolled her eyes, then stared at Choi Kum and said, "And besides, you are learning how to read. Who would want to marry a girl who knows what her husband is reading? I feel sorry for you because you will never find a husband with status."

"I like to read my father's books. I love being in his study. He has so many beautiful things." Choi Kum turned away from the deformed feet and looked into the garden.

"I would never be caught dead in my father's study. Those are men's things. Who wants to walk like a peasant? A girl with proper upbringing is carried by her maid till her feet stop growing. Then she will learn to walk in her lotus gait, like a branch of willow blowing in the wind. That is what a girl should aspire to." Yim Fong looked down, admiring her own shriveled feet and leaned back on a pillow with satisfaction. She looked at Choi Kum and said, "You are so stupid. Well, at least you have one good thing going for you. You do beautiful embroideries and draw fine patterns."

"I like everything the way it is. I trust my parents to do the right things for me," Choi Kum said with confidence.

"Aiya! Go away!" Yim Fong suddenly screamed, pushing the maid away. "Don't touch my feet. You are hurting me. Come back when I call you." The maid scuttled out of the room.

She turned her attention back to her cousin, saying, "That is not what I heard from my parents. They say your parents are extremely stupid to raise a girl doing all boys' things. How are they ever going to marry you off? I worry about you." She glanced at Choi Kum's feet and smiled, satisfied with her own position.

"Stop worrying about me. I'm going to the kitchen and get us some teacakes. We can't wait for your maid to come back from washing that stinking cloth for your feet." Choi Kum ran outside grateful that she didn't have to sit in a room and wait for someone to cater to her every need.

Every morning, as Choi Kum woke up her personal maid, Ah Ying, brought in a basin of warm water for her to wash up with. Ah Ying was only three years older and was sold to the family when Choi Kum had outgrown her nanny at the age of four. Ever since, Ah Ying had taken care of her.

"Your teacher is not coming today," Ah Ying informed Choi Kum while she cleaned the basin and toothbrush. "A few of your brothers are away to the city with your father. He thought it would be a waste of his time to come just for the younger boys and you."

Ah Ying followed Choi Kum to the dresser and waited for her to sit on the chair in front of it so she could comb her hair.

"Mr. Wong is such a bookworm. His glasses make him look so funny, like his eyes are swimming inside them. I wonder if he knows we all call him four eyes Wong," Ah Ying joked. But Choi Kum wasn't listening, she was looking out the large window facing the garden and the morning sun. She delighted in watching and listening to the birds singing on the branches of her favorite plum tree.

Her room was decorated simply, yet elegantly. The table and two chairs across the room were carved from the finest rosewood. The cushions of the chairs were covered with lavender silk. On the other side of the room, the bed was covered with a thick soft comforter with matching pillows and a bed skirt made with the same color silk.

"What would you like to wear today? Your blue jacket with the pattern of bamboo branches or the yellow one with lilies?" Ah Ying asked Choi Kum as she finished combing her hair.

"I want to wear my favorite pink jacket with the gold buttons. I am going to Yim Fong's house with Mother today. She's having a get together with a few girls to play descending spirits with a well-known clairvoyant from our village. She is actually very good and it's a fun game," Choi Kum said as she checked the embroidery on the slippers she was working on. "Maybe you should come with me to visit my cousin."

Ah Ying walked over to the cedar chest and fetched Choi Kum's ensemble for the day. She helped her dress while Choi Kum checked herself in the mirror.

"Shall I set up the stretcher for your embroidery?" Ah Ying looked at the pink chrysanthemums and multicolored butterflies on the white silk satin with admiration. "I love to be with the girls and watch you play. But I don't think your mother will allow me to go. I still have to air out your winter clothes and clean out the chests." She put away the toiletries and started to wipe down the mirror.

"I will ask my mother. You know she usually gives in to my requests. You should have fun once in awhile, too. When you get to Yim Fong's house you can catch up on the gossip with her maids. My mother always enjoys what you tell her afterwards. She said the only way she knows what really goes on in that house is to get the stories from the servants." Satisfied with her embroidery, Choi Kum got up to look for the silk scarf that she'd bring to play the spirit game with.

"Your cousin is fourteen years old and her feet haven't stop growing yet. She hasn't even learned how to walk on them and she is already dreaming about her marriage," Ah Ying said wistfully. She found the scarf and helped Choi Kum thread it through the buttoned closure of her silk jacket.

"Ah Ying," Choi Kum said and let out a sigh, "Yim Fong has nothing better to do. She doesn't even try learning to sew. She doesn't know how to do anything but to look as good as she can for her future husband." Choi Kum checked herself in the mirror one last time before going to meet her mother for breakfast.

"Your cousins always talk behind your back about your big feet and how you learn to read and write. Doing all the wrong things. They bet you will never land a proper husband." Ah Ying stared down at her own feet.

"I trust my father to choose a suitable husband for me. I am Governor Chan's only daughter. Any family would give anything to have Governor Chan's daughter as their daughter-in-law," Choi Kum said matter-of-factly.

"Yes, I envy your position. My fate is without marriage and to serve you for the rest of my life, unless your future husband's family have enough servants and don't need me to stay with you," Ah Ying said, trying to restrain the thin mist of tears in her eyes.

"Ah Ying, cheer up. I trust my father to choose a suitable husband for me. Chances are that they already have enough servants. In that case, my father will marry you off. I think that will happen for sure. I know my father will do the right thing," Choi Kum said reassuringly and put her hand on Ah Ying's shoulder. "Now I am going to ask my mother if I can bring you to my cousin's house."

As the girls walked towards the dining room through the garden, they heard a loud commotion. Just outside of the garden walls, a noisy crowd was passing by. Someone was banging on a gong. The girls climbed onto a stone bench under a window that looked out into the street. They saw a large group of people. Some spit and some threw stones in the direction of the man banging on the gong at the head of the procession. Behind him, there were two other men carrying a pig market basket woven with shaved bamboo. The basket was wrapped with a thick sea grass rope. It hung from a long bamboo stick with each end balanced on the men's shoulders. Through the large holes of the basket, they saw a woman. Her hands and ankles were bound with cotton ropes. She was choking on her own tears.

"Shameless whore!" a man yelled as he threw a stick towards the basket.

"Pig basket is going to the river! Pig basket is going to the river!" a crowd of children chanted, while throwing stones and whatever else they found on the road at her.

"Oh no! It is Ah Wun. The maid from the Jiang family." Ah Ying shook involuntarily and tears ran down her face. "She was having an affair with Mr. Lum next door."

"She knows what the consequences are. She made a bad choice," Choi Kum said coolly. "She should know her place and accept her fate. She went against her fate and this is what she gets."

A woman came forward and spat on Ah Wun's face and said, "Have you no shame? See what you have done? Your family's name is ruined forever. How are your parents going to live out the rest of their lives in this village? You dirty whore, may you stay with the ghosts for a thousand lifetimes."

The people got louder and more stones were thrown at Ah Wun.

Both of the girls knew what was going to happen to her. They watched the angry crowd move toward the riverbank. Ah Wun was to be drowned.

"There you are!" Ah Ying stuck her head out from the doorway of the dining room into the garden. Choi Kum was sitting under the gazebo, engrossed in a novel. She did not bother to look up.

"I have urgent news!" Ah Ying ran to Choi Kum and pulled on her arm.

"I am not interested!" Choi Kum said, annoyed and still didn't look up. Ah Ying sat down next to her, grabbed at the book and said, "I just spoke to your mother's maid in the kitchen. She told me that the matchmaker is coming for tea this afternoon!"

Choi Kum slammed the book shut with her brows raised and said, "The matchmaker is coming today? We better hide behind the screen to hear what she and my father have to say." The girls ran inside the house to the room where the matchmaker would be meeting the governor to find a spot out of sight before her arrival.

Governor Chan sat in the great hall with his wife. The walls, lined with red silk brocade, were sparsely decorated. A large painting of a family ancestor hung on the back wall. A beautiful antique four-paneled screen inlaid with gold and mother-of-pearl was placed in front of a sidewall. Ah Ying and Choi Kum sat on carefully placed chairs behind the screen, their legs folded under them so no one would see their feet from the other side. Oversized windows looked out onto a magnificent garden. The rosewood and marble chairs were covered with red silk cushions. Between every two chairs there were tea stands for guests to put their teacups on.

"It is an honor to be of your service." The matchmaker bowed her head and backed into a chair as the governor waved his hand gesturing her to take a seat. A servant brought them tea and left the room quickly.

"My daughter is approaching the age of marriage. I'd like to know if there are suitable families for me to choose from," the governor said and took a sip of his tea.

"Lo Yeah, as you know," she began, "the judge from the next village is your friend and his son is available. He is well groomed and I am sure he will take over the judgeship one day." The matchmaker kept her head bowed, not daring to look directly at the governor.

"I do not want to match my daughter with anyone who has anything to do with the government. This is the reason why I summoned you to search for someone who is outside of the political circle," the governor said patiently. His wife looked at him and smiled.

Choi Kum looked at Ah Ying and rolled her eyes knowing her father had little patience with people who missed the obvious.

"You mean you are interested in families that have no status? Lo Yeah, are you sure?" the matchmaker asked incredulously, her eyes wide, openly staring at the governor.

"I am looking for families that have good backgrounds but do not hold any titles. I am especially interested in families that have ties to the Golden Mountain," the governor replied and looked critically at this petty and provincial woman.

"Oh, Lo Yeah! Why don't you just come out and tell me in the first place? Aiya! Do I have a perfect match for you!" the matchmaker exclaimed, squinting her eyes and smiling, showing her gold tooth.

"Leung Sing Tai of the next village just came home from the Golden Mountain with his son. He is looking for a suitable wife for him. I heard the son was educated there." The matchmaker picked up her teacup and slurped on the tea loudly, enjoying the moment and continued, "They came home with a fortune. Mr. Leung just built a grand house and purchased land for a big farm. He also opened a fine china store at the market."

"Hmmm, is that so?" The governor raised his brows and glanced at his wife. She smiled and nodded.

"Bring me more information. If I like what I hear about them, I'll negotiate the match," the governor said to the matchmaker, who by now was sitting on the edge of her chair overwhelmed by excitement.

"Yes, Lo Yeah. I will contact the Leung family immediately. Thank you for your trust in me to bring the best possible match to your family." The matchmaker got up and bowed to the governor and left quickly.

Choi Kum and Ah Ying waited for everyone to leave the room. They stretched out their aching legs and looked at each other. "What is my father thinking? Matching me with a merchant's son? I must talk to mother immediately!" Choi Kum said incredulously.

"I don't understand the governor!" Ah Ying, too, was thoroughly puzzled.

Choi Kum ran into her father's study while the governor was reading some of his official documents. She didn't wait for him to greet her. She pulled on his sleeve and said angrily, "Father, mother told me that you have made a match for me with the son of Leung Sing Tai in the next village. He has no title and is only a merchant's son. He also was educated in the Golden Mountain of the Western Barbarians. How could you think he is suitable for me? Why did you agree to the match?" She stared at the governor. Her face flushed and almost started to cry. "I trust you to bring me a good future. This does not look good to me."

The governor put down his paper, looked lovingly into his daughter's eyes and said, "My dear daughter, trust your father to do the best for you. You are my most precious jewel." He held her hand and offered Choi Kum the chair next to him. He stood up and walked over to the bookcases and sighed, "The political wind now is extremely unstable. We have just gone through the Boxer Rebellion and the Kwok Ming Tong is having an uprising. The future of the government is unknown. I am looking for a way out for you." He turned to look at his daughter. "You will have a chance to leave China when the political wind changes. Our family has our roots too deep in this province. We have to honor our position. But you, my dearest, will be married to a family that has a way out."

Choi Kum felt her father's sadness and suddenly realized how sheltered her life had been and how oblivious she was to the outside world. Her whole life had been so carefree. She was bathed in refinements and everyone catered to her every whim. The only change she knew was her impending marriage to a complete stranger.

The Chan Household was busy arranging the newly acquired furniture for the dowry. Everything was neatly displayed in the great hall. Close to a hundred lacquered food boxes were stacked in the dining room in preparation for the wedding day. Ah Ying busily gathered and packed the personal belongings Choi Kum had chosen for her future husband's household.

"Do you think they will need me to be your personal maid when you get there?" Ah Ying asked Choi Kum anxiously as she filled the carved cedar chest with clothes.

"You will find out soon enough. I will come home for the traditional visit three days after the wedding. If they don't need you, you will be told to stay in our house and not go back," Choi Kum said as she put her favorite outfit into the same carved cedar chest Ah Ying was packing.

"I pray that I get to come home and be married off, even if just as a concubine. I don't want to be a servant all of my life. I want to raise children of my own." Ah Ying gazed out into the garden.

Choi Kum pulled at Ah Ying's sleeve to get her attention. "Let's get this done. I still have to put the soles onto the slippers I made for the wedding."

"Are you scared?" Ah Ying asked as she closely watched Choi Kum's reaction.

Choi Kum looked away and said, "Mother always told me that I must accept my fate. If I marry a chicken, I have to follow the chicken. If I marry a dog, I have to follow the dog. I have to do what is expected of me."

The evening before the wedding day, Choi Kum's mother supervised the last details with Ah Ying. Then she sat Choi Kum down, looking deeply into her eyes and said, "Dear daughter, be prepared to live your new life as a member of the Leung family. They have different habits and ways of dealing with everything. Be obedient to your mother-in-law and your husband. You have a charmed life here at home and have been allowed to do what pleased you. It will be different once you are a wife and a daughter-in-law." She held her daughter's hand and looked at her soft, tapered fingers, lingering on them as if she was seeing them for the last time. She continued, "Silence is a virtue; accept your fate and don't fight it. You will have a much easier time when you know how to bend with the wind. You belong to your husband. Do what he tells you, especially in your bedchamber. A happy man makes a happy household."

Choi Kum listened without moving, beginning to understand the immensity of the change to come, beginning the next day.

"Mother, I will miss you and father so very much. All I know is the wonderful life here with the both of you. I don't know if I can be a good daughter-in-law to a stranger," Choi Kum said tearfully.

Her mother squeezed her hand and said, "This is your life's passage. Every girl has to go through it. I have gone through it and look how well I have done. I am sure you will do as well, if not better." She forced a smile and said, "We raised you as a good representative of the Chan family. I have full confidence in you, and you must accept the fact that you are now a member of the Leung family. Mother and father are only your guardians for a very short time. Your life actually begins in your married household. They are your family for the rest of your life."

"But I will never spend time with you and father again," Choi Kum said and started to sob.

"Hush my daughter," her mother said soothingly, rubbing Choi Kum's shoulder to console her. "Remember to accept your fate and don't let your emotions rule you. Life will be much easier if you just surrender to your own fate."

After breakfast the next day, Ah Ying and Choi Kum's mother were busy getting the bride dressed for the wedding. The musicians and helpers for the procession were already in the courtyard. Outside the main gate, the wedding sedan waited for the bride. The servants rushed to get the last of the food into the lacquer boxes. Choi Kum wondered if it was the busyness of the household or the enormity of the change taking place that made her feel so restless and uneasy.

Ah Ying put the red embroidered slippers on her feet. Choi Kum's mother admired them and said, "My dear daughter, I am so proud of you. This is such a fine example of your work. Your new family surely will appreciate that they are getting such a true prize." She held the phoenix crown out to Choi Kum, the wedding headdress that was passed on to her from her great grandmother. She put it on her daughter's head. "How beautiful it looks on you." She stepped back and took a good look at Choi Kum.

"Now you are ready to get into the sedan and be on your way to your new life," she said with tears in her eyes. Ah Ying brought over the red silk that would cover Choi Kum's head until the ceremony began.

"Summon the governor and tell him our daughter is ready," Choi Kum's mother said, gesturing with her hand for Ah Ying to go. Ah Ying ran out of the room as the mother draped the red silk over her daughter's head. As the silk settled over her, Choi Kum realized the world as she knew it had ended. She could see nothing but red in front of her. When her husband lifted it from her face at the wedding, it would be a new world before her. She heard the familiar sound of her father's footsteps.

"My dear daughter, today is your happy day and we will see you in three days when you come home for the traditional visit. I have no doubt that you will find your new family agreeable," Governor Chan said to his daughter happily and admired how beautiful she looked as a bride. Tears streamed down Choi Kum's face. She would miss his gallant voice.

Her mother noticed the slight heaving of her daughter's shoulders. "Choi Kum, stop crying. You have to look good for your new family and your husband. Nobody wants to see red and swollen eyes," she said quietly and took Choi Kum's hand. Ah Ying came over and took the other hand and they led her to the main gate and into the wedding sedan. After Choi Kum was seated, Ah Ying lowered the red silk curtain in front of the sedan and two men in red jackets lifted it onto their shoulders. The musicians started to play and the procession began.

Choi Kum was mesmerized by the rhythmic sounds of the wedding music and the red silk swaying in front of her face. It was as if she was on a mystical journey into another world. She had never been to the village of her new family before. It seemed to take forever to arrive at the front gate of the house. She heard fire crackers popping and cheers from a big crowd. The sedan stopped and someone lifted the curtain. She felt Ah Ying's hands on hers and was led out of the sedan. Then Ah Ying carried Choi Kum on her back into the house and to the wedding chamber.

Ah Ying led Choi Kum to a chair covered with a red silk cushion especially embroidered for the wedding with a pair of gold dragons and phoenixes.

"Do you want some tea? It has been a long journey. I'll go and fetch you some and be right back." Ah Ying scurried out to find the kitchen.

Choi Kum was anxious to see her new environment. She lifted the red silk just enough to take a peek. At a glance, the room was gaudy and ostentatious. An exact replication of how she imagined a peasant with a lot of money would decorate a house. Her heart dropped, disappointed that this family lacked refinement. She let the red silk fall quickly. At that moment, she made a firm commitment to herself to accept her fate as her mother had advised and not to let her emotions rule her. If she started to judge her new family, it would be the beginning of a long, difficult life. She sat back in the chair, surrendering herself to fate, and waited for Ah Ying to come back with the tea.

On the third day after the wedding, Choi Kum went home for the traditional visit with boxes of food and gifts from her husband's family. Ah Ying was told not to go back.

It was strange for Choi Kum to come home as a visitor. The entire household treated her as a guest. She was now a family member of the Leungs. Though her parents greeted her warmly, Choi Kum felt a faint distance from them.

Within a month, Choi Kum got word that her father had matched Ah Ying up with a hard working man in their village. He was poor but would be good to Ah Ying. Choi Kum was pleased that her father had married her off as a proper wife to a poor family rather than as a concubine to a rich man. Ah Ying was almost like a sister and she knew Ah Ying would be very grateful to her father.

Choi Kum found her new life as Hong Kai's wife pleasant enough, as long as she kept her promise to herself that she would do what she was told like a good wife should. Her husband was ambitious. He told her that he was determined to go back to America as soon as possible to make enough money to surpass his father's wealth.

Still getting used to being the wife of a stranger, Choi Kum began preparing for her next voyage to the unknown. Her husband had decided to set sail for the Golden Mountain on the next ship.

Choi Kum had never set foot on a ship before. She shared quarters in the hold with nine other female passengers, while her husband stayed with a group of men in another room. They each occupied a tiny bunk. Choi Kum had never had to share anything with strangers and hated the fact that she had no privacy. Being a young woman of seventeen and from a wealthy family, the other women openly stared at her every move.

For dinner, she met Hong Kai in a big hall with portholes looking out onto the ocean. She noticed the tables were bolted to the floor.

"What is this?" Choi Kum asked, picking up a metal prong on the table.

"Ha! I forgot to warn you. It is a fork! White ghosts eat with this. You can forget about chopsticks on this ship." Hong Kai laughed and picked up his own fork to show his wife how to use it.

She found a knife next to the fork. "They cut their food at the table and not in the kitchen?"

"You'll get used to the barbarian ways soon enough." He looked around to check on the other passengers. "I wonder if anyone here from China is going to Boston. It will be nice to make a few friends."

Choi Kum tried to learn how to use the fork with the beef stew a waiter had already placed in front of her. Staring at the food she was appalled by the grayish color and the nondescript vegetables.

"You just scoop the food up from the plate? There is no bowl to hold the food with," she said to her husband timidly. Hong Kai shoveled the food into his mouth and just nodded. She looked away. She had a lot to learn about the barbarian ways.

Before the food could reach her mouth, it fell right back onto her plate. Choi Kum turned red with embarrassment. She glanced at the next table, then she stabbed a piece of meat with her fork like other diners. She had her first taste of beef stew. After she chewed on it a few times she had to spit it out.

"Ha! Ha! You'll get used to the food soon enough too," Hong Kai said. He swallowed a mouthful of his stew and laughed.

"I never knew beef could be gamy." Choi Kum took a large gulp of water and reached for a cracker.

She watched her husband walk around after dinner striking up conversations with fellow passengers. He had informed her that he would see her in the morning for breakfast. She went back down to the hold.

During the night, the rocking of the ship made Choi Kum a little dizzy. She vaguely heard gagging sounds around her. She sat up and was horrified to see that a few women had vomited all over the floor. Across the room, partially digested food dripped down the wall from the top bunk. She covered her head with the rough wool blanket and prayed that the woman who slept on the top bunk of her bed was not seasick.

On the third day, they passed through a storm. Anything that was not bolted down sloshed from one side of the ship to the other. Choi Kum did not dare get out of her bed. She had joined her fellow roommates. She was weak and sick to her stomach. They lay in the hold for days, like rotting food in the belly of the ship.

By the time they disembarked, Choi Kum could hardly walk and had lost a great deal of weight. She hadn't seen her husband much, but to her surprise, he looked robust and jovial.

The sun was bright and hot as Choi Kum carefully descended the gangway. The noise and dust from the loading and unloading of the passengers and cargoes overwhelmed her. As she set her feet on dry ground, she felt disoriented. The smell of horses and sweat was suffocating. People spoke loudly in a foreign language. Their voices mixed with sounds she had never known, the rattles of horse drawn carts and the clanging bell from a nearby church. Men wore funny hats and western suits like the one she had seen her husband in. Women wore ridiculously big skirts and puffy blouses. They had hats so big that they cast shadows on their faces. Besides their bone structure and height, their gestures were also very exaggerated. Choi Kum felt dwarfed and intimidated by the foreign women who were much bigger than the men in China. She felt light headed and wondered if she could ever get used to being in this place that her husband preferred. She held onto Hong Kai's arm tightly, terrified that she would be lost forever in this foreign land.

By the time they arrived in the city of Boston, Choi Kum was exhausted. She could barely keep up with her husband when they came to the building Hong Kai's brother had rented. Hong Guay had come to Boston a month before and found this location in the heart of the city. The street was paved with cobblestones. It was noisy and crowded with horse drawn carriages and venders with carts full of wares. The brothers planned to open a restaurant on the ground floor and live in the apartment directly above it.

"Welcome! First elder brother and first elder sister-in-law! I hope you both had a good journey," Hong Guay greeted them warmly. "Set down your luggage and let me show you the storefront and the floor plan of our restaurant." When he stepped forward to take their bags, he took a closer look at Choi Kum who stood behind his brother. She looked ill and tired.

"Maybe first elder sister-in-law wishes to take a rest. Shall I take you up to our living quarters first?" He looked to Hong Kai for his approval.

"I am excited about our new venture and want to get started as soon as possible. You can take Choi Kum upstairs and I am going to take a look around." Hong Kai walked toward the back of the store.

Choi Kum was grateful for her brother-in-law's thoughtfulness. She followed him upstairs through a steep stairwell. Hong Guay opened the door and stepped aside to let Choi Kum enter the apartment first. She walked in not knowing what to expect, and was devastated to see what greeted her. The apartment was long and narrow, like the restaurant below, and consisted of three rooms each leading into the other and only separated by a thin wall and a doorway without any doors.

The first room was Hong Guay's. His belongings were strewn everywhere. They stepped around his things to get to the next room. A sheet hung haphazardly across the doorway. Choi Kum followed her brother-in-law, cautiously pulling aside the sheet to peak into the other room, afraid to find it in worse condition. It was empty except for an old rickety bed. The wallpaper was faded and peeling. The floor was encrusted with dirt. There was no window in this middle room since there were buildings on either side of it. The next room was empty and had a large window facing the street. Hardly any light came through the thick layer of grime. She could hear the noises of the street below, the strident voices of people and the clack and clatter of horses and carts.

"Welcome to the Golden Mountain. First elder brother told me that we are going to make our fortune here. He also told me that many people have started with much less than we have and they went home with a ton of money," Hong Guay said hopefully.

"I am glad." Choi Kum forced a half smile and retreated to the room where the old bed was. "If you don't mind I will lie down for a few minutes. I don't feel too well."

"Please rest. I'll check in with you later," Hong Guay said, and went downstairs to find his brother.

Choi Kum crawled into the bed and covered herself with the dusty blanket. As she lay there, she noticed big brown spots all over the ceiling. It must have been old leaks that came through the roof.

She closed her eyes and made no effort to stop the tears that streamed down her face. Father, if you could see your daughter now, would you think you have given her a way out? Why am I here? I am the governor's daughter. I am supposed to be having the best life of anyone in my village. How can I endure this?

She wept bitterly and then remembered her mother's advice. I must take what comes and accept my fate. I have to make the best of the situation. I have to regain my strength and start making this my home. She took a deep breath and fell asleep.

The brothers worked at least eighteen hours a day to get the restaurant ready for business. As they painted the ceilings and papered the walls, Choi Kum would ask them for leftover materials to freshen up the apartment upstairs. She scrubbed the walls and floors as she had learned from watching her servants. She was heartened when she saw the grain of the wood begin to emerge like amber behind the thinning layers of dirt. She washed everything that was washable. She asked her husband to buy her a bolt of fabric so she could sew curtains for the windows and interior doorways.

Choi Kum washed the window facing the street. At least now this room was a little more cheerful. It was clean and sunlight streamed through the new curtain each morning. She had decided to move the bed into this room and was glad for the space between her husband, herself and her brother-in-law.

After several weeks, Choi Kum became puzzled that she remained tired and nauseous after the ocean journey. Soon she noticed her swollen belly and knew she was pregnant. The idea of delivering a baby in a place where she knew no one and did not speak the language made her anxious. She could not rely on her husband because men were usually not good at, or interested in, this sort of thing.

She remembered going to Yim Fong's house for the birth of her brother. Choi Kum's mother had helped the midwife deliver the baby and Choi Kum was allowed to help. She had been in charge of bringing in the basin of warm water and a stack of clean cloths. The midwife spread a thick layer of cloth under the mother and when the baby came out, she cut the umbilical cord with a pair of sharp scissors and tied a knot as close to the baby's body as possible. Then she cleaned the baby off with the warm water and wrapped him in a nice bunting. Choi Kum decided she could do it by herself. It was better than the embarrassment of exposing herself to a foreigner. This decision calmed her. She would tell her husband after dinner that she was expecting their first child.

The restaurant opened for business. Choi Kum had to help in the kitchen throughout the day. She washed dishes, prepared large pots of rice, and cut up meat and vegetables for Hong Guay to cook. Hong Kai was in charge of the front as he spoke fluent English. Choi Kum and his brother did not know the language at all and seldom went into the dining room.

Every morning before the restaurant opened, Choi Kum went down to the dark basement to tend to the sprouting of mung beans. She pulled on the chain that was connected to a single bare bulb. She then put on a pair of big rubber boots and waded through the water that had spilled from the large iron tubs on the floor, each of which held beans in various stages of sprouting. Choi Kum emptied the water from the soaking beans, washed and rinsed them and filled the tubs up with water again. Sprouting beans was the first lesson Hong Kai had taught her about the restaurant business.

One afternoon, Hong Kai came into the kitchen visibly upset.

"A white ghost came in for lunch. Someone told him that I have a wife helping out in the kitchen. He offered me a nickel to let him take a look at the chink woman. I told him that this is a restaurant and not a zoo. He can keep his damn nickel." Hong Kai spit on the floor and said, "When I get enough of what I want from here, I will go back to China to live like a king."

Choi Kum was eight months pregnant and exhausted from the long days of hard work.

"I am very tired. And I need to buy some things for the baby. Do you think you can take me to a shop before we close?" she asked her husband timidly, knowing very well that he would not be happy to hear that she wanted to take any time off work.

"The day is almost over. Just finish up with what you need to do and go upstairs. If you need baby clothes, make some out of the leftover fabric from the curtains. Everything costs money. You should make do with what we have around here. I want to save every penny to take home to China," Hong Kai said, annoyed.

She continued her work and said nothing. Her silence lasted for three days. She worked and tended to household duties, each day retreating further into herself.

Choi Kum was resourceful. She made diapers and a few sets of clothes for the new baby out of soft cotton rice bags from the restaurant. To make a bassinet, she took apart a big laundry basket and lined it with an old blanket. She felt as ready for the birth as possible. Keeping busy somehow helped lessen her anxiety.

"What are you doing?" Choi Kum asked when she saw her husband drilling a hole in the floor at the entrance to their room.

"I am installing a bell so you can stay up here with the baby." He hung a bell on the doorjamb of their room. It was attached to a wire that ran through the floor of the bedroom and out into the ceiling of the kitchen downstairs. "This way, when I need you, I'll just ring the bell. You come down right away and leave the baby here. It should work out well," he said while pushing the wire through the floor. He did not even look at his wife. Choi Kum held back her tears.

"I might need a few days to rest after the birth of our child. I remember my aunt stayed in bed for seven days after her son was born," Choi Kum said, almost inaudibly.

"This is not China! You have work to do. This is the Golden Mountain. Everybody works here. I'll tell you what to do after our child arrives. I should be able to tell by how you look. The restaurant cannot run with only two people. I am not going to close it just for the birth of a baby." Hong Kai gathered his tools and stomped downstairs. Choi Kum retreated back into silence for the rest of the day.

Choi Kum went into labor early in the morning. She cleaned the apartment immediately after the birth of her son. She had been taught that men do not like to see any sign of blood from birth or from menstruation, or anything else relating to women's needs. The only sign of it was that a baby slept in the once empty bassinet.

Choi Kum knew her husband had to do without her for the day and would not be happy about it. She watched him walk into their room while she nursed their newborn child. He looked grumpy.

"Is it a boy or a girl?" he asked nonchalantly.

"It's a boy," Choi Kum replied without looking at her husband.

"I will name him James." He bent down and peered at her closely. "You don't look tired. You can start working in the kitchen tomorrow. Just come downstairs when I ring the bell." He turned to take a look at his son. Choi Kum saw his brother rushing into the room with a plateful of food.

"Congratulations! Do I have a niece or a nephew?" Hong Guay asked earnestly.

"It's a boy," Hong Kai said, and stepped aside so that his brother could take a closer look at the baby.

"What a handsome boy! He looks just like you, first elder brother." Hong Guay turned to Choi Kum and said, "Please eat while the food is still hot. You must be starving. I know giving birth is hard work." He moved a small table next to the bed and set the plate of food on it. Choi Kum was grateful for his thoughtfulness. She hadn't eaten since the evening before.

The baby woke several times during the night. He had a good appetite. By mid morning, Choi Kum was exhausted. The adrenaline from the excitement of dealing with the unknown had finally worn off. She dozed off nursing the baby and was startled by the bell ringing. She decided to finish nursing before she got dressed to go downstairs. It rang every two minutes. As soon as she finished nursing the baby, she put him in the bassinet and rushed downstairs without dressing properly.

"What took you so long? When the bell rings, I expect you to get down here immediately!" Hong Kai said angrily.

Choi Kum tended to her work without replying. She knew life now would be regulated by the sound of that bell. From then on, when it rang, she would stop everything, lock the door to the apartment and rush downstairs.

By now, Choi Kum had seven children, none more than fifteen months apart. She climbed laboriously up the stairs to the apartment after her morning's work in the restaurant. Her entire body ached with the flu. She needed to take her cough medicine. She unlocked and opened the door to the apartment.

The older children were playing cowboys and Indians. One of the boys had taken the hand off the clock, which was shaped like an arrow. He was shooting it at his sisters with a rubber band while they squealed and covered themselves with sheets and towels and threw whatever they could find back at him. The younger boys were playing with a sack of flour on the bed. They had poured water and her cough medicine all over it and told their mother they were making apple pie just like their uncle was baking downstairs.

She sunk to the floor by the door. For the first time in years, she thought about her parents and her brothers' families. Her heart ached for the days she spent with her father in his study, her intimate talks with Ah Ying and her mother's gentle and caring touch. She looked at her hands, wrinkled and white from soaking in water all day, her fingertips chapped and cracked. They once were fine and tapered, prized for their nimbleness in guiding embroidery needles through fine silk and satin to form beautiful images. She started to sob and then quickly stopped herself. She knew if she remembered her life as the daughter of Governor Chan she could not go on with her present life.

She took a deep breath, stood up, gathered herself and mustered all the strength she could to clean the apartment. She had to accept her fate. The children scattered to various parts of the apartment, pretending nothing had happened. Choi Kum kept her eyes on her cleaning and did not say a word.

A few years before, a friend of Hong Guay's had introduced him to opium. He showed Hong Guay how the drug relaxed him after sixteen hour days in his laundry shop. Choi Kum cautioned Hong Guay about the highly addictive drug. She had seen and heard too many cases of ruined lives within her family in China. Hong Guay said that he found it helpful and he would be careful not to take too much of it. But as time went on, he stopped working several hours at a time to tend to his addiction. Eventually, he missed work altogether. Choi Kum watched him slip from being a caring and considerate brother-in-law into a hopeless addict. She felt his hollowness, inside and out. His life was about his next fix. Sometimes he didn't remember her name.

"I have decided that I am ready to go back to China," Hong Kai said to Choi Kum as he pulled the cash out of the drawer at closing. "With what I have saved, we can go back and invest my money in properties. I hear Hong Kong is an up and coming place. Some of my friends have already moved there and bought buildings. My money will have a better chance to appreciate in a city," he said, straightening the dollar bills. "James is fifteen. He will be ready to marry in a few years and we have to find him a wife. He is getting interested in girls and I don't want him running around with white ghosts and half breeds."

Choi Kum had known this time was coming. The restaurant floundered without Hong Guay's energy. She was ready to leave, too. After the restaurant was sold, they headed for Hong Kong with their children.

Choi Kum was surprised when she arrived in Hong Kong. She had expected the city to have some similarity to her village in China but it was more like Boston with a Chinese flavor, tall buildings packed closely together with motorcars rumbling on asphalt paved streets. People spoke Cantonese instead of the dialect from her village. Most women in her position were well coifed and had personal tailors, which made Choi Kum feel provincial.

Once again, she felt displaced, a foreigner in a new land.

As soon as she arrived in Hong Kong, Choi Kum sent word to her relatives to learn about her family in China, anxious to reconnect with them. After a few weeks, which seemed like years to her, one of her nieces finally came to visit.

"Aunt Choi Kum," she began quietly, "I am very sorry to tell you that no one in your family is alive. A few years after you left for the Golden Mountain the communists came and put them through a public trial. They claimed your father was the running dog for the imperial court and executed your entire family. Your brothers and their wives also perished. I am so sorry." Her niece bowed her head and dabbed her eyes with a handkerchief.

Choi Kum was stunned. She stared through the window behind her niece. The hope of reuniting with her family in China had enabled her to withstand the hardships in America. The devastating news left her motionless. Now she understood her father's foresight in marrying her into the Leung family. This was how he had gotten her out of China. But was it worth it to live her life without her family? The world she had longed to re-experience had been taken from her forever.

Again she retreated into silence, this time for weeks. Nothing would penetrate her heart. She had closed it off for good.

Hong Kai bought two buildings in a very desirable location and at an excellent price. The family moved into one of them. They occupied the top floor and the rest of the apartments were rented out. It was expected that people in their position would have servants. Reluctantly, her husband hired a maid and cook. Choi Kum was relieved that she didn't have to work sixteen hours a day but she rarely saw any friends or relatives. Socializing took money and she was never given permission to handle cash. She did not even have a small allowance. Her husband said she had everything she needed and was well provided for. She should be grateful to be served by servants.

In Hong Kong, Choi Kum gave birth to two more children. She relied on her older children to take care of themselves and their younger siblings. She found it much easier not to be involved and buried herself in books to relive some of the pleasant memories of her earlier times when she lived at her father's house. If she did not care about her present life, there would not be any pain.

By this time, Choi Kum's in-laws had fled from the communists and joined them in Hong Kong. They settled on the ground floor of the same building and were invited upstairs to dinner with the family every evening. There was always tension between her mother-in-law and her husband's concubine. Choi Kum removed herself from the situation and stayed out of everybody's way. She hardly spoke and spent as much time as she could in her room, living in a world of fiction.

When James turned nineteen, Choi Kum was surprised to hear from Hong Kai that a matchmaker was coming over to the flat in a few days to show them a possible match for their son.

One afternoon, a woman with hair like dried seaweed came to visit. She wore a gaudy white and blue flower jacket and pants. Before Choi Kum had a chance to sit down next to her husband, the matchmaker had pulled out a package wrapped in wrinkled brown paper and held together by two rubber bands like a cross. She snapped them loose, took out a big stack of photographs of eligible girls, and fanned the pictures out on the table like a deck of playing cards. Choi Kum tried to sit closer to take a look.

The woman's hand swooped down to the table and picked out a photograph. With great exaggeration, she waved it in front of them and said, "This one is not to be missed!" She shoved it under Hong Kai's nose and continued, "She just came back with her family from America and they are WEALTHY! She is the last unmarried daughter of a widow. Her mother will put everything she has into her wedding."

Choi Kum noticed the shine on the matchmaker's lower lip. She knew she was drooling over the fees she would make from both families. Choi Kum watched Hong Kai look at the picture with great interest probably thinking of the significant dowry he would get from her family. "She is pretty," he said. "Did you say she is from America? How perfect! I will take her for my son."

"I don't know if James is ready for marriage," Choi Kum said quietly, "I told him the other day that you are looking for a suitable girl for him to be his wife. He just ran out of the house and did not want to hear about it."

"These American boys, they have no sense of tradition and obligation. I don't care what he wants. I will make sure he understands that it is his duty to do so." Hong Kai looked at the matchmaker and shook his head. Then he turned to his wife and said thoughtfully, "If worse comes to worse, his brother John is seventeen. He is old enough to get married. If I can't talk James into marrying this girl, I will have John marry her. One way or the other, she is going to be my daughter-in-law."

Choi Kum resigned herself to sit back and listen half-heartedly to her husband making plans with the matchmaker for the negotiation of the dowry.

After they received the list of what was coming with the bride, Choi Kum watched in silence as Hong Kai sold their shabby furnishings in preparation for the new furniture that would fill the entire flat.

The prize her husband most anxiously awaited was the one hundred American one-ounce gold coins promised by the bride's mother. Choi Kum found it distasteful of Hong Kai to prance like a rooster, so excited by the mere mention of money. She believed a person with refinement should not be easily impressed by just wealth.

After the arrival of the dowry, everyone was busy arranging the new furnishings and preparing for the wedding. The house was filled with excitement, but Choi Kum remained aloof. She was pregnant again. She felt embarrassed to be at her son's wedding carrying her own child but was thankful that she was only two months along and not yet showing. She didn't tell anyone.

The wedding was a big event. Choi Kum was unwilling to get involved, allowing her husband to make all the decisions. As she accepted the tea from her new daughter-in-law during the ceremony before the banquet, she looked at the young woman and shuddered, knowing this was the beginning of the bride's life in the Leung family. The bride was barely seventeen as she had been when she married.

⋐⋗

Shortly after the birth of her tenth child, Choi Kum's daughter-in-law, Margaret, became pregnant with her first child. At the same time, James landed a job as the chief inspector of the police department, a high position for a young man. Choi Kum had always thought James was her smartest child.

"We are going back to America," Hong Kai announced one evening during dinner, "I want to make more money by investing in New York. A friend told me about the new Chinatown there. It is just starting to bloom and I can still easily buy a couple of buildings."

He turned to James and said, "Since you are settled now with your own family, you can take care of my business here. Collect the rent and send it to me in New York."

James stared at the dishes in front of him, swallowing hard, without saying a word.

Hong Kai turned to his other teenage sons and said, "You are old enough to help out. I'll open a restaurant and all of you will work with me."

The family ate in silence. Choi Kum had just re-acclimated to not working sixteen hours a day. The thought of going back to America almost made her gag on her food.

In America, Choi Kum found herself back to the grindstone. In Hong Kong, she had become used to having servants. Now, she felt suffocated. No longer could she escape into the fictional world of her books. The household demanded her attention. In order to escape the relentless chores, she decided to take a job in a factory assembling clothes with a sewing machine. At least there she could set her own pace. Choi Kum stayed at work as much as possible. She felt uplifted by the freedom of having her own spending money and talking with new friends. She had not experienced such feelings since before her marriage. Choi Kum often returned home after dinner. No one seemed to miss her. Hong Kai was busy working in the restaurant with two of their sons. The other children had long ago become accustomed to taking care of themselves and each other.

One evening after work, as Choi Kum was getting ready for bed, her husband walked into the room and sat in front of her. She knew he must have something important to say. He put his hands on his knees, leaned forward and said, "James hasn't been sending the rent money from Hong Kong for almost a year."

"Did you write and ask him why?" Choi Kum asked anxiously. She sensed his annoyance.

"I wrote him numerous times and he's never responded." He looked at his wife and continued, "I'll let the two boys take care of the restaurant. I am going back to Hong Kong and find out what is going on. I will leave next week."

"I hope everything is all right," Choi Kum said. She slipped into bed and covered herself with the comforter. The unknown always unsettled her.

Six months went by. Life went on as usual. Choi Kum had not heard from her husband since he sent a letter to her the first week he had arrived in Hong Kong. He told her that he was straightening out the business with James. She did not bother to find out what was delaying his return. She enjoyed her freedom.

After a year had passed and Choi Kum had not heard from her husband, she became curious about what went on in Hong Kong. She was aware of her sons' waning interest in running the restaurant by themselves. They had expressed to her that they wanted to get into other ventures on their own.

When Hong Kai had been gone for two years, Choi Kum suspected her husband was having an affair. It was unlikely that he would tolerate living a celibate life as he had been extremely demanding in the bedroom. Yet, Hong Kai was a well-known man in the community and she would have heard about an affair but there was absolutely no gossip on her husband. She decided to write him, inquiring about his return but she received no reply to numerous letters. Not until his sons wrote Hong Kai that they were quitting the restaurant did he return to New York.

Within a month, he came home with James' oldest daughter.

"Margaret has asked me to bring her daughter here to get an American education. She'll stay with you. I am going back to Hong Kong in about two weeks," Hong Kai said to Choi Kum as soon as he came into the apartment.

"Why are you going back to Hong Kong? Your business is here and all of your children are here except James."

"I want to retire. I am tired of working," Hong Kai said, sitting down and leaning back on his chair. "You are fine here with the children. They can help you out if you need it. I want to take care of the business in Hong Kong and I like living there. I finally have enough investments for them to make money on their own," he said thoughtfully and looked directly at his wife. "You stay here and keep an eye on the properties and I will take care of the ones in Hong Kong."

Choi Kum felt weak. She reached for the nearest chair gasping for breath. She thought the purpose of working so hard most of her life was to retire in Hong Kong and live a comfortable life as a wealthy woman, to have a leisurely lifestyle and to be served by servants. At least that was what her husband had told her when she was putting in sixteen to eighteen hours a day in the restaurant. The thought of living in America by herself with her children was not acceptable to her. She could put up with almost anything from her husband but this betrayal was too devastating. Normally Choi Kum would not say a word but she could not see herself being abandoned with her children in this foreign country.

"I want to live in Hong Kong, too. I would like to go with you," she said firmly.

"No!" Hong Kai snapped and stared at her fiercely. That was the end of the conversation. He left for Hong Kong two weeks later.

Choi Kum quit her job as an assembler for a clothing manufacturer. She went back to her books, the fictional world she could live in and not have to face her own life. She spoke even less and retreated more deeply into herself. The world beyond her apartment existed, but she only ventured into it to shop for necessities. She read or sewed new clothes for herself, the two activities she most loved as a girl living at home with her parents, but the books she read now were not classical literature and the materials she used for her clothes were not fine silk and satin.

Two years passed.

Choi Kum did not hear from her husband and didn't bother to write him. She lived with her two unmarried daughters and her granddaughter in the apartment. They took care of the household chores. She saw her other children on Sundays. Her daily routine was to take a nap, sew or read. She found it a tolerable life. Most people told her that she had a good life. From the outside, she had successful children, a wealthy husband and a life of leisure. No one knew that her husband had abandoned her and her isolation was almost too much to bear.

"A telegram from Hong Kong," her daughter said to Choi Kum one morning before she went to work.

"What does it say?" Choi Kum asked without interest.

"Father passed away yesterday!" her daughter cried.

"Tell your sister to pack and we will go back to Hong Kong tomorrow to arrange for the funeral," Choi Kum said quietly.

The minute she set foot in the flat in Hong Kong, Choi Kum surveyed the situation. The sight of James horrified her. He was a skin-covered skeleton, nodding away in his room in a heroin-induced stupor. Obviously, his wife did not share this room with him. The grandchildren occupied a large room next to the living room. Her husband's bedroom was cleared out ready for her to move into.

At the end of the apartment near the kitchen, she saw Margaret's belongings and her clothing piled haphazardly in a tiny room where the maid used to stay. A cold chill ran down her back. Her husband's mistress was her daughter-in-law! She was frozen by the realization of this truth. Never had she felt so alone. She was the only survivor of her family and now the total betrayal by her husband and his family knocked her further into emotional numbness. She turned her head and walked away.

After the funeral, Choi Kum felt relieved. She had hoped the ache in her body would be buried with her husband. She decided to make up for what she had missed and went on a shopping spree spending thousands of dollars on fine jade and gold jewelry, intricate ivory carvings, antique vases, porcelain figurines, cedar chests and beautiful handicrafts from Mainland China. She shopped in a frenzy, intoxicated by her new freedom.

James' third daughter was strong and always willing to please. She took on the task of dyeing and setting Choi Kum's hair, shining her shoes and carrying packages for her when they shopped together.

"Your father was the smartest one. If he hadn't gotten hooked on the white powder he would have been a big shot by now. Maybe the chief of police or something, and he would be able to provide for his mother the best life any woman could wish for. I would be living in Hong Kong in style and never have to go back to America," Choi Kum said to her granddaughter while they shopped, as if talking to herself. She bought crates and crates of goods to be shipped to New York. Despite the sad occasion of the funeral Choi Kum was having one of the best times of her life.

Choi Kum hardly spoke to her daughter-in-law. She knew her coldness would send the message that she knew what had gone on between her husband and Margaret.

Barely three weeks after Hong Kai's funeral, James was sent to the hospital. He could no longer sustain his feeble body from the long exposure to the toxicity of heroin. He died quietly. Choi Kum knew it had just been a matter of time, but nonetheless, it was devastating to bury her own child.

Choi Kum took Margaret's second daughter back to New York for an American education with her own two daughters. She had decided to make America her home and to be with her children. She left Margaret with her two younger daughters to take care of Hong Kai's mother and the rentals in Hong Kong.

A few weeks after they'd returned, the crates arrived in New York. Choi Kum was excited to get everything out and begin beautifying her environment. She opened the first crate of ivory carvings, porcelain vases, and figurines, looking around the apartment for a place to display them. Instead of the red silk brocade walls and fine carved rosewood furniture of her childhood home, the walls of the apartment were painted with a shiny coat of cheap apple green paint. Their ancient couch was draped with a homemade checkered cover she had made a few years before, its legs digging into the worn linoleum. She looked out the window of her apartment and was greeted by the gray façade and windows from another building across the courtyard. The birds singing on her beloved plum tree with streams of sunlight shining through were irretrievable.

She put the lid back onto the crate, went into her room and began to read. She no longer desired to chase the life she had longed for and which had eluded her: to be the wealthy woman who lived a proper life like her mother, a woman with stature and dignity, admired by the members of her community.

When her children came to visit the following Sunday, she gave them everything. From that moment, Choi Kum never allowed herself to go beyond her books and the apartment. She had finally accepted her fate and no longer hoped for anything else.

Choi Kum had left Margaret to collect the rent in Hong Kong and send it on to New York. For two years, the rent money arrived like clockwork on the tenth day of each month. By the third year, it started to arrive late and sometimes rent payments were skipped for several months. Eventually, it stopped coming altogether. Choi Kum also heard a rumor about Margaret having a highly visible affair with an herbalist. Choi Kum did not want to deal with it. Everything was going well in New York. Her children were taking care of business and she did not need to attend to anything.

"Your mother is a whore and you are no different. If you ever come home pregnant you better go kill yourself," one of Choi Kum's daughters said and spat in the sink, sneering at Margaret's eldest daughter who was washing dishes.

"We won't tolerate having our names dragged through the mud. We have already had enough of your mother's dirt. Your whole family has no shame," Choi Kum's other daughter chimed in.

"Mother, you have to go back to Hong Kong and put a stop to Margaret's stealing our money," she exclaimed, turning to Choi Kum. "She is pouring it away and we're tired of hearing rumors about her disgusting affair with that damn herbalist!"

"If you are not going to do it, we will make arrangements for the three of us to settle the business with Margaret," her other daughter insisted.

After several months of their nagging, Choi Kum reluctantly agreed.

"What happened to the rent money?" Choi Kum asked Margaret the day she arrived in Hong Kong.

"I lost it," Margaret said with her head bowed.

"How did you lose it? Mr. Wong told me that you borrowed money from him because your wallet was stolen. I also heard from friends that you have incurred a large debt by borrowing from them throughout the years. How do you explain that?" Choi Kum asked coolly.

Margaret said nothing, fixing her gaze on the floor. Choi Kum looked at Margaret's sheepish expression. She had no stomach to go through pursuing the truth and exposing the dirty business. As long as her daughter-in-law knew that her time for playing and using her had ended, she would be satisfied. She decided to pay off Margaret's debts. To keep her out of trouble, she would send Margaret and her remaining daughters to New York.

She took Margaret's youngest daughter with her on an airplane. Margaret and her third daughter would travel by ship the following month after they'd rented out the flat and crated all their belongings.

"Hong Kai's mother passed away two weeks after you left Hong Kong," Choi Kum said to Margaret when she and her daughter arrived at the apartment in New York.

"We waited all this time for her to die. She was fine and as soon as we left she decided to go. What a terrible life she chose to live and then to go without any kin at her side. She must have owed some big debt in her previous lifetime," Margaret replied.

Choi Kum did not say anything. She had no interest in her mother-in-law's fate. She felt that Wong Oi had sided with her son in abandoning her in America. She felt Wong Oi should have talked to her son and put a stop to the sordid affair between Hong Kai and Margaret. Instead, she chose to condone his action by looking the other way. She felt Wong Oi deserved what she got.

On her seventieth birthday, Choi Kum's children arranged an elaborate banquet to celebrate. She was delighted to see everyone together in the restaurant. There were well over a hundred members of the immediate family, her children and their spouses and the grandchildren with their spouses. It was a happy occasion and she felt some contentment mix with her pervasive sadness.

She had already buried three of her children. James had withered away with his addiction. One daughter died when her ship sank while traveling to Southeast Asia during the war, and another daughter died of colon cancer. She missed them greatly whenever all of her remaining children were present.

A few weeks later, she asked one of her sons to accompany her to Hong Kong to sell off the rest of the properties. She gave all the money from the proceeds of the sale to her children to be divided among them equally.

While she was in Hong Kong, she went to a fabric shop famous for their fine silks from China. She came across a beautiful silk brocade of midnight blue that had small patterns of pale pink peonies and yellow chrysanthemums with tiny green leaves. Her heart stirred. It immediately brought back the memory of the outfits she wore on her wedding day. How appropriate for her to pick this pattern for her funeral robe, her outfit for another life of the unknown. She bought enough of the fabric to make a skirt and a jacket for her last journey.

During a Sunday visit with her children and grandchildren, Margaret's third daughter, Oi Ling, announced that she was going to London to pursue a master's degree in art. She would be the first one in her generation to pursue a higher education. Choi Kum was dismayed.

"You should not seek more education. I know from experience when you are over educated your expectations will be too high and no man will seem good enough for you. Most men don't want a woman who is smarter than they are." Choi Kum sat on her sofa, looking at her granddaughter while shaking her head. "And look at your shoes, these four inches heels make you look like a piece of tall bamboo! You are already as tall as most Chinese men without them. Get rid of those shoes. Don't be like your aunt who is too choosy and still not married."

Her granddaughter, sitting on a low stool, smiled broadly, looked up to her and said, "Grandmother, I thought being smart is good."

"Being smart for a boy is good. Being too smart for a girl just creates a hard life. It will be difficult for you to accept your fate if you have too many options. Be a good girl, get married and have a family." Choi Kum tried to be patient with this young girl.

"Yes, grandmother. I will when I come back with my master's degree," her granddaughter said and smiled again.

At this moment, Choi Kum knew that her granddaughter was just too ambitious. She was too inexperienced to know most men wanted a wife who would follow orders. She shook her head and sighed.

"I heard mice squealing all night behind the walls," Choi Kum said to her only unmarried daughter.

"I heard them too. They kept me from sleeping. We should get an exterminator because I really need to sleep on work days."

Choi Kum looked at her daughter's exhausted face, "Don't worry, they will be quiet soon."

"Don't throw away any of my things. You will find my final writings in the safe and my skirt and jacket in the closet," she said softly.

"What? What are you talking about?" her daughter asked exasperated. She turned away, walked toward the door and left for work.

A week later, Choi Kum didn't feel well and went to see her doctor. He asked how old she was. She told him that she was seventy-eight. The doctor said there was nothing he could do about her condition. At her age, she had to accept ailments as part of her life.

The next evening, Choi Kum took some over the counter Chinese remedies to calm her system and went to bed. As she waited for sleep, she felt a sense of detachment and relief. She felt light and knew her time had come. She had no desire to have any of her children witness her passing. She wanted this moment to be as private as the inner world she had never shared with anyone.

MOTHER

❧

1924-1935
Braddock, Pa, U.S.A.

⸺

1935-1965
Hong Kong

⸺

1965-1979
New York City, N.Y., U.S.A.

⸺

1979-1994
Adrian, Mi. and Los Angeles, Ca., U.S.A.

t's a girl," the midwife spat out with disgust. She walked down the stairs huffing, wiping her hands vigorously with a thick towel as if to wipe off some trace of contamination. Her heavy footsteps echoed angrily down the dim hallway. With her bag under her right arm, she used her left arm to brush back the mousy brown hair matted to her sweaty forehead, careful not to touch her face with her hand.

"I wish I didn't need the money, so I wouldn't have to take this damn job," the midwife muttered to herself. She walked toward the smiling father and threw the towel into a large basket full of dirty laundry. She looked toward the door and extended her palm saying, "Give me my fee and I'll be on my way."

The father bowed slightly and reached into his pocket. He pulled out a roll of bills and carefully counted the correct amount for the midwife.

As he handed the money to her, he bowed slightly and said, "My lucky day today. Thank you for your help in bringing this gift from heaven to my household."

The midwife pressed her thin lips tight, narrowed her steel blue eyes, glanced at the money and then the father. She cautiously picked the money from his hands, stuffed it into her purse and walked quickly toward the front door of the laundry shop without saying a word. The father followed her quietly to the door. As soon as she was outside, he closed and locked the door, hurrying upstairs to greet his new daughter.

To come to America, Mah Wah had paid a handsome fee for his American citizenship papers in China. He had been lucky that men of greater means had not known about the available papers for sale. At the time, most immigrants to America acquired a common laborer's paper which allowed for a single male, or, if one was lucky, a father and a son. Mah Wah's merchant paper included a wife and a son. Even so, it was rare for a woman under any circumstance to accompany a man on the voyage across the sea to the Golden Mountain.

Mah Wah and his wife were in their early forties and had five children. Lim Fung, their youngest child and only son, was nine years old. Each of Lim Fung's four sisters were married. Three of them already had children of their own. The Wahs left their daughters behind in China. Once they were married, they belonged to their husbands' families and had little more to do with their parents. Mah Wah's hope was to build a better life for his wife and son in the Golden Mountain.

They opened a laundry business in a small town outside of Pittsburgh, Pennsylvania and enrolled their son in the local school. Every Sunday they visited Chinatown in Pittsburgh to catch up on the news of their friends and relatives in China and to bring home Chinese supplies. The few stores were small and crowded. Baskets full of kitchen utensils, dry vegetables, herbs and spices crammed the front of a restaurant. People lingered to gossip after their meals, grateful to have a day to re-connect with their homeland. Thus, the Wahs settled into the routine of a new life in America.

After school, Lim Fung helped out by sorting laundry. Mah Wah lifted and dumped heavy baskets of dirty laundry into the wash while his wife ironed and folded clothes and linens. The work was laborious, but it was a steady income during an unstable time. Their family came from a farming community in the south of China. Revolutionaries and bandits continually robbed farmers and no one knew what would happen next. Mah Wah knew he had been extremely lucky to come to the United States.

By their third year in America, Lim Fung spoke fluent English and excelled in school. Since he spoke the language much better than his father, he now helped out at the front counter after school. As for his mother, she had not learned even a few words of English. She stayed in the back and was never seen. Mah Wah struggled to learn English and managed to get by when his son was in school.

"I don't understand why I am so tired. I hope I am not ill," his wife said one evening while she ironed a stack of handkerchiefs. Mah Wah was packaging orders, preparing them for customers to pick up the next day.

He looked up from his work. "Maybe you should pick up some herbs from the herbalist to boost your energy. You have to take good care of yourself." He put the shirts away and said, "Come sit down. I'll make you some tea. It's time for you to take a rest. Those handkerchiefs can wait till tomorrow."

He went over to the ironing table and took the heavy iron away from his wife. "Don't feed the coal for the iron." He set it down on the thick metal plate at the side of the table. "You should stop for today," he said gently and led his wife to the stool their son used to sort laundry. She sat down and rubbed her legs briskly with her hands as if she could rub the fatigue away. He hurried to the kitchen at the back of the shop and a few minutes later brought his wife a cup of her favorite tea.

She looked up at her husband and said, "I don't understand. At my age it is not likely for me to be with child but it feels like I am. I will see the herbalist on Sunday to make sure that I am not sick."

On Sundays, Chinatown brimmed with families who traveled from neighboring towns on their day off. By the time they got off the streetcar, Mah Wah noticed his wife looked pale. He took her arm and quickly guided her through the crowds toward the Chinese pharmacy where they would find the herbalist. She was dizzied by the buzzing of people congregated in front of the store. Two walls of the small shop were lined with over a hundred small wooden drawers. Each contained herbs imported from China. Dozens of glass jars, crowded on the counter, contained numerous varieties of remedies. Customers waiting to see the busy herbalist occupied the few chairs. Mah Wah asked the proprietor if he could find a small stool for his wife while they waited. The man took a close look at her and quickly went to the back, an area separated from the main shop by a curtain that hung across the width of the room. In a few moments, he motioned Mah Wah to bring his wife into the back. Mah Wah was grateful for his thoughtfulness and helped his wife to the back room.

The room was jammed with boxes of dried goods and herbs. The herbalist sat on a chair next to a small table with a tiny embroidered cushion on top of it. He gestured for her to sit down on the chair opposite him. She lay her hand on the cushion with her palm up. He gently placed his fingers on her wrist, then nodded and asked for her other hand. He felt for her pulse again, smiled and said, "Congratulations! You will be a proud mother in about seven months. I will give you some herbs to ease your morning sickness and please take plenty of rest."

She opened her mouth as if to cry out in disbelief. She felt her husband's hands rubbing her shoulders and remotely heard him say that he was honored to have a gift from heaven.

"What a beautiful child." Mah Wah picked up his daughter from the bed where she rested with her mother. He looked at his wife and said, "Our daughter looks just like you. Since we are in the Golden Mountain, I will give her an American name. We will call her Margaret and her Chinese name will be Mei Yuk, for beautiful jade. My beautiful precious jade."

His wife smiled and said, "She is precious indeed. I am so happy that she has come into our lives."

Her husband put their daughter down next to her and said, "You must be hungry. Let me go down to the kitchen to get you some food and don't worry about a thing. The customers can wait. I will attend to everything with our son. You just take good care of yourself and our daughter." He walked downstairs with lightness in his steps to prepare a meal for his wife.

Lim Fung ran breathlessly upstairs and rushed to the bedside. "Mother, father told me my new sister is here. Let me see her." He pulled excitedly at the folds of the bunting and peered in at the baby.

"Wow! She is so tiny. Don't worry mother. She can trust her big brother to keep her away from harm," he said proudly and looked to his mother brightly.

She smiled, patted him on his head and said, "Your sister is lucky to have you as her big brother."

"Today is a very good day, our family is happy and Margaret brings joy to us all," Mah Wah said as he walked into the room with a tray of food.

"Sit up, my dear wife, eat some food to give yourself strength. I can't wait to tell everybody at our family association in Chinatown next Sunday that Mei Yuk is here." He set the food down on a small table next to the bed and watched her eat heartily.

"Maggie the maggot! Maggie the maggot!" a few boys yelled across the schoolyard, laughing at the small girl walking home from school. She had a slight frame compared to most of her American schoolmates. She knew she looked different from them. Her eyes were almond shaped instead of round. Her skin was darker and her face was wider than theirs. But with her short cropped hair and a nice red wool coat with matching mittens she felt like them all the same.

"My name is Margaret!" the girl yelled back defiantly.

"A Chinese maggot!" the boys called and laughed again.

"Go away and leave me alone!" Margaret cried, but her anger only encouraged the boys. They threw snowballs at her and she started to run. She bent to gather some snow and packed a snowball, turned around and threw it at them. One of the boys packed snow around a small rock so that the teacher nearby wouldn't see it and threw it at Margaret. It hit her in the head. She screamed and fell. The boys scattered in different directions before the teacher could react. Margaret got up, picked up her books from the sidewalk and ran home crying.

"What's wrong! Why are you crying?" Margaret's mother exclaimed. Margaret sobbed louder, threw her books on the floor and ran straight into her mother's arms.

"Let me look at you. Oh my, you have a big bump on your forehead. What happened?" her mother asked and gently rubbed the bump.

"A stupid boy threw a snowball at me with a rock inside it," Margaret sobbed.

"Shhhhh," her mother said, still rubbing Margaret's head. "Everything is going to be fine." She picked her daughter up and cradled her on her lap. "You are home now and mother is going to make your favorite hot cocoa and slice you an apple. Come sit with me while I warm some milk." From experience, her mother knew there was nothing she could do about the incident. As the only Chinese student in his class, her son was also picked on at school.

"As long as you do well in school, you have to let things like that go. These children don't know better and you cannot let them bother you."

"It's not fair! They hurt me. I didn't do anything to them," Margaret protested.

"Sometimes you just have to be the better person. That makes you strong and builds your character." Her mother put a small pan of milk on the stovetop and turned to look at Margaret to emphasize her point.

"That sounds stupid to me. Not fighting back only shows them that I am a weakling," Margaret pouted.

"You don't want this to continue any further. You could get hurt worse the next time. You did the right thing not fighting back. Come eat your apple." Her mother put the sliced apple on the table. Margaret tentatively munched on her favorite snack.

"After you eat, be a good girl and come to the front to help me sort the laundry," she said to change the subject, and to remind Margaret to do her usual chore.

Margaret ate slowly, but soon grew bored and went to join her mother who was ironing. She sat on a small stool and picked out the stiff snotty handkerchiefs and smelly socks from a big pile of dirty laundry.

"This is yucky. These guys are so dirty. I hate sorting their stupid filthy handkerchiefs and socks. I'd rather fold the clean ones and pair the socks up."

"We don't mind them because they are our customers. They won't need us to clean them if they are not dirty. You like your hot cocoa and warm coat in the winter? Our customers give us the money we need to clean their dirty clothes. Be grateful," her mother said.

"Grateful or not, I hate snotty handkerchiefs," Margaret said wrinkling her nose.

"Where is everybody?" Margaret called when she came home from school. The shop was empty and everything appeared untouched since the morning.

"Mother? Father? I am home! Where are you?" she called louder, heading toward their apartment.

"Don't come upstairs!" Lim Fung ran down the stairs and stopped Margaret.

"Why not?" she asked.

Her brother stepped closer to her, held her tight and said, "Father died this morning."

Margaret wrenched free from her brother's hug to look into his face. Tears welled in his eyes.

"No!" she wailed. "He can't do that."

"The people from the funeral home are upstairs. The doctor said a vein in father's brain burst and he died instantly. Mother wants me to keep you here so you don't see father's body. She doesn't want you to be scared."

Margaret curled up on the floor in a pile of dirty laundry and cried.

"Margaret, listen to your brother. Be a good girl. Sit up and get yourself something to eat in the kitchen. I am going back upstairs to help Mother talk to the people about the funeral."

He pulled Margaret up to a sitting position and watched her as she dried her eyes. "I'll be back down soon," he murmured.

Margaret stood up and watched her brother start upstairs. She walked to the kitchen obediently and looked in the icebox to see if there were any leftovers from the day before, but she didn't like her food cold. Her mother usually warmed her food up or cooked her anything she wanted. She listened to the muffled voices and scraping of chairs upstairs. She closed the icebox and turned around to open the cupboard, remembering they'd had her father's favorite apple pie for a late snack the night before. She stared at the half-eaten pie and sat down on the floor and cried.

A month after their father's funeral, Margaret's brother helped their mother negotiate the sale of the laundry business.

"We are going back to China," her mother announced one evening as they closed the store. "Your brother needs to get a wife and I don't want to stay here without your father." She counted the money from the drawer while Margaret locked the front door.

"When are we leaving?" Margaret asked, thinking this was a way to get out of school and away from the bullies.

"Soon, we are waiting for the money from the people who bought our store. Your brother has already reserved a stateroom on a ship for us."

Her mother tidied up the counter and headed for the stairs. Margaret followed, looking forward to the coming adventure.

The long journey on the ship to China did not bother Margaret. Unlike most Chinese passengers who slept on bunks in the hold of the ship, they had a stateroom with a private bath. They took their meals in a dining room with their own table, served by the same waiter daily. The passengers from the hold ate in a large hall and had to share a long table with others.

Margaret loved to sleep in the white linen on her bed. The only time she'd seen bed linen like that was watching her mother iron them for their customers.

"I learned to play shuffleboard on the top deck with a girl named Alice. It was great fun," Margaret said to her mother, popping a sugar cube into her mouth and looking for the waiter to bring her the menu.

The dining room was lined with portholes on both sides and was painted soft green. It was decorated with wall sconces that emitted a glowing amber light. Crisp linen covered each table with perfect settings of fine china and silverware. A vase of frilly white carnations was placed next to the silver containers for condiments. A small plate of butter shaved into curls sat on a silver bowl of ice in the middle of the table. Almost every day, Margaret had her favorite apple pie and ice cream after dinner. She was fascinated by the well-groomed waiters in white jackets and black trousers. They served the passengers politely and with great attention to details. Before Margaret had a chance to think about anything, like magic, the glass was always filled and empty plates were whisked away.

Except during meals, she seldom saw her family. Her brother kept their mother company, for she still did not speak English. Margaret made friends with other Americans on the ship. They played shuffleboard on deck and cards in the library. When alone she'd sit on deck reading magazines and watching the ocean. She stayed away from the Chinese passengers in the hold. Margaret felt superior because she had a stateroom and spoke English.

Margaret did not know what to expect. The voyage on the ship had been exciting. It was her first taste of luxury and she looked forward to more adventures. However, the moment she stepped off the gangway, stifling humid air and the stink of raw fish and vegetables sold by hawkers near the piers nauseated her. The streets by the port were packed with stalls and baskets full of utensils, tools, pots, dried fish, herbs and bolts of cloth. These additional foreign smells bewildered Margaret. All around her were Chinese in country clothing, homemade loose tops with twisted cloth buttons and wide pants with handmade sandals. Margaret had only seen a few people dressed this way in Pittsburgh's Chinatown — the fresh off the boat immigrants who had not yet learned to dress properly. But here everyone dressed the same. They spoke so fast and loud, she had a difficult time understanding what they were saying. For once, Margaret felt out of place. She walked gingerly and held tightly to her brother's hand, afraid of getting lost or stepping on something she would regret. The roads were nothing more than dirt. Rotting produce was strewn all around. She had never seen such a dirty place in her life and how she hated the smell.

"I want to go home!" Margaret screamed. It was their third day in her mother's small house in the village of Dik Hoi.

"This is your home, silly girl. This was our house before we left for the Golden Mountain," her mother said while she rubbed Margaret's back.

"No! This is not my home! My home is in America. I hate this place! I want to go to the bathroom in a toilet and not a stinking hole outside in that windy shed!"

"My feet are always dirty, dirt floors are everywhere and I don't want to share my food with the stupid flies!" Margaret cried.

The house was stifling. The few windows were small and poorly placed so that hardly any air flowed through the house. It was furnished with the bare necessities. A rough hand-made table and four hard wooden stools were placed near the kitchen. On the other side of the room was a row of low stools for visitors. As was the custom, the main room of the house was reserved for important occasions. Red plaques with the names of the ancestors on them were displayed on a table. On major holidays, the family burned incense and candles and made offerings of food and rice wine to their ancestors.

Margaret shared a room with her mother. Her bed was two pieces of hard board balanced on two wooden benches and softened by a thin comforter. The bed was placed barely a foot away from her mother's bed. There wasn't any room for anything else.

"Margaret! Come meet your aunts and cousins," Lim Fung called, urging his sister to join them for tea. Margaret walked slowly into the room thumping loudly on the floor. She pressed her lips tight and refused to make eye contact with anyone.

"Poor girl, she is not used to the climate and the food yet," her mother said apologetically to the relatives.

"Aiya! What a pretty girl," one of her aunts said solicitously, "Come, sit down and have a sweet tea cake I made for you."

Everyone fussed over Margaret. She reluctantly sat down and reached for the plate of sweets. She turned to her brother and asked, "When are we going to leave? I want to go home." Before he had a chance to answer, Margaret noticed the children across the room openly talking and laughing at her funny accent and odd clothes. She stood up, threw the sweet back on the plate and left the room.

One warm evening, Margaret sat inside the house pouting as usual, refusing to join her family outside enjoying the cool evening breeze. She hated the sticky humid air. As she methodically kicked the legs on her chair to vent her frustration, she overheard a conversation between her brother and their mother.

"Mother, I think you should go to Hong Kong. Buy a building with the money you made from the business. Margaret needs to go to school and this is not a place she wants to be," Lim Fung said.

"I thought I came home to stay here for the rest of my life. All I know is this house and your other sisters and their families

are here," his mother replied. She hesitated, and then continued, "But I know Margaret is very unhappy. I have relatives in
Hong Kong and Margaret will have a few cousins her age to go
to school with. Your other four sisters have done without us for
such a long time anyway. I suppose it would be good to get
Margaret to a city and a life she is more used to. She is such a
particular girl and hard to please."

"Let's make arrangements to go to Hong Kong. I am sure
Margaret will be happy to know." Lim Fung said with a sigh
of relief.

Everyone in Hong Kong spoke Cantonese, the official
dialect of the city. Growing up in the United States, Margaret
had been taught Toisanese by her parents, a dialect from their
village in China, but she had never been taught to read Chinese.
She had a difficult time adjusting, especially in school. She came
home with a big stack of books. Each of them had English
transliterations in the margins to give her clues on the sound
and the meaning of the words.

"Jung kwog lig tse," Margaret struggled to read. "History in
China. I hate this!" she screamed in frustration, and threw the
book on the floor.

"Mother, what is the point of me going to school? I hate it,"
Margaret said to her mother one day after school. She sneaked
a look at her mother and added, "You are going to marry me off
soon anyway."

"All of your cousins go to school," her mother replied as she
sliced ginger for the steamed fish she was preparing. "Don't you
want to be with them?"

"I am fifteen, almost old enough to get married! Why do I
have to go to school?" Margaret pressed on, while picking at the
ginger and scallion on the counter.

"As you wish. You should finish up this semester and maybe I really should look into getting a good match for you."

"Take your time mother and make sure you find me a good match," Margaret said and smiled. She sat down and waited for her mother to serve her dinner.

A few months passed, the school year ended. Margaret began to enjoy living in Hong Kong. Her mother had found a tailor to make her Chinese dresses so she would fit in more with the girls her age in Hong Kong. She discovered American romance magazines like True Confessions and ordered several from an exclusive bookstore. When she was not busy visiting her cousins, she pored over her magazines fantasizing about passion and intrigue.

Unlike her cousins, who didn't dare hope for anything more than a happy marriage within their own class, Margaret dreamed of finding real love.

"Don't you think cousin Kwok Sing is good looking? I think you have your eye on him," her cousin Quai Fun teased Margaret at lunch. They had taken their food into a room out of earshot from the adults.

"Speak for yourself. I see how you look at him every time he comes over!" Margaret shot back playfully.

"I saw him touch your hand the other day and you thought no one was watching! I caught you!" Quai Fun laughed.

Margaret turned red and said, "That isn't fair. Let's change the subject."

Her cousin was not going to let her get off so easy. "Hey, no one is here. You can tell me and I'll keep the secret. Do you really like him?"

Margaret glanced at her cousin, smiled shyly and said nothing.

"Oh, I get it! If I am to be a good cousin of yours, I will get out of your way every time he visits. You can count on me being your friend. I like a boy in my class better anyway," Quai Fun said, sipping her tea.

"Really? Tell me more about him!"

Just as Quai Fun began describing the boy, her mother came in to ask if they wanted dessert. The girls gathered their empty bowls and drifted into the dining room where the adults were just starting on bowls of red beans and lotus seeds in syrup.

One morning at breakfast, Margaret's mother told her to change into her best outfit.

"You're going to the salon to get your hair done," she said, serving Margaret a bowl of rice gruel with thin slices of beef. "I have contacted the matchmaker and she will be coming to our house to pick up a photograph of you in a few weeks."

"You have already spoken to a matchmaker? Why can't I pick my own husband like the Americans? I am an American, Mother." Margaret watched her mother's reaction, expecting her to give in to the wishes of her youngest child, as always.

"You are Chinese. Americans are foreigners and don't you forget it. I have to do what a proper mother should. With our status, I must find you the best match available in Hong Kong. I will have no relatives of mine make fun of me," her mother replied sternly. "We are going to the photographer this afternoon," she continued, ignoring her daughter. "He is supposed to be the best in the business."

From the authoritative tone Margaret knew nothing could change her mother's mind. There were customs in her culture that her mother would never forgo. They showed the world where you stood socially and economically. Margaret felt a sudden constriction over her entire body.

Despite her shock at this turn in her life and a future out of her control, Margaret still wanted to be the prettiest girl in the matchmaker's pool of eligible girls. She spent several hours at the hair salon with her hair crimped into waves. A few strands fell softly above her eyebrows. She picked her favorite pale blue silk dress with piping and knotted buttons in the shape of lilies on the collar and down the side. Even the photographer complimented her on how pretty she looked.

"Aiya, what a pretty daughter you have!" said the woman with hair that looked like seaweed. She looked at Margaret's picture, nodding her head in approval and snapping the rubber bands on a small package to open it, exposing a stack of photographs of eligible girls.

Margaret's mother smiled. "I am sure you'll find an appropriate match for my daughter."

The matchmaker slid Margaret's picture into the stack, looked up and said, "Trust me to bring you the perfect match. My ears are specially tuned to families from the Golden Mountain." She pulled on her gaudy outfit of big pink flowers on a green background, to show Margaret's mother that she was a successful woman.

"I will contact you when I find a match." The matchmaker stood up and headed for the door just as Margaret walked in.

"Aiya, is this your daughter?" She stared at Margaret from head to toe, and said, "She is even prettier in person. Good! I will be back soon." She turned back to Margaret's mother, smiled broadly and hastily departed.

"Who is she? She's so rude and ugly," Margaret asked her mother, annoyed.

"A matchmaker. She came to collect your photograph," her mother said while clearing the table of empty teacups.

"Mother, I don't really want to get married. I am only sixteen," Margaret said desperately.

"You will be seventeen in two months, a perfect age for marriage. When I was seventeen, your eldest sister was born. The matchmaker will find a good match for you."

"I can't do this," Margaret cried and stomped her feet like a little girl.

"You better learn to act properly for soon you will be a bride. I won't hear of your nonsense," her mother scolded.

Margaret knew her mother would not give in. Tantrums no longer brought about the desired result. She had to accept the fact that she was going to be married to a stranger. The prospect of an unknown future was frightening. Her only hope was that her future husband would be a good husband, catering to her and possessing looks that matched her prettiness. Most important was the hope that she would find romance like in her stories. She sat down to read her American magazine and resigned herself to hoping for the best.

Two days later, Margaret saw her mother busily rummaging through the dresser trying to find a desirable outfit. It was unusual for her mother to do this on an ordinary day.

"The matchmaker has found a very good family. The boy was born and educated in the Golden Mountain and he came home with his parents." Her mother picked a silk top with matching pants in deep blue. She turned to look at Margaret and continued, "They have two buildings in the better part of the city. A match like this is hard to find. We are meeting the family tomorrow."

Margaret was mortified and called her cousin to tell her the news. Quai Fun assured Margaret that she would find a way to be there for her support.

The future groom's family picked the most exclusive tea parlor in Hong Kong in which to meet Margaret and her mother. In this setting, both families could assess the future bride and groom. At least they would know what the other looked like before their wedding day.

When Quai Fun learned of the date and time, she talked her mother into going to the tea parlor and pretending to be there by coincidence so they could get a good look at Margaret's future husband.

"He is ugly compared to Kwok Sing," Quai Fun blurted out as soon as she saw Margaret.

"Don't tell me that, I am already feeling very bad about this," Margaret replied, tears welling in her eyes.

"I can't help it, he is just not as refined as our side of the family. He has big bones and thick lips. I just don't like the way he looks," her cousin went on.

"Mother is already preparing for the negotiation of the dowry. I have no choice," Margaret said, choking back her tears.

"I feel very sorry for you. I hope I have better luck myself." Quai Fun squeezed Margaret's shoulder in commiseration.

"After your wedding, I am going back to China to live out the rest of my life," her mother informed Margaret. She turned away from her daughter to instruct their relatives who wrapped teacakes and fruits to be distributed to the guests before the wedding.

Margaret stared at her mother in disbelief.

"I have no reason to stay in Hong Kong once you belong to the Leung family," her mother said, still engaged in making sure everything was wrapped correctly.

Margaret couldn't move. She watched her mother supervise her cousins and aunts from her stool.

"What if I want to see you after I get married? You will be so far away!" Margaret cried.

Her mother motioned her to be quiet.

She looked directly at her daughter and said, "Remember this. Once you are married, you belong to your husband's family. You should never wish to come home." She explained that she had put most of her money from the sale of the laundry business into Margaret's dowry. The world would see that her daughter was from a family of good standing. After Margaret's wedding, she would sell her building in Hong Kong and return to China to live a quiet life. She had done her last duty as a mother. Her life was complete.

Margaret knelt in front of her mother and put her head on her lap.

"Mother, I will miss you." Tears filled her eyes as she tugged her mother's sleeves.

Turning away, her mother said, "This is life. When you live as a member of the Leung family, you are no longer a family member of the Mah. That is how life is, accept it."

Margaret was shaken. She had never experienced her mother's coldness. A marriage that she did not even want had completely altered her life. All because of a custom built into the Chinese culture. She could not understand how her world had so quickly shattered.

On the morning of the wedding day, Margaret dressed with the help of her cousins. She sadly watched her mother, already preparing to leave her for China. Soon she would be starting a new life with a stranger in an unknown environment. How she wished she could get out of it. She would gladly go to China with her mother but she knew this was not possible. The car for the newlyweds would arrive at the door any minute.

When she looked at herself in the mirror, she knew it was every girl's dream to wear such a gorgeous wedding gown. Though her cousins thought her future husband ugly, she could see the envy in their eyes that she was marrying into wealth. She studied her reflection, turning and checking herself from head to toe and knew she was a very pretty bride.

She felt a great weight sink through her body. She sighed. Her mother, at least, would be honored when the friends and relatives of her new family took their first look at her.

"Margaret, are you ready? The car is here," Quai Fun yelled from the front room.

"The groom is waiting for you!" another cousin taunted.

She picked up the bouquet of white lilies and ferns. They matched the garlands of flowers on the car and the lapel of the groom's jacket. She took a last glance at her reflection in the mirror, smiled and bravely headed out the door.

The chauffeur held the door open for Margaret and helped her get into the car. The groom, seated in the back seat, looked at her, nodded and stared straight ahead for the rest of their journey to City Hall.

Although Margaret had been nervous and distraught since learning about her marriage a few months before, she had also fantasized about the wonderful romantic life she would have with her new husband, full of passion and unending love, as in the romance stories. She studied the groom from the corners of her eyes. He looked like a wooden puppet, expressionless and remote. She hoped he would be different once they were in the privacy of their room and not on display.

It was a long and exhausting day. By the time the bride and groom got back to their room in his parents' flat, it was past midnight. Margaret changed into a pair of pink silk satin pajamas embroidered with red peonies, which matched the canopy, pillowcases, bed skirt, the silk comforter and the curtains that her mother had sent as part of her dowry. She sat on the bed with her head bowed as her husband undressed. He came over to the bed and motioned her to get under the comforter.

A little later, Margaret sat up in bed, turned to face the wall and said to her husband angrily, "You hurt me! This is not what it is supposed to be. You should be thoughtful and caring. I hate this!"

"I hate this as much as you do, so let's just get on with it the best we can under the circumstances. I was just starting to have some fun since coming to Hong Kong and now my parents got me into this with you," James said, speaking to her as her husband for the first time.

"I wish I was going to China with my mother." Margaret glanced at her husband, and pouted like a little girl.

"Don't I wish," James said and turned to face the window.

Margaret was furious. How dare he find her undesirable! She bounced back on the bed to slam her head on the pillow and yanked the comforter past her shoulders, hoping her husband would offer her a few words of comfort but James didn't respond. Soon, he started to snore. Tears rolled down Margaret's face. How she wished she could go back to the laundry shop. There was nothing she could do. She had to find a way to make her life in this family bearable.

It was customary for well-to-do married women to have their hair and nails done in a salon, take afternoon tea with female friends at a British restaurant and play a few games of mahjong. Since Margaret did not find romance with her husband, she adopted this lifestyle and shared her good fortune with cousins and friends.

Time passed, Margaret now had two daughters who were cared for by a nanny and she settled into the life of the privileged class.

"My in-laws are going back to the Golden Mountain," Margaret said to her cousin Sui Ping during tea at her favorite restaurant, The Silver Palace. She often met her friends and cousins there to gossip and pass time when James was away. She picked up a cube of sugar with silver tongs and dropped it carefully into her red tea with lemon.

"Your in-laws are going back to the Golden Mountain to obtain more wealth? Aren't they wealthy enough?" Sui Ping asked, stuffing her mouth with a forkful of butter-cream icing.

"No one ever has enough money." Margaret said averting her eyes so she wouldn't have to watch her cousin's provincial behavior. How one acted revealed one's roots.

"I guess not," her cousin mumbled. Margaret was repulsed by the icing clinging to the corners of Sui Ping's mouth.

She looked around to see if any friends were around. Usually Margaret didn't mind being with Sui Ping in public as she made Margaret appear more sophisticated, but today Margaret had little patience. She suspected James of having an affair but it was too early to tell and she didn't want to make an issue out of it before she could confirm it.

"You seem angry. What's wrong?" Sui Ping asked, slurping her tea.

Margaret rolled her eyes and said, "Let's just finish up and go home. I don't want my cake anymore."

"Can I take it home?" her cousin asked, eyeing the cake, oblivious of Margaret's annoyance.

"As you wish." Margaret waved to the waiter for the bill. She graciously paid it and walked toward the door without looking at her cousin.

Before James' parents left for America, they gave him the responsibility of collecting rent from their two buildings and sending the proceeds to them in New York. He also obtained a job with the Hong Kong police as a chief inspector. Wealthy, tall, and well groomed, he was one of the very few men in Hong Kong who drove a big American car. He was seen as a man of the world. Although married, women threw themselves at him wherever he went. He loved his position and openly enjoyed the adulation of women. Margaret watched with disgust.

As soon as his parents left, James started to stay out through the night.

One day, Margaret confronted her husband when James made to leave the house again. "Where are you going? Don't tell me that you have official business at the station again. When we are out I see how you flirt with all those women."

"Why pretend anymore? You have known this for a long time. A man in my position has his privileges. When women throw themselves at me, I might as well take advantage of it," James said matter-of-factly.

"I forbid this. You can't just openly sleep around with those women." Margaret's shrill voice filled the flat, "I am your wife! You should have some respect for me."

"Ha, this is China. My grandmother is living in the same building with my grandfather and his concubine. You should feel lucky that I don't bring them home!" James mocked, and headed for the door.

"I hate you! I hate this family! I hate my life here. I wish I never married you in the first place," Margaret wailed and ran into the bedroom.

"I feel the same," James said nonchalantly and walked out, slamming the door. He began to stay away from home for several days at a time.

In time, James no longer came home on a regular basis. Margaret accepted her role as the wife of a well-to-do man of a Chinese family. She bought expensive American clothing and shoes for herself and her two daughters, played mahjong with friends and associated herself with the privileged set of neglected women. She kept the cook, the maid and the nanny for herself and her two daughters. She had everything a woman of her status could have asked for, but she was extremely unhappy. Growing up, her parents had doted on her and catered to her every whim. Now, abandoned by her mother and her husband, she felt completely alone. Worst of all, the dream of sharing her life with a loving man had never materialized. Margaret felt herself falling, tumbling into the abyss.

"Margaret, how are you doing? How are your in-laws in New York?" a man in a western suit greeted Margaret while she waited for friends at The Silver Palace.

She looked up, surprised to be greeted by a man. "Mr. Wong?" She vaguely remembered him as one of her father-in-law's friends who had made a fortune in America. He had sold his Chinese restaurant there and returned to China to acquire a wife. They already had three children and had settled in Hong Kong. He had purchased a building just a few doors down from Margaret's flat.

"My in-laws are doing well. And how are your wife and children?" Margaret asked cordially.

"You should come over to visit. My wife took the children back to China to visit her family. Her mother is not well." Mr. Wong took a step closer and said sincerely, "Since we live so close by, you really should come over. It is quiet there and my family will be gone for months. It would be good to have someone to talk to."

A tinge of loneliness came over Margaret. "I know what you mean. It is nice to have someone to talk to," she replied. It would be a change of pace to socialize with a man, especially a man from America. He might be sympathetic to her situation.

"Maybe I will visit in a couple of days. Is that ok with you?" Margaret asked.

"I am delighted! Of course! How about ten o'clock in the morning on Tuesday? Come over and have tea with me," he said enthusiastically.

Margaret noted his pleasure and felt flattered.

"Yes, that would be fine. I'll see you on Tuesday at ten o'clock," she said casually and stood to greet her friends who had just arrived.

Mr. Wong was from America. None of Margaret's female friends could share that experience with her. She dressed as usual in the morning and looked forward to spending time with an American friend.

She walked up the stairs to his building and rang the doorbell. A maid dressed in a white jacket and black trousers opened the door. A faint scent of cologne wafted over Margaret. Chinese men did not customarily wear cologne. It was more a custom of the American male. Until now, she had only smelled it on James.

The maid led her into the living room, which was decorated with an overstuffed brown leather sofa and chairs, grouped around a mahogany coffee table. On the table, steam from a fragrant tea wafted up from two cups and saucers made of bone china. Next to them, a crystal vase held a dozen freshly cut red roses, Margaret's favorite flower. She appreciated the elegance of the décor. It was rare to encounter Western style furnishings in Hong Kong.

"Margaret, welcome. I am so glad to see you. Please sit down and have some tea," Mr. Wong said, extending his hand and coming forward to greet her. Margaret admired his dark olive-green suit and the pale yellow shirt with gold cufflinks.

The maid disappeared into the back room. The scent of cologne became more pronounced. Margaret smiled and sat down on the sofa. She let her hand glide over the buttery leather. These trappings of American culture made her realize how much she missed the freedom of life in the United States. She felt that Mr. Wong would understand her and soon began to describe her grievances and despair. He listened with intense interest.

"I wonder if I could have stayed in America and married someone I had chosen, would life be different? James is such a womanizer, he doesn't even bother to come home anymore,"

Margaret complained, staring out onto the balcony, wishing that she hadn't married her husband.

"Margaret, you poor thing. James is absolutely in the wrong. What can we do about it?" Mr. Wong asked, taking one of Margaret's hands in his and wrapping his other arm around her shoulders.

Margaret was taken aback. She looked away, wondering if she should leave. It didn't take long to decide. She would seek this opportunity to even the score with her husband. Margaret waited, anticipating Mr. Wong's next move.

Encouraged by her stillness, he kissed her neck and cheek, and then her lips. She responded and he promptly pulled her up from the sofa and led her into his bedroom.

Margaret walked into Mr. Wong's building in broad daylight, not caring if anyone noticed, hoping someone would tell James. She wanted him to know that she too was desirable.

After James came home to visit one day, Margaret noticed her ruby necklace and bracelet were missing. She soon realized that every time James visited, another valuable piece of jewelry would be gone.

Margaret waited for him to show up one evening.

"I want you to stop taking my jewelry and giving it away to your whores," she began before she noticed James' glassy-eyed look and tremendous weight loss.

"What has happened to you?" Margaret looked at him more carefully. James did not say a word and rummaged through the drawers of their dresser, looking for something of value.

"What are you doing?" Margaret pressed.

James did not answer. He opened Margaret's purse and took out all the money she had in it and left without saying a word.

Nearly a year passed when Margaret got word that her father-in-law was returning to Hong Kong. She made sure the house was in order and prepared for his arrival.

Mr. Wong also knew that his friend Hong Kai was coming home. Margaret and he both understood the unspoken rules of the culture. When the cat appears, the mice disappear into the walls. They stopped seeing each other without a word between them. James had not been home for quite awhile and Margaret had no way of contacting him, nor did she wish to. She wanted her father-in-law to see her situation and hoped he would be sympathetic. But she also knew she could get into serious trouble if he found out about her affair, and that her lover was one of his friends. Hong Kai was a prominent member in his community in Hong Kong and New York. He had a wide circle of business associates. Most people knew of him if they didn't know him personally and the family name was not to be tampered with.

Margaret had some idea what the consequences might be and she didn't want to face any of them. Not long ago, women were drowned for having affairs with married men. She could become an outcast, perhaps be sent back to her mother in China, and branded for the rest of her life as an adulteress. Margaret had learned to enjoy her life in Hong Kong and could not imagine living under the conditions she had experienced in China, particularly as an outcast. If she remained on her best behavior and strove to please her father-in-law, she hoped to escape with only his wrath.

As soon as Hong Kai set his foot in the flat, Margaret greeted him sweetly. "Lo Yeah, you must be tired. It is such a long journey. I will tell the cook to prepare dinner early today and I will draw your bath for you while you rest."

He smiled and said, "Margaret, it is good to see you. I am tired," he walked toward his room. Margaret followed him and quickly pulled up a chair with a soft cushion.

"Please sit down and rest. I will give you a shoulder rub before drawing your bath." She already had a hand on his shoulder as he began to sit.

"Sure is nice to be taken care of," Hong Kai murmured, and stretched out his legs and closed his eyes.

Margaret knew Hong Kai had learned of her affair. But whenever he prepared to question her, she either began massaging his shoulders or attending to him in some other way.

As time went on, Hong Kai became accustomed to Margaret's willingness to please. One evening after dinner, while the children played in their room, Hong Kai and Margaret were alone on the roof catching a cool breeze. He sat on his favorite white canvas lounge chair with Margaret sitting close to him. As always, Margaret reached over to give him a soothing massage on his hand. Hong Kai suddenly withdrew his hand, grabbing hers to put on his erect penis. Margaret was taken aback. She stood up and pretended she needed to attend to her children and ran downstairs.

Hong Kai was relentless. Every chance he had, he pursued Margaret. Eventually, she gave in. Margaret shared her father-in-law's bed with him after the children went to sleep.

James walked into the flat while the family was having dinner. Hong Kai put his chopsticks down and said, "You have not been home for the three months I've been back. Is this how you take care of my business and your family?" He looked at his son critically.

"I have another household," James responded immediately, as this was the most acceptable reason for him not to be home.

"My grandson is a successful man," Wong Oi said. She looked at her son and set her rice bowl on the table trying to defuse the tension.

"I heard all about that from everyone around here. That does not explain the missing rent money and the way you look." Hong Kai was determined to press the issue. "You look terrible. What have you been taking? You better not go your uncle's route!"

Margaret watched in silence.

James turned away and walked toward his room. Within a few minutes, he emerged, hands jammed into his trouser pockets, and hurriedly left the flat. He brushed by his father, not giving him a chance to confront him again.

After dinner, Margaret approached Hong Kai while he was having a cigarette in his room.

"For more than a year he has been taking my jewelry and money every time he comes home. I don't have anything of value left," she cried.

"He is addicted to some kind of drug. This is a sad situation." Hong Kai shook his head and took Margaret's hand, squeezing it gently. Margaret knew the issue of her affair was safely forgotten.

For a time, James began to come home at night. Margaret resumed her position as his wife. He continued his claim that the reason he was away was another household, which was partially true. He had two children with one of his regular mistresses. Margaret was now pregnant with her third child.

One evening during dinner, Margaret's grandmother-in-law said, "I heard my grandson has two boys from another household. Why don't we bring the woman home with the boys to live in this house as his concubine?" She slurped the last of her winter melon soup and looked at Margaret, "Since his wife has only two girls, it would be a great opportunity to legitimize the male heirs."

"I will have no whore coming into my house to share my husband's bed!" Margaret fumed. "What if I am carrying a boy?" She glared at Wong Oi with hatred.

"Let's wait and see," Hong Kai said, trying to calm the situation. To end the conversation, he turned his attention to the cook who was bringing out the steamed fish, sautéed hearts of winter green, sliced beef with bitter melon and rice.

But his mother was adamant, "We'll see if your next child is a boy. The boys from the other household will come home if you have another girl."

Margaret slammed her bowl on the table and went into her room.

On an unusually hot day at the beginning of summer, Margaret rushed to the birthing clinic a few doors down from her flat as her child pushed its way through. Flushed with anticipation, she eagerly climbed onto the birthing bed. Less than an hour later, the midwife announced the arrival of her third daughter. Margaret was crushed. The midwife saw the disappointment on her face and said, "Maybe better luck next time."

She whisked the baby off to the next room to get her cleaned up. A surge of anger and hatred rose in Margaret and she started to cry in frustration. Life would be so different if this child was a boy. She would go home in triumph, bringing the prize with her to keep her grandmother-in-law's mouth shut. She dreaded the mockery that she would have to endure from Wong Oi and the continued demands of Hong Kai. Exhausted from sustaining her position in the household, she did not need another strike against her.

The midwife returned with the baby wrapped in a light bunting and said to Margaret, "Take a look at your new daughter, Mrs. Leung. She is a cute baby."

"Put her somewhere, anywhere. I will ask for her when I am ready." Margaret could not bring herself to even look at the infant. The mere sight of it brought on a nauseating sensation in her throat. How she wished her baby was a boy. The humidity and the heat made her even more agitated. She got up, gulped down a large glass of water and splashed a handful on her sweaty face. She walked over to the stack of clean towels to dry her face and caught her reflection in a small mirror above the shelf as she reached for a towel. She saw a woman with greasy matted down hair, a tired and angry face. Who was this awful looking woman in the mirror? This was not how she remembered herself. Since marrying at sixteen she had endured a cruel and demanding life. Nothing had developed as she had hoped. She merely wanted someone to care for her, to acknowledge her awful existence, to hold her close and tell her everything would be all right. Exhausted and overwhelmed she sat down and wept. Between sobs, she cried, "Mother, where are you?"

Each step she took toward the fourth floor felt like a monumental task. With the new daughter in her arms, she reached her flat in no mood to see anyone.

"Is this our new daughter?" James asked casually.

"Yes," Margaret answered. She walked past James without looking at him, clutching the baby to her chest, and headed for their room.

"I'd like to name her Oi Ling, after my grandmother, and her American name will be Irene," James said, following Margaret into their room. She knew there would be an uproar with her grandmother-in-law with the birth of this child. It was ironic that "Oi" means "love" in Chinese.

"Whatever," Margaret said without interest. She wished she had another life, one without the pressures of being Chinese. Her daughter started to cry. She watched the infant crying on the bed. The mere sound made her cringe with revulsion. She couldn't bring herself to pick her daughter up. The thought of feeding the child from her breast, the creature that had just ruined her life, was sickening. Margaret knew then that she hated her life.

All the more, Margaret catered to her father-in-law's desires. She and her grandmother-in-law would have a confrontation and she needed him on her side.

It came one evening during dinner. Hong Kai's mother said to him casually, "My new granddaughter is almost a month old. When are you going to arrange the homecoming of James' concubine and their sons?"

A heavy silence hung over the room.

Before Hong Kai could think of an answer, Margaret slammed down her chopsticks, looked directly at her grandmother-in-law and barked, "No whore is coming over this threshold. Did your husband get himself a concubine because you had no sons?"

Margaret saw Wong Oi's shaken face. The act of slamming chopsticks down on the table was unthinkable and the way Margaret had spoken to her was absolutely out of order. The fact that Hong Kai did not intervene meant that Margaret had more power than her grandmother-in-law. Margaret relaxed. Wong Oi never spoke to her again.

Despite not having to deal with James' mistress coming home, sometimes Margaret just wanted to scream. The only way to vent her anger and hatred was to take it out on her children. They were easy targets when she was in a bad mood.

Two years passed. In the early summer, Margaret gave birth to another girl. James also had four children with his mistress, three boys and a girl. They were the same ages as his children with Margaret. Fate was not to favor her and she resigned herself to having four girls and a marriage that was almost non-existent. Margaret turned her attention to the newborn child and doted on her because she knew this would be the last of her children. James removed himself more and more from the household because no one cared if he came home or not.

During dinner, Hong Kai announced, "I have to go back to New York to attend to my business." Throughout the years of his stay in Hong Kong, Hong Kai received numerous letters from his wife inquiring about his return. He glanced around the table, turned to his mother and said, "I will be back shortly. Margaret has asked me to take her eldest child with me to get an American education and I plan to do so. She will live with her grandmother. We will leave in a few weeks."

His mother went back to her meal and ate without response. Margaret smiled, pleased that her daughter was going to America at her request.

The younger girls looked at their eldest sister with envy. Everyone believed that going to America was the best thing that could ever happen to you.

Hong Kai came back to Hong Kong a month later with a big suitcase full of gifts for Margaret. The household developed a rhythm of ease.

One afternoon while the children were scattered throughout the house playing, James appeared after an absence of more than three years. Margaret was shocked to see him. He was skin and bones, filthy, needed a haircut and the clothes he wore looked as if they had been on his body for months.

"I am coming home to live out the rest of my life. The children from my mistress are taken care of," James said, looking at Margaret through lifeless eyes.

Margaret was silent.

"Please let me come home," James pleaded.

Margaret summoned her father-in-law before she would let him through the door. Hong Kai was saddened to see his son in such condition. Without saying a word, he nodded at Margaret to let James in and went back into his room. He never spoke to his son again.

James was never seen outside of his bedroom. At first, Margaret would send one of her daughters to deliver food to him but he had deteriorated to a point that he only ate chocolate occasionally. She also reluctantly went to the drug store to get supplies for his injections of heroin.

In less than a month, they had a big row. Margaret refused to have anything to do with him and assigned Oi Ling to take care of his needs.

One early morning, Hong Kai called Margaret from the bathroom. She rushed to see what he needed. He was trying to hold onto the side of the bathtub but he slid onto the floor and lay down in the blood he had just vomited. A big pool of blood spread across the floor. Margaret couldn't help him up by herself. She called an ambulance and went to the hospital with him.

It was the monsoon season. Hong Kai had been in the hospital for a few days before Margaret decided to take the children to the hospital, braving high winds, heavy rains, and flooding. She began to take them every day. She pulled and carried the children through the high waters with the help of her niece, determined that her father-in-law would die honorably with his descendents at his bedside.

On the sixth day, when Margaret and her daughters arrived at the hospital, another niece pulled Margaret aside and whispered, "Your father-in-law is dying. If you have anything to say to him, do it now."

But Margaret looked into the room and saw Hong Kai sitting up, humming.

"He looks fine, maybe he is getting better," Margaret said with a ray of hope.

"Aunt Margaret, listen to me. Just before someone is ready to go, he always looks his best and is in good spirits. I am afraid he is dying," her niece insisted.

Margaret looked at her and knew what she was telling her was common knowledge. She broke down and cried.

Her niece consoled her and held her arms until she collected herself. Margaret went into the room with her daughters and greeted Hong Kai warmly.

"I just saw Hong Guay and Lo Tsoa. They were happy to see me and called to me from the other side of the river," Hong Kai said animatedly. Margaret held back her tears. The people he had mentioned were deceased.

"I am going home! I feel great. Dee-dee, dee-da-dee." Hong Kai hummed happily.

"Lo yeah, please rest." Margaret held his hand, trying hard not to cry.

Suddenly, he struggled for breath. He sat up, terrified, his eyes bulging. He gasped for air and tried to grab Margaret. Then he lost his strength, fell back to bed and fought to draw in another breath.

Margaret and her daughters knelt by his bedside crying and calling out to him.

Choi Kum, Margaret's mother-in-law, returned from New York for Hong Kai's funeral with two of her unmarried daughters. Margaret sensed her coldness and wondered if Choi Kum suspected her affair with Hong Kai. She tried her best to be a compliant daughter-in-law.

Less than a month after the funeral, as the family began set-tling back into a routine, James became too frail to force choco-late down his throat or to give himself injections of heroin. He asked Margaret to admit him into a hospital.

One day, Margaret and her daughters went to see James at the same hospital in which his father had died. He was fed intra-venously and needed oxygen to help him breathe. Too weak to speak, James motioned Margaret to come closer to him. She leaned over him and turned her head so that her ear almost touched his mouth.

"I just want my last fix to exit this world. Please let me go in peace," James whispered with great effort.

"I will tell the nurse to give you your last wish," Margaret said, looking at her husband with disdain.

She went outside and spoke to the nurse on duty. "My hus-band requests an injection of heroin. Since he is so weak, just give him an injection of saline solution. He will never know the difference." She could punish him at last. She followed the nurse into the room and watched as she gave James his injection.

He closed his eyes. After a minute or two, he looked at Margaret and his daughters for the last time and closed his eyes again. Margaret was expressionless. Her daughters looked at their mother puzzled. They remembered their grandfather's death just a month before. They turned back to their father, knelt down and called out to him and cried as his final breath slipped from his gaunt lips.

After James' funeral, Choi Kum went back to New York with her two daughters and Margaret's second daughter. At age twelve, Margaret felt that her daughter was old enough to go to America to receive an American education. It was important to her that her daughters had a chance to experience American cul-ture. Her mother-in-law had given her the task of collecting rent from the tenants.

The house was quiet with everyone gone. Margaret suddenly found herself in a vacuum. She was not prepared to face a life of peace and quiet. Boredom to her was as oppressive as a life of chaos. She resumed her life of socializing with the set of neglected women, taking tea in fancy tea parlors and playing mahjong.

For years, Oi Ling had been passing blood every time she went to the bathroom. An acquaintance of Margaret's took her third daughter to an herbalist. It took only two doses of the herbal extract to stop her daughter's bleeding. Margaret was amazed. She thought if he could cure her daughter in just two visits, maybe he could help her with her frequent headaches and the pain in her shoulders.

"Oi Ling, do you know how to get to the herbalist by yourself?" Margaret asked her daughter after dinner.

"Yes, it is a long walk over the big hill behind my school. He lives in one of those seven-floors buildings. It is really dirty," Oi Ling answered.

"I'll pick you up after school tomorrow and you will take me to see him," Margaret told her daughter as the maid collected the empty bowls.

"I will meet you in front of the gate?" Oi Ling asked timidly.

"Yes, where else do you think I will meet you? Sometimes you just ask the stupidest questions," Margaret said impatiently. Oi Ling looked down, slipped out of her chair quietly and left the table.

It was a long and dusty road over a steep hill. Oi Ling walked with a steady gait. Margaret panted, trying to keep up with her daughter in her nice dress and fine leather shoes with heels.

"Walk slower. Where are you rushing to?" Margaret called out to her daughter and wished she had taken a taxi but Oi Ling only knew how to get there on foot. As they got closer, Margaret smelled the open sewers. A wave of nausea came over her. In her adult life, she had never before associated with the lower echelons of society and certainly would never have chosen to go to such a dilapidated neighborhood.

Oi Ling pointed to a huge cluster of cheaply built large cement buildings and said the herbalist was in the fourth one on the second floor. It was one of the complexes the government had built for the poor. An open sewer ran in front of the building. Margaret gagged and began coughing and spitting as if to get the smell out of her throat. As they climbed up the stairs, a group of children no more than three years of age played around the stairwell in dirty shirts and no pants. One boy urinated on the floor without turning his back to them. Margaret held her breath and tiptoed around the rivulets of urine. How she wished she hadn't come.

They turned the corner and Oi Ling led Margaret into the herbalist's tiny box. Margaret stepped in and was greeted by a man with small beady eyes, a smiling wide mouth, big nose, pockmarked face, and slicked back hair. Now she was sure she shouldn't have come.

The living space was no more than ten by ten feet. In the front of the room was a tiny table with a chair on two sides set against a cheap piece of thin board. Centered on the table was a small pillow for patients to rest their wrists on. To the left, there was another table crowded with dishes and bowls stacked together with chopsticks, ladles and spoons. A kerosene stove, a dirty oil-coated wok and two tin pots covered with soot were shoved underneath the table. A little beyond that, there was an entrance to a room just big enough to accommodate a homemade bunk bed. She could see stuff packed solidly under it.

"I am Doctor Lai. You must be this fine young lady's mother," the herbalist said with a twinkle in his eyes. "It is nice to meet you. Did your daughter tell you she was bleeding from her stomach? I am sure she is much better now, isn't she?" he asked, smiling at Oi Ling. She smiled back, but Margaret couldn't reply. She was too overwhelmed by the poverty of the setting. Instead she inspected a chair to see if it was clean enough for her to sit on.

"Mah-mee, do you want to go first?" Oi Ling asked her mother, oblivious to her mother's concern.

"No, I'll just stand here and wait till you are finished," Margaret said to her daughter, thinking that if Oi Ling went ahead of her, she would at least wipe off some of the dirt from the chair by sitting on it. The pillow on the table was gray and brown from years of use. Margaret tightened her mouth in a grimace and looked away. Oi Ling sat down on the chair across from the herbalist and flopped her wrist down on the dirty pillow. He placed three fingers lightly on her wrist and concentrated on her pulse. When he was done feeling Oi Ling's pulse, he gestured for her to change her hand.

After a minute or two, he took out a piece of rice paper, a brush and an inkpot and wrote the formula of herbs on the paper. Margaret glanced over at the table and was impressed with the beauty of his calligraphy. When he was finished, he stood up and walked a few steps out the door to the hallway. Leaning on the cement railing he called down to the clerk in the herbal shop in the building next door. He threw the formula down to the man, who took it into the shop to measure out the different herbs and wrap them individually in paper.

Oi Ling got up from the chair and offered the seat to her mother.

Margaret sat down on the chair and reluctantly put her wrist on the pillow. The herbalist asked her to relax. He stared straight ahead, concentrating on her pulse. When he was finished he continued to study her. Margaret felt uncomfortable. She had never experienced such a penetrating look from a man before.

"I will give you herbs to make your headaches to go away," the herbalist said to Margaret, looking deeper into her eyes.

"How do you know I have headaches?" Margaret asked, amazed.

Doctor Lai smiled slyly, "Your pulse tells me everything."

Margaret turned to look at her daughter outside in the hallway, the way he stared at her made her feel strange. She was not sure what it was. She shifted nervously on the chair.

The man from the herbal shop delivered the two packages of herbs. Margaret paid him and called to Oi Ling that they were ready to leave. She paid Doctor Lai and thanked him for taking care of her daughter. As she took the few steps to get to the door, she felt his eyes on her. Margaret turned and looked uneasily back at him. She forced a smile and left with her daughter.

Margaret went with Oi Ling to see Doctor Lai every other day. After two weeks, they were feeling much better. She continued to go to him accompanied by her daughter. Although Oi Ling didn't need the herbal infusion anymore, Margaret told her daughter that she needed remedies to boost her own energy. Margaret began to find the herbalist charming.

"You live in such a spacious flat with only two daughters, where is the rest of your family?" Dr. Lai asked Margaret, since she told him her address a few days before.

"Most of my family is in America," Margaret said smugly. To impress him further, she continued, "We also own the two buildings on Tai Po Road."

She saw his lips and eyes glisten.

"I want to take you to Tsuen Tsueng Guey, the restaurant famous for its chicken baked in rock salt. Would you like to come with me tonight?" Dr. Lai asked, looking intensely into Margaret's eyes.

"You have such good taste. I have never been to the restaurants that are known for their specialties. My friends and I always just frequent the few places that we know," Margaret said, excited to find him worldly.

During the next few months, Margaret told all of her women friends and relatives about an amazing herbalist she had found and brought them to see Dr. Lai for their ailments. She wanted to show off his herbal skills and drum up business for him. She began to go to his place early in the morning and to come home late at night. Dr. Lai and Margaret went to fancy restaurants almost daily and she paid for a tailor to make him new suits. Her children seldom saw her at home. Margaret was in love. She felt special in the herbalist's presence. He doted on her.

One morning, Margaret went to Dr. Lai's place early to surprise him with a special breakfast.

"Look what I have brought you! Pastries from our favorite cake shop." Margaret held the box out as soon as she saw the herbalist emerging from the tiny bedroom.

"Let's go to our special tea parlor to have tea instead," Dr. Lai said and grabbed Margaret's arm and pulled her toward the door.

"You are still in your pajamas, silly. Let's just make some tea and eat here."

"No, let's go now," he insisted.

Margaret set the box down on the table and reached for the kettle. She heard a faint shuffling sound behind the thin wall. She stood still and waited for the noise to stop and sat down on a chair, folded her arms and stared at the herbalist. "I think we should have breakfast here," she said angrily.

She had heard rumors that a friend's daughter was pregnant by Dr. Lai. Margaret had tried not to believe it. Now she was in the same room with another woman who had just spent the night. The herbalist tried to reassure her but Margaret would not give in. She sat rigid in the chair for hours until the woman had to come out of the room.

Choi Kum's niece sheepishly emerged from the bedroom, her face flushed. "Aunt Margaret, I came to get some herbs for my headaches. How nice to see you." She tried to keep her composure as she rushed for the door.

Margaret stood up to leave.

Doctor Lai immediately took Margaret's arm, pulled her into the other room and didn't give her a chance to utter a word. He threw her onto the bed, kissing her passionately. Then he yanked her panties off and forcefully made love to her.

Margaret had never been so taken by a man and had never felt so wanted. She was completely intoxicated.

Afterward, Margaret lingered in bed, thoroughly confused. Must she accept his behavior as she had accepted her husband's womanizing? Was this the life a woman had to settle for? Would she rather be alone or enjoy his affection and put up with other women?

In less than a month, Margaret moved the herbalist to a big apartment in a ritzy neighborhood. She furnished the place and paid for everything he wanted with the rent money she collected from the tenants for her mother-in-law. She fired the domestic help so she could use the money to support him. Margaret didn't even bother to go home and only saw her daughters once or twice a week to leave enough money for them to buy food.

"You haven't brought money for next month's rent," Dr. Lai said to Margaret while they munched on pieces of roast duck from a famous restaurant.

"I have already given you all the money I collected this month from my buildings," Margaret said uneasily. She wanted to do everything she could to keep him happy.

"We better find a way to make more money then," the herbalist said thoughtfully. "Lo Muk runs a very lucrative opium den. It is easy money and I know how to set one up. Matter of fact, we can run it right here." His eyes brightened.

"You go raise the money and I'll set it up," Dr. Lai said, excited by his decision. When he was happy, she complied.

Margaret went to friends of her in-laws to borrow money. In less than a week, the business was in full operation. Four narrow beds were set up in a room. Each was supplied with a long bulbous pipe. Customers came to the apartment to purchase a small container of the opium paste. As a courtesy, they could stay and smoke it while reclining on the beds.

Margaret became part of his scheme. Sometimes she allowed men who worked at the den to cook the opium in her own home using one of her daughters to portion it out in small containers. There was only one thing on her mind, how to compete with other women for the herbalist's affection and win.

It had been a year since Margaret last sent the rent money to New York. She was informed that her mother-in-law was coming back to Hong Kong. Margaret quickly hired a maid and told her children not to talk to anyone about anything under any circumstances.

The day Choi Kum arrived with her two daughters, chills swept through the entire flat. The daughters had come to even the score. Margaret knew they wanted her to be punished for what she had done but Margaret's greatest defense was denial. As in the past, if she denied everything and they could not find hard facts to prove it, they couldn't accuse her of the deeds. But her mother-in-law was not interested in pursuing Margaret's dirt. She had decided to put a stop to the mess by moving Margaret and her two remaining daughters to New York.

Choi Kum left for New York with Margaret's youngest daughter. Oi Ling stayed behind to help her mother empty out the flat and bring whatever they could to New York by ship two months later.

Instead of consolidating and packing everything to be sent to New York, Margaret spent all of her time with the herbalist. She hastily packed two suitcases the night before she set sail with her daughter and left everything behind.

"Oi Ling, go up to the deck or stay in the lounge. Don't come back till the ship starts moving," Margaret said to her daughter as soon as they entered their cabin. The herbalist was already sitting on one of the chairs next to the beds. Oi Ling scurried out obediently and Margaret locked the cabin door behind her.

"It is so hard to say goodbye. As soon as you get to America, write me immediately," Dr. Lai said tenderly. "I am sure you'll find a way to get me there to join you." He pulled Margaret toward him and gently led her into bed.

"Sure, I'll write you," Margaret said half heartedly, knowing this was the end of her affair. She was bound to her family and she could not and would not consider jeopardizing her own tenuous position.

"You are the one for me. You have to start the process of my application for immigration as soon as you get there," the herbalist said, stroking Margaret affectionately. "You know I love you."

Margaret closed her eyes to relish her last moment of intimacy.

"All visitors please leave the premise immediately. The ship is to depart in five minutes." Margaret was startled by the loud announcement through the speakers in her room. She turned to look at her lover. With tears in her eyes, she said goodbye, knowing she would never see him again.

New York Chinatown was not what Margaret had remembered America to be. Fruits and vegetables in wooden crates spilled out onto the sidewalks as if the street was a giant outdoor market. She hated the smell. The streets were buzzing with people. She was surprised to find everyone spoke Chinese.

They had no need to assimilate into the American culture. The immigrants could survive by not speaking a word of English if they stayed in the confines of the community.

Margaret was annoyed to find most people in New York were of working class. Everyone, it seemed, had a job. Choi Kum owned two buildings in the heart of Chinatown and she had assigned a small apartment for Margaret to live in with her second daughter, Teresa, on the fourth floor. Oi Ling, now called by her American name Irene, and her younger sister, Louise, lived with their grandmother and her unmarried daughter on the second floor. Margaret's eldest daughter, Virginia had married a Chinese man as soon as she'd turned eighteen. They owned a Chinese restaurant in a small suburb.

This was the first time in Margaret's life that she had to consider finding a job. Her mother-in-law told her that everyone in the Golden Mountain had to work. Margaret would be no exception. Choi Kum was willing to help her by not charging rent but she would not give her an allowance.

Everyone in the community knew Margaret was a newcomer and needed a job. Although Margaret had no skills she had the greatest asset: she spoke English and Chinese. Soon, Margaret landed a job as a bookkeeper at a butcher shop in Chinatown. It was a small store with glass meat cases in the front, with a small office, walk-in freezer and refrigerator in the back. Customers from the suburbs packed the store on weekends to get their weekly supplies.

Margaret loved her job. She was the only female employee and was surrounded by a dozen men. She went to work before seven in the morning and did not come home till after eight in the evening. Not long after starting the job, Margaret could be found at the retail counter socializing with the male employees instead of tending to her bookkeeping in her office.

"Mrs. Leung, you are so smart. You speak such good English," Mr. Chui, Margaret's co-worker said to her during lunch.

"Oh, thank you," Margaret said glowingly.

"I wonder if you can help me to fill out some official papers. My wife and sons are waiting for the American consulate to grant them entrance to the United States." Mr. Chui smiled and waited for Margaret's response.

"That is easy. I'd love to." Margaret glanced at him, seeing that special look in his eyes that she by now knew so well.

"I'll see you at my apartment after work," he said, lowering his voice.

She smiled and nodded.

Margaret and Teresa had to move out of their apartment for remodeling. She then rented one from her brother-in-law on the outskirts of Chinatown. Irene and Louise painted the new apartment and moved everything in while she was at work. All three daughters now lived with her.

Margaret spent most of her time at Mr. Chui's apartment and returned home only when necessary to fend off any gossip that would reach her mother-in-law.

"Look at your skirt! Don't you have any shame?" Margaret yelled at Irene as soon as she came into the butcher shop to pick up a package for her.

"Only whores wear skirts that short!" Margaret snorted, staring at her daughter. Ever since Irene started going to some art high school uptown, she behaved differently. Margaret just hated the way she looked. She wore strange clothes and had makeup on her face. A proper woman should not be seen with a whorish looking girl as her daughter.

"You better go home and change into something decent," Margaret ordered. "And look at your hair! A beggar's hair looks better than that."

Mr. Chui came into the office. He walked over to Margaret and whispered, "Don't yell at her anymore. Why do you pick on her all the time? She'll go crazy if you keep this up."

"She just has a face that begs to be hated," Margaret said, dismissing his advice and walked out of the office.

Irene looked down on the floor, picked up the package and left without a word.

Margaret's affair with Mr. Chui was very low key. She found comfort in sharing time with him to ease their mutual loneliness. Unlike Dr. Lai, he did not manipulate her or drive her to dizzying heights of desire.

Managing her affair with Mr. Chui was a simple task – as long as her daughters covered for her, the family would never know.

"Mom, I want to get married," Teresa approached Margaret after she came home from work one evening. Teresa had met an American-born Chinese man less than a year before. Since moving to New York with her grandmother when she was twelve, she had quickly adapted to Chinese-American life in Chinatown. Teresa was proud to pass as an American-born Chinese and refused to associate herself with immigrants. She felt superior because she spoke fluent English. However, the Chinese from Hong Kong felt that American-born Chinese lacked the depth of the ancient culture and the art of subtle manipulation. They called the American-born "empty bamboo stick without ends," for they could not hold anything and had nothing inside.

"We better start planning soon," Margaret said thoughtfully, knowing the groom's family background was similar to her own. A wedding from the Leung family must not be shabby. "I have to shop for my own dress. I'll go to Lord and Taylor's and see what they have that's suitable for me."

Margaret put everything she had into Teresa's wedding. It was important to her to show the world that a widow from a good family could still provide a grand wedding for her daughter.

In her powder blue and white brocade suit, Margaret watched tearfully as the priest performed the ceremony. To see her daughter in an ivory satin gown and veil, holding a bouquet of gardenias while standing in front of the altar with her new husband, reminded Margaret of her own grand wedding. She thought about her mother. This was her proudest moment and she was happy realizing that her mother probably had felt the same.

Margaret's help in filing immigration papers for Mr. Chui had brought them together but had also speeded up the arrival of his wife and children. After seven years, her affair had ended. She had also changed her job. Most of her co-workers now were female. She had no interest in establishing friendships with any of them.

Irene had left for London to pursue her master's degree in art. Louise had married her junior high school sweetheart and moved to Michigan. Her daughters had taken care of cleaning and tidying. Margaret had never lifted a finger for domestic work. She also was used to having people around to take care of whatever she had failed to pay attention to. Margaret found herself alone in the apartment. It became cluttered and she had no interest in cleaning it. Soon, Margaret found an additional job as a night cashier in a well-known restaurant in midtown Manhattan so she didn't have to go home to face the mess and her own emptiness.

Margaret came home from work, exhausted, and in no mood to sort out her bills from the stack of mail. But she found a letter from London.

Dear Mom,

I am inviting you to my graduation in July. If you choose to come to London, I will let you have my flat for yourself

*and I'll stay with my boyfriend. Please let me know soon so
I can make the arrangements.*
   Love,
      Irene

Margaret was surprised. She never thought Irene would
amount to anything and had never paid much attention to her.
She had actually stayed in London for three years to finish her
master's degree.

London was fabulous, it reminded Margaret of her leisure
days in Hong Kong. Irene took her to tea at Fortnum and
Mason. Margaret felt like a fish released back into its own pond.
   "Madam, what tea would you prefer?" the waiter in a white
jacket, black bow tie and trousers asked her politely.
   "Earl Grey, please," Margaret answered and smiled with satisfaction. She leaned back on the chintz-covered chair. She
glanced around and loved being in the company of all the ladies
taking their afternoon tea in their dresses with matching hats
and lacey white gloves.
   The waiter came back with a lovely pot of fragrant tea and a
silver three-tiered serving tray with tiny sandwiches and petite
pastries on white lace doilies.
   "I hope you like London," Irene said timidly, fiddling with
the teacup.
   Margaret noticed five different colors of nail polish on her
fingers. She had shaggy hair, tight jeans and a flimsy silk shirt,
a direct contrast to her demeanor.
   "How I miss Hong Kong," Margaret said as if talking to
herself.
   The graduation ceremony started at ten o'clock the next
morning. Margaret was left in the audience while Irene joined her
graduating class of fourteen in the section reserved for the school
of graphic design. After a lengthy speech by the provost, Margaret

watched her daughter in her black cap and a gown trimmed with ermine fur, walk up to the podium to receive her certificate. Margaret was proud. Even though she never thought much of this daughter, Irene was the first one in this family to receive a master's degree. Margaret now had a bragging right.

Two years passed. Irene had quit her job as an instructor at Penn State University. She went to California and got married. Like her younger sister, she did not bother with a proper Chinese wedding. More importantly, she was the first to break the family tradition of marrying Chinese only by marrying a Caucasian. Nevertheless, Margaret was relieved that Irene was legally married and glad that someone actually took her peculiar daughter as his wife.

Louise and her husband opened their own restaurant in a small town in Michigan. One day, on her day off, she received a telephone call from Louise.

"Guess what? I am pregnant!" She didn't wait for her mother to respond and continued, "I need to go back to work soon after the birth. I'd like you to come help me with my baby."

"I don't know. I have two jobs," Margaret said, but she was relieved to know that she didn't have to be alone any longer.

"Mom, why do I always have to convince you to do the obvious?" Louise said patiently.

Margaret played coy and replied, "I'll let you know when the time comes."

A few days before the birth of Louise's son, Margaret took two weeks off from work and joined all of her daughters and their families at Louise's house in Michigan for the happy occasion. Virginia was there with her son. Teresa came with her husband, their two sons and daughter. Irene arrived with her husband.

"Mom, why don't you stay and help me with my baby?" Louise asked with her newborn son in her arms, sitting at a picnic table in her back yard, bathed in the setting sun of late summer.

"I don't think I can. I'll have no income if I quit my jobs," Margaret said. She took a sip of her tea. Irene came over to the table and sat down to join them.

"I'll give you spending money each week. Why do you want to keep two jobs?" Louise asked.

"I want to keep my own apartment," Margaret insisted.

"Not one of us is living in the city anymore. You are there alone. Is that what you want? To be alone for the rest of your life?" Irene asked her mother, direct, as always. Margaret never liked her bluntness.

"Come here to stay with Louise. She needs you," Irene finally said. It was what Margaret wanted to hear. She was needed.

"All right then, I'll go back to New York to put in my notices at work," Margaret said to her daughters, relieved that Louise was going to take care of her. "I'll be back in a few weeks."

Margaret left the New York apartment the way she usually left her residences. She packed two suitcases of personal belongings and left everything else behind.

At first, Margaret was delighted to take care of her grandson. Louise was her favorite child. Taking care of her favorite child's son was like raising a son of her own which she had wanted so much when she was raising her own children. She doted on the baby.

They lived in a small town. Margaret had never learned to drive and relied on Louise or her husband to take her places. Otherwise, she was confined to the house. Both Louise and her husband worked long hours at their restaurant.

"I'd like to go to the mall and look around. I think they have a sale today," Margaret called Louise at the restaurant.

"I'll take you Monday, on my day off. I am really busy right now," Louise said patiently.

"Forget it. I won't go then." Margaret pouted and hung up. She was irritated to find herself not the center of attention and her children would not cater to her wishes as she demanded.

She felt increasingly isolated.

In less than a year, Irene gave birth to a girl. Since Irene ran a business with her husband, Margaret offered to stay with her and help take care of the baby. She also wanted to take advantage of being in Los Angeles away from the small town. She stayed for six months.

When Margaret returned to Michigan, she cried to Louise, "Irene's husband is exactly like your grandfather, stingy and controlling. Every time Irene came back from the market or errands, the first thing her husband did was to inspect her checkbook making sure every penny she had spent was accounted for. What kind of life is that? I feel so sorry for her."

"Butt out! It is her life and she likes it. Her husband is nice to us. I like him," Louise replied.

"You just don't know. You have to live with them to see what is going on. Her husband is so sweet on the surface but he has this mean streak in him that sends chills to my bones," Margaret said, drying her eyes with a piece of tissue.

"Quit that nonsense. Irene is a big girl. If life is so miserable for her she will put an end to it. After all, she is the one who traveled around by herself for years and did so well." Louise rolled her eyes to emphasize the pointlessness of her mother's concern.

Margaret saw the futility of continuing the conversation. Her other daughters would never have a chance to see the whole picture. To her amazement, Irene had changed from being a rebel to a docile woman. Perhaps Louise was right. It was better to leave it alone.

Louise gave birth to another boy shortly after Margaret returned from California. As usual, Margaret had to pick a favorite. As Louise was her favored child, her youngest grandson became the untouchable in that household. He could do no wrong in Margaret's eyes.

"Waaah! Pau Pau! Michael hit me! Waaaah..." Jason, Louise's younger son cried and ran to Margaret's side.

"Michael! What did you do? Picking on your brother again?" Margaret scolded the older boy, not bothering to find out the facts.

"He messed up my picture with a crayon. I spent hours on it and he pinched me!" Michael defended himself tearfully.

"You always pick on Jason. Now go to your room and don't come out till I let you." Margaret looked at Michael fiercely and turned to Jason and said, "Show Pau Pau where he hit you. Does it hurt?" She patted Jason's head and gave him a hug.

Michael was furious. He ran into his room, slammed the door and called his mother at the restaurant to tell her about the injustice.

Louise talked to her mother numerous times about being fair with her children but Margaret never grasped the concept of fairness. Tension in the house built over time and soon became unbearable. Margaret complained and cried to Irene on a weekly basis. Irene finally offered Margaret to stay with her in California.

Two more years passed. Irene gave birth to a boy. Margaret now stayed in California year round and only went back to Michigan for a short visit once a year. She loved the fact that Irene worked hard with her husband and they'd established themselves in the business world. They lived in a large and elaborate house in a well-to-do neighborhood. They also had a full-time housekeeper who chauffeured Margaret wherever she wanted to go.

"Don't tell Mommy," Margaret said, shoving a piece of candy into her grandson's mouth. He looked at his grandmother with wide eyes and smiled. They shared this secret of sneaking candies when Irene was not looking, as she didn't want her children to have excessive sugar.

"Pau Pau, you are my friend." He gave his grandmother a hug and played with his toys nearby.

"And we don't want to get yelled at." Margaret winked at her grandson.

"Irene, is breakfast ready? I'm hungry. Tell me when it's on the table," Irene's husband Bob yelled from their bedroom upstairs. For years, she'd had breakfast ready before her husband got out of bed. He liked waffles, sometimes bagels, bacon and eggs. His latest fancy was Irish steel cut oats, which took half an hour of stirring to cook properly.

"Get it yourself. I'm assembling the necklace that you ordered me to make yesterday," Irene grumbled.

Margaret immediately chirped, "I'll make it for you Bob. I'll tell you when it is ready." Irene stared fiercely at her mother and turned back to her work. Margaret was taken aback.

She started to see more signs of trouble. Well into the night, she heard quarrels between her daughter and son-in-law. She also noticed Irene spending more time alone in different parts of the sprawling house, isolating herself from everyone.

"I can't stand your daughter. She is such a domineering bitch to her brother and she has a big mouth. If she talks back to me one more time, I will slap her face," Margaret complained to Irene who was sitting by the pool in the garden. She expected Irene to look away and say nothing as usual or to tell her mother to do what was necessary but this time Irene stared at her so hard it sent chills down Margaret's back.

"You had your chance at raising your own children. These are my children. This is my time. If you dare to touch my daughter, you will never be allowed to set foot in this house again. If you don't think you can handle it, don't bother to come back to my house after you go back to Michigan," Irene said calmly and firmly. She had fire in her eyes, a flame Margaret had not seen in her daughter for years. When she felt threatened, Irene usually went into a hysterical rage and lost control. After calming down, she would submit herself to whatever was expected of her. Margaret's face grew ashen.

"You have changed. I hope you know what you are doing. I don't like where you are heading," Margaret said with little confidence. She was used to being the aggressor and had never been challenged by Irene in this way. There was a quiet strength and determination that Margaret had never known from her.

"I know you have an airline ticket that is close to expiring. You have to use it in a few weeks. This time when you go back to Michigan, you better think clearly if you can handle relinquishing control over my children. This is my house. The only way you can come back to stay is to learn to live as a guest and respect my rules," Irene said, refusing to relent.

"I don't know if I want to come back. I will let you know after I get to Michigan." Margaret responded, hoping that a display of indifference would soften Irene's stance. Irene had always given in to her pouting.

"It is your choice, you know the rules," Irene said coldly.

Margaret was crushed.

Two weeks after Margaret returned to Michigan, Irene called her on the phone and informed her mother of her divorce. Margaret refused to believe Irene was willing to give up her lifestyle just because she was unhappy. After all, didn't everyone forgo everything else in order to acquire wealth and status? Weren't wealth and status the main sources of happiness everyone died to pursue? Through Irene, Margaret had lived the lifestyle she wanted and now her daughter was going to throw all that away. Where did that leave her? Did that mean she could not go back to Irene's house? Margaret felt her lifeline was being severed.

A week after Margaret found out about Irene's divorce, she suffered a heart attack. Margaret came home from the hospital, sitting by the kitchen table and sat staring at the pills. Blue ones, white ones, pink and orange ones. She was completely overwhelmed by the schedule of her medication. She also had a machine to help her breathe. She kept it close by, never knowing when the next asthma attack would come. Margaret was frightened and wished she had taken better care of her health.

Irene had stopped calling regularly. Louise and her husband had to work, and their sons were in school. Margaret, alone during most of the day, was distressed about her steadily weakening body. She became depressed, which only made her condition worse.

One morning, Louise was startled to find her mother standing at the foot of her bed.

"Take me to the hospital," Margaret uttered laboriously, her face turning blue.

Louise rushed out of bed, put Margaret into her car and raced to the hospital. The emergency crew tried to revive her but she was already in a deep coma. She had suffered a massive heart attack.

The doctors put Margaret into the intensive care unit. A respirator breathed for her and food was supplied intravenously. The staff knew that Margaret had daughters from out of state and were trying to give them an opportunity to say goodbye.

They told Louise the chances of recovery were very slim. If Margaret started to breathe on her own, the best they could hope for her would be to live the rest of her life in a coma. Her brain had been deprived of oxygen for too long and was no longer functional.

When Irene arrived at the hospital, Virginia had already visited and returned to New York. Teresa and Louise filled Irene in about their mother's status. None of them expected Margaret to recover. Margaret's doctor came in and asked for their permissions to take her off the respirator, again explaining that their mother had almost no chance of survival. He assured them she would go quickly.

The nurse removed the tubes that connected Margaret to the respirator. To everyone's surprise, she started to breathe. The doctor and nurses were amazed. Margaret breathed evenly, as if sleeping. The sisters lingered by her bed for a few hours until the nurse told them to go home, assuring them she would inform them if any changes occurred.

A day went by. The sisters sat by Margaret's bedside, hoping she would awaken. The doctor discussed putting Margaret into a nursing home if her status remained stable for another day.

At five o'clock the next morning, the nurse called Louise. Their mother's blood pressure was erratic and she was having difficulty breathing. She suggested that they come see her right away.

The sisters rushed to the hospital and found Margaret laboring to get air into her lungs. They watched and listened in silence as her breath became shallow. Her daughters congregated around her bed as she exhaled her last breath. Margaret would have been pleased to know that she was not alone.

OI LING

1950–1965
Hong Kong

I t is another girl, Mrs. Leung," announced the midwife, looking up from between Mother's legs as she drew me into a
new world of light and loud clear sound. Swiftly, she pulled
me up by my ankles and gave me a good swat on my butt. I
cried and sucked cold air into my lungs. She whisked me off to
the next room and plunged me into a basin of warm water. Ah,
that felt much better. She wrapped me in a light bunting,
brought me back to Mother and held me out to her. Mother said
something in a gruff voice and turned to look away. The midwife quickly walked to the far corner of the room and put me in
a cage-like contraption with a soft pad on the bottom. I peered
out between the white iron bars. I watched Mother get up from
her bed and stomp towards a stack of towels. I studied her
reflection in the small mirror above them. Her face was twisted
with rage. I saw her shoulders shake violently and heard an
awful groan. She turned and gave me a burning stare. I felt a
sharp pain in my belly.

151

Mother's heart beat fast against my face as we moved outside. The light was blinding. I squirmed, and her grip tightened around me. Then we were inside again, going up. Mother breathed heavily. Doors opened and closed and I heard a new voice, low and pleasant. Then mother spoke again. She walked to the bed and set me down roughly. I cried to protest, but there was no response.

This was my homecoming, a matter of tension in the household. My two sisters certainly did not want another sibling to compete for the little attention Mother deigned to give. They had little to worry about, quickly discovering that I was not wanted by anyone in the house.

"Stop your crying! You cry for every little thing. You just have a face that begs for hatred," Mother said to me after one of my sisters grabbed a toy from my hands.

"Can't you accept life as it is? You can't have everything you want. Be quiet and learn to take it."

I had a lump in my throat and knots in my stomach. Sometimes if I cried, it seemed to feel a little better but I was told that crying was not an acceptable behavior. If I ran to Mother crying about an injustice, I got in trouble. She gave me the nickname "Crying Bag," because she thought I cried too easily. This provided more ammunition for my sisters. They would taunt me and if I cried they would call me Crying Bag righteously.

It was disrespectful to call elders by their names, so the younger ones addressed those older by rank. I called Tsuen Tseen first "elder sister" and Meew Ling "second elder sister." Whenever one addressed a cousin, an aunt, or an uncle by naming their ranks one immediately knew whether he was a maternal or paternal relative and his birth order in his family. Only the youngest members were addressed by their names.

My first elder sister, who was seven years older, had little interest in me. She had her own issues with my parents. But my second elder sister, who was only two years older, had quickly deduced that if something was done to me, I couldn't go to my mother for support. Since birth, Mother assigned me the role of punching bag. I learned early on to take a hard punch.

"She is the ugliest one in the family, look at her big forehead and the wide mouth. I don't know who she resembles. No one in this family is that ugly," Mother said with a little snort to one of her friends. Just a few months before, she had come home with my younger sister. Everyone commented what a cute baby she was and Mother seemed to be in a better mood.

"Your daughter doesn't look too bad. She looks different than your other three daughters, that's all." Mother's friend looked at me and smiled. I wondered why I was ugly. I tried to compare myself with my sisters and could not figure it out.

"She is not only ugly, but she is stupid as well. She's two years old and still won't utter a word. I sometimes wonder if she is dumb." Mother looked at me with disdain, turned back to her friend and went on, "My other two daughters did everything faster and better than she does. My youngest daughter is already doing better and she is the best looking one of all." I sat on the floor next to her playing with a strip of cloth, accustomed to Mother's comments.

"Different children do things in their own time. I am sure she is fine," her friend reassured her.

"I hope so. She better learn to talk soon," Mother said impatiently. She turned to me and rolled her eyes.

When both of my older sisters were in school, I was once playing by myself and I suddenly became conscious of looking out into the world through my eyes, hearing sound through my ears. I looked at my hands and knew there was something inside of me that was commanding my fingers to wiggle as if my body was my tool. I ran into the other room excited by my discovery. I found Mother and asked, "Mah-mee! Why am I in me and not in you? Why am I not in anybody else's body and only in mine?"

Mother looked at me sharply and said, "Don't be ridiculous. You always say stupid things. Go play with your toys and leave me alone."

I walked away not knowing why what I had said was stupid, but I learned that was a subject that I should not talk to anyone about. I was three years old.

One hot and humid day after dinner, everyone was on the roof hoping to catch an evening breeze. I walked into the kitchen to get some water. I surprised my second elder sister stealing Mother's homemade pickled daikon. I was aghast that she dared to steal, but she quickly stuffed one into my mouth and said, "You better not tell! You have stolen, too, and you'll get into big trouble if you do." I learned to keep secrets to protect the ones who told me not to tell and to feel guilty about being a part of the secrecy.

I lived in a general state of confusion.

Once my mother yelled, "Why did you tell your father where the money was?"

"You told me to always to tell the truth! You didn't tell me not to tell," I responded, close to tears.

"Do I have to tell you everything? You should know what to do. You are as stupid as a pig," Mother ranted on. "Don't you know how to turn corners? You only know how to walk a straight path. You are the dumbest idiot I know."

I looked down at my feet. My face was hot and twitching from fright. I bit my lower lip and stood as still as I could, not wanting to give her any reason to hit me.

To avoid future troubles, I learned to keep my mouth shut and to not answer any questions. Whenever someone asked me something, I looked down or away and either didn't respond or answered that I didn't know.

Mother usually entertained guests in the living room. Once a friend of Mother's came to visit. I walked through the room as quietly as I could, trying to make myself invisible. We were taught not to be noticed when adults were present. They sat on our carved rosewood chairs, steam spiraling between them from the teacups full of fragrant tea. Her friend was remarking about the quality of calligraphy on our silk paintings on the wall. She saw me and asked, "How are you doing in school, Oi Ling?"

I just looked at her and then to the floor. I saw my mother's exasperation. I knew she wanted me to answer.

"And how is your father?" her friend added.

That question gave me more reason not to answer. I often evaluated situations and responded to them silently. In this way, I didn't have to engage the world directly and I escaped getting in trouble for saying the wrong thing. I never knew what to say. To not to get in trouble, I continued to stare at the floor and then watched her expression change from politeness to confusion. Mother's lips tightened and she glared at me until I walked out of the room. In her eyes, I was a hopeless case.

The friend turned to Mother and laughed, "I can't even pry her mouth open with a spoon."

To demonstrate that we were from a family of proper standing, we were taught to hold our bowls and chopsticks a certain way at the dinner table. We were not supposed to chew food with mouths open or to slurp soup. We ate in silence while adults conversed freely, their mouths full of food. Sometimes, when we were alone, we laughed, mimicking the sounds the adults made when they ate.

We only ate chicken on special occasions. It was often called the phoenix and was offered on happy occasions, special holidays, birthdays and the New Year. The best parts of the chicken were reserved for our great-grandmother, then our grandfather, my mother and my younger sister. She came before us because she was the favorite, as the youngest usually were. Mother always offered her the heart and liver, both prized as the best parts of the chicken.

One day during dinner, I was tempted by a nice piece of chicken. The adults seemed engrossed in a discussion about the tenants. I watched for the best moment, and then leaned across the table to get the piece of chicken with my chopsticks. Then, WHACK! My hand was hit by Mother with her ivory chopsticks and mine nearly fell out of my hand. The piece of chicken fell back onto the plate.

"You take what is in front of you. Who told you that you could reach over to get that piece of chicken?" she hissed. My hand throbbed with pain and I fought to hold back the tears not wanting to get into more trouble.

"Don't you dare to cry in front of the food, that is bad luck. You should be happy with the food in front of you."

I tried to wipe away my tears and continue eating but I couldn't swallow. I sat in my seat and tried to let go of the cramps in my stomach and the lump in my throat. But Mother said impatiently, "Go away if you are not eating, I don't want to see your sorry face."

I slipped out of my chair with my head bowed and left the dining room.

"Oi Ling! Bring me the green stick!" Mother yelled from her bedroom.

The green stick was the element of fear in our house. It was a flexible green rattan stick about three feet long and three quarters of an inch thick. It was kept behind the door between the living room and the dining room. Whenever we got into trouble or when our mother was angry, she would tell one of us to fetch it. She would grab it in her hand and order us to stand still. She'd raise it above her head and whip it with such force that we feared the whizzing sound before we felt the sting on our flesh. Afterwards, welts swelled to more than a quarter of an inch high on our legs and butts. They quickly turned black and blue at the edges and a dead white in between. Later, the middle part turned green. I usually could not sit without pain for a week.

When I heard Mother ask for the green stick I began to cry. I was playing in the living room and did not know what I had done wrong. I obediently brought her the stick.

"Why are you crying? I am not even going to hit you. You are such a stupid child," Mother said as I handed the stick to her.

She was going to hit my first elder sister. I was relieved but the anxiety of anticipation made me almost as afraid as when the stick was raised high above me. Most of the time, we didn't know why we got hit. She found reasons I didn't understand. I tried to read her moods, for they could determine whether or not I would be hit.

We lived on the fourth floor and our balcony faced the street in front of the building. I often climbed into an indentation in the balcony wall and looked down at the street to watch the passing cars and buses. I counted cars by their colors and sometimes by their styles. I'd pick a color, like blue or green, and when a car of that color approached I'd count by trying to spit on it while it drove by. This entertained me for hours.

One afternoon before dinner when I was five or six, I was crying about something my second elder sister had taken from me.

"Why don't you just jump out of the balcony if you feel so sorry for yourself? End your life now so that it will be better off for everyone," my mother said to me angrily.

She often said this to us when we cried. I usually didn't take it seriously. But this time I thought it might be a good idea to end everyone's misery. I climbed onto my spot on the balcony and peered down to the street. There weren't many cars. I pulled myself closer to the edge, balancing myself on my tiptoes. The people crossing at the corner looked small. I remembered my recurring nightmare of falling, the weight of my body rushing through the air, sinking fast. I thought of the green stick, the whizzing sound before the sting. Hitting the ground after falling four stories must hurt a thousand times more. I got dizzy. My legs got weak. I was afraid of losing my balance and falling onto the street. I turned to look down at the floor of the flat and quickly climbed down. From that moment on I could not look down to the street from our balcony.

"Go get me a pencil! I have to do my homework," second elder sister ordered as usual, expecting me to do what I was told.

"No! Get it yourself," I spat out gruffly. She raised her eyebrows and looked at me in disbelief.

"You go get it right now!" second elder sister yelled and had her hands on her hips. I turned away to dismiss her. That just incensed her more. She charged forward and grabbed my collar to drag me into our bedroom. She shoved me onto the teak bed using both of her hands and I fell on the smooth hard surface of the wood.

"This is what you get when you don't listen to my orders!" second elder sister shouted while throwing a thick blanket over me. She stood over me on the blanket so I couldn't get out. I heard her laughing. I couldn't breathe. Every time I tried to get to the edge of the blanket, she would stomp in front of my head so I had to find another way out. I panicked. I screamed and cried. She laughed louder. I finally collapsed in exhaustion and stopped moving. I couldn't fight anymore. I gave up. At that point, I thought if I die, I die. Second elder sister yanked the blanket away and looked at me closely, thinking I was dead.

"My baby spider girl," my grandfather cooed affectionately to my younger sister, while he bounced her on his knee. I climbed onto his other knee, wanting the same attention.

"Go away, you are too heavy," he growled, pushing me off and pointing to the door for me to get out. I left without question. By this time, I knew what was good for me. I didn't want to get hit.

My grandfather had a habit of taking an afternoon nap everyday. When he slept, we all knew to tiptoe around the house. I once made something fall and woke him up. He gave me a good whipping with the green stick.

One afternoon, my younger sister decided that she wanted to play the popular game of jumping steps with a rope of rubber bands hooked together. She tied one end to the arm of a chair and asked me to hold the other end. She jumped too hard and I reminded her that Grandfather was napping and she had better be quiet. She laughed and went on jumping.

The door of Grandfather's room opened. My mouth went dry. My face twitched involuntarily. My hands and feet were numbed, frozen from fear. Grandfather came out with his vest unbuttoned. One look at his fiery eyes, and I knew we were in trouble. He looked at us, his lips pressed tight with the corners turned downward and walked over to reach behind the door for the green stick.

I let go of the rope, stood still and waited for his wrath. I held my breath for my sister, and scrunched my eyes tight, waiting for him to hit her. Without warning the stick landed on me. I screamed in pain and shock. He hit again. I tried not to make another sound. If I cried, he'd hit me more. He hit me until he felt satisfied, replaced the stick behind the door, and nonchalantly walked back into his room and shut the door.

I was whimpering, trying to hold in cries from pain when my sister came over to me.

"You should have stuffed a pillow in your pants when Grandfather was getting the green stick," she said sympathetically. I still didn't understand why my sister didn't get hit. Grandfather knew she was the one who made the noise.

When Mother came home, I told her what had happened. I was surprised that she asked Grandfather why he hit me when it was obviously my younger sister's fault. He told her that I was bigger and could take a few lashes. My younger sister was too frail, he said, and besides, she was his little spider girl.

The only time my grandfather allowed me to spend time with him was when he played his magic tricks with us. He started out by using his ivory cigarette holder, pretending that it went into one of his ears and reappeared in the other. I was so happy that he included me in this game. I begged him to play it all the time.

"Grandfather, please show me your magic trick," I asked him eagerly one day when I was alone in his room and everyone was out.

"Bring me one of your small toys," he said with a smile. I was surprised that he didn't shoo me away. I happily obliged, ran out and brought back a plastic toy bowl the size of a coin and handed it to him. He took the little bowl and put it into his shorts.

"Now the magic is that you have to find it," he said, grinning.

I was happy to play any game that Grandfather was willing to play with me. I reached my hand into the leg of his shorts and groped around his penis trying to find my toy. This was the only game he ever played with me.

Routine did have a place in my life. Every morning, the cook made a pot of tea for the day. The red ceramic teapot with a painting of a dragon playing with a fireball outlined in gold was placed in a basket the same shape as the teapot. The basket was lined with a colorful material stuffed with straw to keep the tea warm. She also filled a big thermos with hot water so when we ran out of tea we could refill it with the hot water from the thermos. The teapot and thermos were placed on a cabinet next to a tray of glasses for us to use throughout the day.

I often sat in front of Mother's vanity table in her room on a low soft stool. It had a big round mirror and she kept her jewelry and make-up in the drawers. When she was out, I tried on different pairs of earrings and rummaged through her makeup, being very careful to put everything back how I found them.

Occasionally, I played a game with my second elder sister. We dared each other to jump down from the cement staircase. The loser would be the one who quit first. We would start from the second step, and jump down to the ground. She jumped first and I followed, then we progressed to the third step and so on, until one of us gave up. Oftentimes, we would get to the eighth step. One time I jumped from the eleventh step and landed on the concrete floor. The shock went straight up my feet to my thighs. My feet and legs stung and throbbed all day, but I had won.

The tenants in our buildings and the next building over had girls about my second elder sister's age but I rarely had the opportunity to play with them and my sister. When I asked if I could join them in a particular game, they would say, "We have enough kids already." Sometimes they told me flat out, "We don't want to play with you."

Mother and Grandfather were usually busy doting on my younger sister and seldom included me in their activities so I would go into the kitchen to watch the cook prepare our meals.

"Go away... I said get out of my way," she would say, shooing me out of the kitchen. I was intrigued by how she cut up the vegetables, slaughtered a chicken and prepared the live fish. It was interesting to see which condiment was to go with each dish, how much to use and the method of cooking with each combination. I would stand on my tiptoes by the kitchen door, out of her way with my back to the wall. That kept me out of trouble with everyone.

I slept on a huge teak bed with my second elder sister and my younger sister. It was two slabs of four-inch thick wood pushed together on big sturdy legs underneath. It was cool and smooth. Every morning, the maid folded all the blankets and stacked them at one side of the bed. I used this bed as a stage and pulled my pajama bottoms through my arms up to my shoulders so I could pretend that they were the sleeves of the costumes worn by actresses in the Chinese operas. I stuck bright paper flowers and headdresses with dangling beads in my hair. I entertained myself by acting and singing the songs from the operas. Sometimes, my younger sister joined me and we'd play for hours.

I was Grandfather's helper when he went around the buildings to do minor repairs. I carried his toolbox behind him and handed him tools when he told me what he needed. We also played the magic game when no one was around.

"Bah-ba! You are home!" I was so excited to see my father, I ran to him and stood on his shiny black shoes with my bare feet and held onto his legs tight. He was tall and strong. I had to strain my neck to see his face.

He looked down and frowned, but allowed me to stay on his feet while he walked to Mother's room. When he reached the doorway, he said to me in a monotone voice, "Let go of my leg and go outside to play. I have to talk to your mother."

I reluctantly stepped off his shoes. I was so happy to see him. He rarely came home. Just as I walked down the hallway, away from Mother's room, I heard Father talking to my mother in English so we wouldn't understand what they said. It was never long before they got into a shouting match. In a few minutes, the door swung open with Mother still screaming at Father. I watched him leave the flat in a hurry.

My great-grandmother lived in a small apartment on the mezzanine level of our building and only came upstairs at dinnertime. Though the room was small, she kept it tidy. Her bed was set against a wall across from the window where the recliner was placed. A cabinet and a small table were set against the two opposite walls. During the day I often went to her apartment to visit. Mother warned us to stay away from Great-grandmother, but I loved visiting her. She always shared her food, which she prepared for herself. I washed the dishes and cleaned her tiny kitchen after we ate. I lingered for as long as I dared, playing on her bed and talking to her. A thin gauze mosquito net hung from the ceiling, which I pretended was the curtain of a stage. I sang and acted out scenes from Chinese operas. There was always a smile on Great-grandmother's face when she looked up from the recliner where she often sat sewing. I felt good in that little apartment.

When I passed by Great-grandmother in front of our building, she often reached into her pocket and snuck me a piece of candy. Sometimes when my mother was away, I pulled up a little stool and sat next to her to listen to her stories as she fanned herself with her favorite fan made of a dried palm leaf.

"Are you a good girl and listen to your elders?" Great-grandmother asked me, fanning herself.

"Yes, Great-grandmother. I am a good girl," I said without hesitation.

"That's good. You have to know if you don't tell the truth in this life, you will go to Hell and a ghost will cut your tongue out. If you are greedy, you will be dropped into a pot of boiling oil and if you are lazy, you will be made to slave for other ghosts. To ensure a good life for your next one, you have to do good now." She smiled and looked at me. I nodded, looking up to Great-grandmother with my eyes wide and remembered to try harder to please everyone.

One summer evening after dinner, Mother went shopping with my younger sister. I followed Great-grandmother down to the ground floor and sat next to her at her usual spot in front of the building. She casually fanned herself, watching people pass by. "Look at this shameless woman, her skirt is way up above her knees." Her eyes followed the woman for a while and then she returned to the spot in front of her to see who would next catch her eye. "And look at this one, she painted her face with so much gook that she looks like a witch." Great-grandmother shook her head. I watched with interest, entertained by her comments.

Sometimes Great-grandmother would turn her attention to me. "When you grow up, make sure you keep the honor in this family. How you act and what you wear represents the teachings of our family." She looked deeply into my eyes.

"I will be a good girl. I won't bring shame to our family," I said sincerely to her as an oath.

"That is a good girl and remember Oi Ling, you learn more by traveling for a month than studying from books for three years. Learn from your experiences. Books can only tell you so much." She was distracted by another heavy-set woman walking by.

"Yes, Great-grandmother," I said without really understanding what she meant.

"Look at this woman. She could have a banquet table set on her behind."

She looked over at me and we both laughed.

I finally was old enough to go to school and looked forward to spending time away from the house. To my big disappointment, it was a lot of work and the teachers were mean. I feared the schoolmistress as much as I feared Mother and Grandfather. If I forgot to bring my homework, I had to stand on the stage in the assembly hall with the other offenders. We were displayed in front of all the students during the entire recess. We had to stand in a line and hold out our hands to the headmistress and get four lashes with a four-ply thin rattan whip. If anyone had a greater offense, like stealing a pencil from another student, he got up to twenty lashes on his legs.

The schoolmistress and her rattan whip were a good deterrent to forgetting homework but if I had been traumatized at home that night then I often forgot my work the next day and got whipped in school as well.

One afternoon, I sat in the living room doing homework on the round carved rosewood table. We called it the table with the stone of clouds because of the huge piece of marble set in its center. I made up many stories from the stone's patterns. They were stories of wishing. One of the swirling gray and white patterns looked like a woman climbing a mountain with a child on her back. I imagined she was going into the mountains to look for her husband. They were separated by tragedy and I was sure, one day, he would return. After all, they loved each other.

I wished one day to find someone who loved me and was kind to me.

I was startled from my work by my mother screaming for my first elder sister. My sister ran past me. I saw her frightened face. I didn't know what she had done, but judging from my mother's tone, I was glad it wasn't me.

"How dare you tell the tenants downstairs that I forbid you to get a new pencil when the one you are using was too short to hold? Who told you that you have the permission to talk to the tenants about this household?" Mother's eyes bulged with rage. "You know the rules. We are a respectable family; nothing that goes on in this house goes outside," Mother yelled. "Oi Ling! Bring me the green stick!"

This time I knew my first elder sister was in big trouble. I slipped out of my chair and ran to get the stick from behind the door as fast as I could, afraid that I might get hit if I was too slow. I handed the stick over to my mother. She yanked it from my hand. By this time, my other two sisters were also in the room. My mother always made sure to punish the offender in front of the other siblings so we could learn by watching what would happen to us if we didn't obey the rules.

Mother held the stick high and swung. Her eyes wild, her jaw tight and the whizzing of the stick rhythmically repeated its popping sound when it landed on first elder sister's flesh.

"This will teach you not to lie."

She hit viciously.

"This will teach you not to make up stories about me."

She hit her again and again.

Finally, Mother tired of hitting first elder sister with such force, but she was still angry.

She threw the stick on the floor and grabbed my first elder sister's two braids. She used them as handles to smack her head against the wall. We all got onto our knees and begged our mother to stop. My first elder sister screamed in pain and terror.

I learned my lesson and never told anyone about our household. I learned that Mother had a vision about how she and our household should be perceived by those outside of it. If her actions did not match her vision, we had better stick to her vision and never confront or contradict her. We lived by what she said.

We lived on the top floor. A private staircase led to the roof, which ran the entire length and width of the two buildings. It was paved with terracotta tiles and a four-foot high cement and brick barrier ringed its perimeter allowing us to safely use the roof as a terrace. Grandfather had constructed a huge two tier walk-in cage to raise pigeons and chickens for food. He used the bird manure to fertilize the dozens of plants he grew in large earthen pots on the roof.

I volunteered to feed the birds every day and I spent long hours feeding them by hand. The chickens bobbed up to me, clucking and ruffling their feathers.

When eggs began to hatch, I pulled the shells away from the sharp little beaks and bodies of the babies. I gave them names like Blacky and Pigeon King. Pigeon King was always fun to watch. He had two females and when another male came too close to one, as they always did, he puffed out his neck feathers and beat his wings wildly.

I spent a great deal of my time on the roof when I felt bad or everyone else was busy. I would sit in my favorite oversized rattan chair with my legs folded and stare at the sky. I often spent hours watching the changing shapes of puffy white clouds as they moved evenly across the clear blue sky. At night, I gazed at the millions of stars in different sizes against the pitch-black sky.

One day after I got a beating from my mother, I went to sit in the big rattan chair. I felt so bad that I couldn't even find solace from the sky. I stared into space, hoping the cramps in my stomach and the pressure in my chest would dissipate soon. I knew the pain from the welts on my legs would ease in a few days. I kept staring into space. Slowly, I lost awareness of my body, my thoughts, my pain and my surroundings. The sky and the roof, the pigeons and the chickens, everything started to melt away. I became aware of a very bright light and nothing else. A great sense of peace settled over me. I stayed in this space for a very long time.

"Oi Ling! Come down for dinner," someone yelled from downstairs. I was startled and shocked to find myself back on the rattan chair. I had to face eating dinner with people I feared.

Since then, whenever I felt there was nowhere to go, I found my way back to that rattan chair and that place where I felt safe and in peace.

Great-grandmother was a Buddhist. She taught me to be good so I wouldn't have to pay my karmic debt in my next life. I helped her set up the incense, candles, three small wine cups and offerings to pray to our ancestors or to the different gods, each of whom did different jobs, depending on what Great-grandmother was praying for.

The better schools in Hong Kong were Catholic schools run by the churches. They were prestigious and offered higher standards. In order to get us into the school of my mother's choice, we converted to Catholicism. Unless the family was an active, contributing member of the church, you were placed on a waiting list. Families might wait for years and still not secure spots for their children.

I went to church every Sunday with my mother and to confession every Saturday during our half-day in school. I learned about the Bible and found the stories filled with miracles. I tended to take everything that I was taught, whether in school, at home, or in church, as the absolute truth.

During Mass, I knelt on the wooden bench in front of my seat and watched the sun shine through the three stained glass windows. I was transfixed by the image of Jesus with his crown of thorns staring down at me from his cross. The musky smell of frankincense added an air of holiness to the rituals performed by the priest. When the choir sang hymns in Latin accompanied by the solemn music of the organ, I thought it was the language of God. Maybe if I was sincere and good enough, I would be able to see him. He would grant me a miracle and take me out of my house and set me free.

"Mah-mee, there is blood in the toilet after I go to the bathroom." I had noticed the blood for several weeks before I told her, hoping it would go away on its own.

"Show it to me next time you go to the bathroom," Mother said without looking up from the magazine she was reading.

Off and on for a year I showed the blood in the toilet to my mother. She didn't seem too concerned, so I tried not to be either. One day my nanny said to her, "Sui-nai, Oi Ling is getting skinnier everyday, she only has ribs left and her lips are white. You really need to take her to see a doctor."

"Maybe I should," Mother said.

I was seven when Mother took me to see Dr. Wong, who practiced western medicine. He was a well-known surgeon in Hong Kong. He put me through countless tests and I quickly came to dislike him. I particularly hated the test with the white chalky liquid that went through my intestines, bloating my insides like a big balloon. I wanted to cry from the pressure when I had to hold my breath for what seemed like hours to go through the X-ray. After weeks of tests, he told my mother that I needed to go into the hospital and have my appendix removed.

I was in the hospital for two weeks and Mother was there every day. In spite of all the discomfort and pain, for the first time in my life, I enjoyed attention from my mother.

After the surgery, the doctor wrapped thick sticky bandages around my abdomen. Two weeks later, the stitches were ready to come out. He tried to peel the bandages off.

"Aiya! Mah-mee, it hurts!" I cried and turned to Mother for help. He was ripping my skin off with the bandages. He poured alcohol under the bandages to loosen them, but they were still stuck. Finally, he just yanked them off. I sweated and whimpered in pain. After Mother calmed me, I looked down. The stitches were thick black strings running ten inches down my abdomen like a railroad track.

"This won't hurt a bit," he said and began to pull the stitches out.

"Aiya! Aiya! It hurts too much," I cried in agony. Mother stood and watched in horror. When it was over I looked at the stitches on a metal tray. There was flesh stuck to them and I was bleeding profusely. They wrapped me up again.

As soon as I was well enough to go home, everything returned to the way it was. My bleeding had not stopped. I guessed Mother thought she had done her best and we didn't discuss my health anymore.

"I am taking Margaret's eldest daughter with me to the Golden Mountain. She is going to study in the American school," Grandfather announced during dinner. "I will return shortly. She'll stay in New York with my wife."

I was surprised. I wished I could escape to the Golden Mountain. My first elder sister was so lucky.

"Mah-mee, can I go too?" I asked feebly.

"You are not old enough. You have to be at least fifteen like your sister before we can even consider any of you going to America." Mother looked at me, smiling. I was relieved that it was an acceptable question. Nonetheless, I was envious that my sister got to go and we had to stay.

In the beginning, it seemed to make no difference to me if my first elder sister was around or not. We had little to do with each other as she was always doing the "big girl things" and I was left at home to occupy myself. But as time went by, I became aware that I got yelled at and hit by my mother much more often.

"Oi Ling! Get me the green stick!" The familiar order came from Mother one day after school. As usual, I ran and brought it to her as fast as I could. She told my second elder sister to stand still. As she raised the stick over her head, my sister ran. I was shocked! She dared to defy Mother. She chased after second elder sister and they ran in circles around the house. I saw Mother fuming with rage and the more they ran, the weaker my knees became. I backed up to stand against the wall, afraid to be drawn into the explosion to come.

Mother finally caught my sister and pushed her onto the floor and straddled her and whipped her with the stick until they were both exhausted. My younger sister and I were on our knees begging Mother to stop.

Mother never bothered to hit my second elder sister again. I guessed it was too much trouble for her to force her to comply. I was too frightened to go through more of Mother's rage and was willing to stand still to take whatever she deemed I deserved.

On my eighth birthday, I was glad to be a year older. I already couldn't wait to be old enough to get a job and leave the house. My mother had gone out and I went downstairs to see Great-grandmother. She was sitting in her usual spot in front of the building.

"Great-grandmother! Today is my birthday!" I told her, grinning.

"Good girl, Oi Ling. Do well in school and listen to your elders. Come here, I have something for you." She reached into her pocket and handed me a piece of candy.

"Thank you, Great-grandmother." I took it from her hand and unwrapped it. I needed to eat it quickly so I wouldn't get caught accepting something from Great-grandmother. I popped it in my mouth and turned around to pull up the small stool I always used when we spent time together. I was startled to find Mother standing right behind me.

"What is in your mouth?" Mother asked, narrowing her eyes.

"Nothing," I said, almost choking on the piece of candy.

"Open your mouth!" Mother ordered.

I opened my mouth but before I had a chance to prepare myself, I felt the familiar sting of her hand hitting my face and the salty, coppery taste of blood in my mouth.

"You lie to me, and this is what you get." She slapped the other side of my face, then turned and walked toward the street.

I went upstairs and stood in front of a mirror analyzing the colors on my cheeks. Judging by the tint of her handprint, I knew the imprint would only last for half a day. I opened my mouth to look at my teeth. They were still pink from the blood and I was glad I still had the piece of candy to cover up the taste.

My grandfather came back to Hong Kong after a short time. He brought a large suitcase full of presents for my mother. The things from America smelled dry and fresh, a faint fragrance that only came from American things. It made me aware of the dampness and mustiness of my environment and confirmed my suspicion that America must be even grander and more wonderful than everyone said. I dreamed that some day I might be lucky enough to go there.

I came home after school one day and found Mother and Grandfather talking to a strange man. He wore a cheap black Chinese jacket and wide pants, like one of the poor men on the street. He was desperately in need of a bath and haircut. His eyes were dull and his skin was pasty. My family never allowed people like this in our house. I tiptoed into the other room. I knew better than to stick my nose into something that did not concern me.

"Oi Ling, take this to your father in my room," Mother handed me a small tray of food.

Where was Father? I was surprised to learn that he was home. Why hadn't I seen him if he had come home? I almost dropped the tray when I went into my mother's room and found the man to whom my grandfather and my mother had been talking.

"Bah-ba, here is your food," I said hesitantly. I looked into his sunken eyes, and at the sallow skin on his bare bones. I could not believe that this man with the grimy hair and worn clothes was my father. I had not seen him for years. I remembered him as a suave, good-looking man with his hair nicely combed, nails neatly manicured, his western suit well pressed and fitted, and shoes so shiny I could see my reflection in them.

"Oi Ling, is that you? How big you have grown." Father smiled. "I am not hungry. You can take the food back to the kitchen," he said to me softly.

"At least have some soup. I will take the rest back to the kitchen." I put the bowl of soup and a spoon on the table and left the room.

Father never left his room. Grandfather acted as if he was never home. Mother talked about him, but only when it was absolutely necessary. After a week of Father refusing the food I brought to him, Mother gave up on sending me to his room with meals. He ate only chocolate bars with fruit and nuts, nothing else. It had become my job to buy more candy when he ran out. My reward was a couple of pieces broken off from the big bar.

Everyday after school, I rushed home, eager to spend time with my father in his room. I usually found him asleep, sitting up by the table at the side of his bed. His head would be on top of an open English magazine. The curtains were always drawn and the room dimly lit. I routinely watched him inject medicine into his vein when he was awake. He tapped the white powder from a tiny folded piece of wax paper into an aluminum cap from a bottle of distilled water. He mixed the powder with the water. He then put the tip of the needle into the mixture and sucked it into the syringe. He used the belt from his wool robe to tie around his arm to get his vein to show up and then plunged the needle into his arm. Blood immediately swirled into the syringe and the whitish mixture turned pink. He pushed evenly on the syringe to release the medicine and quickly withdrew the needle. He then closed his eyes. I saw hundreds of tiny red dots following his veins on both arms. I wondered how Father could stand the fear and pain of the needle. Since my stay in the hospital, I hated to get shots. I supposed he was really sick and needed the medicine desperately.

Mother refused to get supplies for Father after they got into a big fight. It became my job to get his distilled water and needles from the drug store just down the street.

"Are you here to get the twenty bottles of distilled water and a dozen of number fourteen needles?" the thin, tall clerk asked as I walked into the drug store. He stood behind the counter filled with western remedies. They all recognized me by now and knew the exact order I came to the store for. As usual, I looked down to the floor and nodded. I stared at the tiny white hexagon tiles that were scrubbed every night before the store closed. I noticed the scuffed black shoes were a little too small for my feet. I could see my big toes bulging on the tips of my shoes. I turned around and passed my time by looking at the funny dried lizards, seahorses, stag horns, jars of snake gall bladders and roots that looked like miniature men that were sold as medicine in the Chinese herbal counter at the other side of the store. Still waiting for the order to get ready, I watched two other clerks precisely measuring herbs stored in little wooden drawers that lined the wall behind the counter. They carefully folded each portion of herbs into little packets in separate sheets of paper periodically checking the formulas written by the herbalists.

"Your order is ready." The tall clerk handed me a bag filled with glass bottles of distilled water. I paid him. Holding the heavy bag with one hand, I leaned all the way to one side to balance the weight. I must look funny to be so lopsided. I saw him shaking his head as I headed to the street.

"You better go do your homework before the Thunder Woman yells at you again," Father would say and smile. Mother always yelled at me for spending too much time with him, so he started calling her the Thunder Woman. It was our secret. It made me feel good to have somebody who was willing to spend time with me.

"I will come back after I have learned my number nine multiplication table. I will recite it to Mother before I come back so she won't yell at me." I would smile back at him then rush outside to do my homework.

When Father was awake, he often told me stories about his experiences.

"Remember the movie star White Light?" Father asked me one day while we shared his chocolate. I nodded.

Chinese movie stars chose names that were meaningful in some way, or, to be fashionable, they chose a direct translation of an English name. White Light was a starlet. She usually played small tart roles in low budget movies.

"One day, your mother met me at a restaurant. I was seeing White Light at the time. Your mother was standing behind me when White Light just happened to walk into the restaurant. Since your mother was short, White Light didn't see her. She stood on her tiptoes and wrapped her arms around me when she noticed your mother standing behind me. She asked who this woman was. I had to tell her that the woman was my wife. White Light slapped my face and walked away. Your mother slapped the other side of my face and they started a shouting match." Father chuckled, delighted at the memory of a starlet and his wife fighting over him in public. I smiled while he laughed, but I didn't know what to make of the story. Would I have to fight for the man I wanted in my life? All the women in the world seemed to.

One evening after dinner, I went to see if Father was awake. He had just finished injecting medicine into his arm and was in a good mood. He gestured for me to sit next to him on my usual spot on his bed and proceeded to tell me a story.

"Before you were born," he began, "I had joined the American Army during the Japanese occupation of China... I had gone to Chung King to fight the invaders as an American soldier. The peasants fled the Japanese who ruthlessly murdered the men, and raped and tortured the women. To compel adults to submit to their will the Japanese routinely butchered children in front of their parents.

"A large group of peasants from several villages were organized by area leaders to relocate to a safer place. They were assigned a guide to lead them out from their homes and villages. None of them knew the way, so they all needed to stay close to the guide. It was a long journey and the villagers packed enough food to sustain them for at least a month. They carried whatever they could in baskets that hung from each end of a long bamboo stick which they balanced across their shoulders.

"A family of five was among this group, a couple with three children, ages ranging from two to seven. The older two children could walk on their own, but the two-year-old had to be carried by his parents. The husband and wife took turns carrying their youngest child and their belongings. The two older children carried their own food on their backs. As the days went on, the weight of their belongings became too burdensome and they dropped them at the side of the road. All they had left were the clothes on their backs and a little food.

"Most people in the group had by now shed all their possessions. They came across a dense forest known to be home to tigers. Everyone was warned not to stray. The guide told them there wouldn't be time to search for anyone who got lost.

"But midway into the forest, the family of five began to lag behind. The parents took turns carrying the youngest child. The rest of the villagers walked empty handed and were anxious to get out of the forest. The family couldn't keep up.

"After a long stretch, they saw the group taking a rest ahead of them. The father told his family that they could rest for a few minutes as well and motioned for his wife to take a few steps away from the children.

"'We have to leave our youngest son behind in order to keep up with the group,' the father said to his wife, looking down and swallowing hard.

"'How could you even think of such a thing? He is our son, our own flesh and blood,' the mother said horrified, 'I can't believe that you are so selfish.' She looked at her husband in disgust.

"'I love my family, that is why we need to do as I say. We will all perish if we are left behind in this forest. Either four of us will survive or five of us will die,' the father said with a mist of tears in his eyes.

"His wife saw that his body trembled. She looked at him and nodded. They dried their eyes and walked back to their waiting children.

"The mother took a sweet bun from the small pack of food and handed it to the youngest boy.

"'Be a good boy and sit here to rest. Mother and Father are going to look for some water with your brother and sister. Eat this bun slowly. By the time you are finished, we will be back to get you.' The mother looked at her youngest son lovingly. The father pulled on her sleeve and gestured her toward the group ahead who were preparing to leave. They left with the other two children. All they could hope for their little boy was a quick death in the jaws of a tiger. They didn't want to think of him being scared for days and then starving to death."

When Father saw me wince at the thought of such horror, he told me that sacrifices had to be made in desperate times. It came down to numbers. "One or five?" he asked me.

I shuddered and wondered what I would do in a similar situation. I hoped I never had to make such a choice.

The cook I had grown up with left to return to her village in China. Mother hired a new cook who claimed to be a Buddhist.

"I will not kill anything that lives," she said, but only live fish and poultry were sold in the market. No one would buy or eat animals if they'd been dead for more than twenty-four hours. Only larger animals like pork and beef were available in pieces.

Mother was not pleased.

"Who is going to do the slaughtering?" she asked. Mother certainly would not do it herself. She looked around and when she saw me sitting at the dining room table her face lit up.

"Oi Ling will do anything. She doesn't care." She smiled at me and said, "Oi Ling! You'll be the one who is in charge of the slaughtering from now on."

I nodded. Protest was pointless unless I wanted to be yelled at or hit.

The day before New Year's Eve, Mother told me to slaughter a chicken. I went up to the roof. The chickens ran toward me and pecked at my hands thinking that I had food for them. I picked out a young fat hen and scooped her up. Holding the hen in my arms, I looked into her eyes and became aware that her job was to feed us and I knew she had had a good life. I had taken good care of her. I carried her downstairs to the kitchen without any resistance. I held her wings and bent her head backward with my left hand and plucked the feather under her beak with my right hand, exposing her neck. I held a sharp small knife, cutting her neck less than three quarters of an inch wide. I found the windpipe and severed it quickly. It was vital to cut perfectly for it was unacceptable to have a dangling head on the chicken - – especially on New Years. It took only a few seconds before she stopped moving. I drained the blood from the neck cavity into a small bowl with a little water. It was saved for later to cook with a different dish. I put the chicken in a basin of boiling water to remove its feathers. I used the same small knife to cut a three-inch slit on the abdomen to remove the innards and wedged its legs into the cavity. After it was boiled, it would look like it was sitting on its nest with its legs tucked under its body. It was essential to cook the chicken and the fish whole. Everything had to have a beginning and an end. It was bad luck to serve something with the head, the feet or the tail missing.

Later, the chicken sat on the table in the living room with its head bent back, a red date in its beak and its wings tucked in. I felt proud. My chicken was doing its job to look perfect on the plate, ready for the New Year.

To celebrate New Year's, we put on our new clothes and something red. We were also careful not to say one bad word. To bring good fortune into the house, the maid swept the floor from the front door inward.

"Gung Hay, Great-grandmother to live over a hundred years, and a strong body and healthy energy," I greeted Great-grandmother when she came up to our flat for the special lunch.

"Good girl and listen to your elders and do well in school." She handed me a red envelope with money inside for good luck. My sisters and I had already wished good health to our Grandfather; and to Mother, we wished good fortune and that her wishes would come true. They in turn, told us to be good girls and gave us red envelopes.

It is customary for friends and relatives to visit each other on the first seven days of the New Year. Everyone wished each other good fortune and wealth and brought boxes of fruit and homemade pastries for the visits and best of all, the red envelopes of good luck money for the children. For seven days, we celebrated. All the shops and markets were closed and the streets were full of children playing with firecrackers. Everyone was in a good mood and I got to wear a new dress and eat dishes specially made for New Year's.

A loud commotion woke me up very early in the morning before school. I ran through the dining room toward the noise and saw strange men in white uniforms walking in the hallway. I heard them say something about a stretcher and ambulance. The activities seemed to be coming from the bathroom. I snuck by the maid in the hallway to see what was going on. I had a glimpse of the blood splattered walls and a huge pool of red on the floor when I felt a hand grasp my arm and I was briskly pulled back into the hallway.

"Stay out of the way. This is not for children to see," the maid said, pushing me back into the dining room. I was scared. No one told me what had happened until almost everyone had left. Grandfather had been taken to the hospital. He had vomited blood.

A few days later, Mother took us to see Grandfather in the hospital. He was lying in a bed in the middle of the room covered with a white sheet. He looked small and frail, not like the towering person I feared. He didn't open his eyes the entire time we were there. I stood around while Mother talked to relatives and the nurse. I knew this was serious because no one would go to the hospital unless it was absolutely the last resort.

Every evening after dinner, Mother took us to see Grandfather. He didn't seem to improve. It was monsoon season and we were in the middle of a fierce typhoon. The wind ripped tin roofs off from the shacks built on the roofs of buildings. They whipped in the sky like giant kites. Torrential rain flooded the streets. Mud water flowed through them like swift yellow rivers. Mother insisted we go to the hospital. An adult cousin carried my youngest sister on her back and second elder sister and I walked behind Mother. The floodwater came up to my waist. I tried to keep up with Mother but the ground was covered with thick muddy water, and I couldn't see beneath it. I stumbled and fell into a hole. The water surged up to my chest. I tried to pull myself out, but I wasn't strong enough. I panicked and kicked around trying to find a spot for a foothold. I didn't dare cry out for help, too afraid Mother would be angry with me for holding everybody up. I finally found a soft spot. I braced myself and pushed with all my strength. I got out and pressed through the water as fast as I could to catch up.

Mother turned to see if we were following her closely.

"Why is your hair so wet?" she asked me.

I bowed my head, not daring to look at her.

"I fell," I whispered, still trying to catch my breath.

"Clumsy ox." She snorted and continued walking toward the hospital.

I stood in the hospital room shivering. For the first time since we saw him in the hospital, Grandfather was awake. He hummed happily. A few of our relatives stood around in the room. Mother was busy talking to them. I thought since Grandfather was better, he might be able to come home soon. My sisters and I huddled together in the corner, rubbing our arms and legs trying to get warm. Suddenly, Grandfather sat up and tried to grab hold of my mother. Everyone backed away from the bed. He had the most frightened look on his face. Mother let out a loud cry and told Grandfather to be happy and to go up to heaven. Our cousin waved to us to come next to the bed. We ran over and got down on our knees like everyone else. I watched him as he tried to breathe. He gasped desperately, his mouth wide open and his eyes wild and terrified. Each breath he took was more labored and shallow until he couldn't do it anymore. He finally stopped, his eyes wide open and his mouth distorted from the desperate sucking in of air.

I cried with everyone else and called out to our grandfather.

My grandmother came home from America with two of my aunts for Grandfather's funeral. Things became much better at home. Mother seemed less angry. She behaved well around Grandmother and my aunts so she wasn't as likely to take her anger out on me.

I became Grandmother's little helper. I shined her shoes and dyed her hair. She tipped me generously and always took me shopping with her. I helped her carry the packages home from her frequent shopping sprees.

Grandfather used to ration everything we ate. As a great treat once in a long while, he would hand out four crackers and measure out half a small glass of soda for each of us.

"You look like you have just gotten released from prison. This is for everyone and you can eat as much as you want," Grandmother said to me when she saw me hesitating to get more food. I looked at my mother to see if it was all right to take more and to my surprise, she wasn't staring at me with her fiery eyes. It didn't take long for me to relax and enjoy this new freedom.

I was walking home from school one afternoon and saw hundreds of posters plastered on buildings. They were part of a huge campaign educating the public on the evil of drugs. The life-size photograph on the poster portrayed a man sitting on a wooden bench in front of a wooden coffin which stood upright against a wall. The man looked like a barely living skeleton. His eyes were sunken into protruding cheekbones and he was pressing his hands against the bench to prop himself up to a sitting position. His lips barely covered his teeth and his feet were severely swollen. When I saw the poster, I immediately felt cramps in my stomach and the heavy pressure on my chest. The man looked exactly like my father! But I said to myself, this man is a heroin addict. Not my father! My father is sick. He might look like this man but my father is not a drug addict. I felt so much better knowing my father was taking medicine to cure his sickness. I walked home and thought about my shopping date with Grandmother.

"Go get changed, girls. I am going to take you to see an American movie," one of my aunts announced one early afternoon.

I was elated. I had never seen an American movie in my life. The theaters that played foreign films were much grander than the cheap Chinese movie theaters. They sold sweet popped corn and sausages that they called hot dogs for some unknown reason. I had never tasted one. I hurried to get a pair of long pants from the dresser and was about to put them on when my second elder sister came in. She grabbed one leg and said that they were the ones she wanted to wear. I refused to let go and she yanked at the material. I usually gave in to escape a beating from Mother but I felt bolder since my grandmother had come home so I fought back. My second elder sister was incredulous. She started to hit me and I ran, still holding the pair of pants in my hands. She was closing in so I headed toward my father's room, since my sister seldom went there. Father was awake, preparing to administer his medicine. I ran and hid behind him. Second elder sister barged in and tried to grab the pants from my hands.

"Stop this instant. What's going on?" Father said sternly, in a tone I had never heard before.

"I had these first and second elder sister tried to take them from me," I said quietly.

"Let Oi Ling have this and go get yourself another," Father said to my sister.

My second elder sister was stunned that Father actually spoke up for me and got angrier. She charged me and pulled on the pants as hard as she could.

"Stop this right now!" Father ordered again but she wouldn't listen still yanking on them. Father stood up and slapped her face for her defiance. We were all in shock. I had never seen Father lose his temper. Since he'd come home to live, I'd never heard him say anything above a whisper.

Second elder sister looked at Father with one of my mother's angry looks and said, "I will never speak to you again and here is your stinking watch. I don't want it." She unbuckled the watch Father had given her for her birthday just a few weeks before. She threw it at him and stomped out of the room. Second elder sister never spoke to Father again.

It was a strange feeling to have someone care enough to defend me. Coupled with Mother's good behavior when Grandmother was around, for the first time in my life I could relax at home.

Less than a month after Grandfather's funeral, Father was whisked away in a Taxi to the same hospital where Grandfather had died. That hospital felt like a death trap to me. Everything there was gloomy and everyone looked grim. I visited Father every day with Mother. He stayed in a much smaller room than Grandfather, with just enough space for a small bed and night-stand. When Mother took both my younger sister and me, one of us had to stand in the doorway. Father rarely opened his eyes and he didn't recognize me when I tried to talk to him. He had a tube running into his nose. Mother told me that Father need-ed oxygen to help him breathe. A bottle was hung upside down with a tube going into a needle that was in his arm. His lips were so shrunken that they barely covered his teeth.

"You should come with me to see your father; he doesn't have much time left," Mother told my second elder sister one day as we put on our shoes.

"No. He can die and I don't care," she said without looking at Mother.

I was stunned that she dared speak to Mother with such defiance, but I was even more shocked that Mother didn't respond. Instead, she started to walk toward the door and motioned for us to follow. I didn't understand. How could my sister dismiss Father on his deathbed just because he hit her once? Grandfather had hit me many times and I didn't hate him. He was my family. Mother had hit us more times than I could remember. How could Mother allow my sister to ignore Father? Great-grandmother had always taught me to honor our family and to be loyal to each member under any circumstance. I was appalled that Father's own daughter and wife were not loyal to him.

I saw Mother whispering to the nurse in the hallway at the hospital before she came into Father's room. The nurse came in shortly and gave Father an injection.

A few minutes later, I watched Father die, so quietly com-pared to Grandfather. It seemed he didn't even try to breathe, as though he accepted or welcomed his death. I cried because that was what everyone was supposed to do. My sister and I kneeled on the floor and called out his name as we had done for Grandfather.

I did not know how I felt. He cared for me in his way and I was lucky to have the short time that we had together. I did not dare feel more than that. After the funeral, I didn't cry for him again. Since I was a toddler I had been taught not to cry when something was taken away from me. I learned the only way to survive was to embrace my fate.

Grandmother planned to return to America with my two aunts shortly after Father's funeral. Mother requested that my second elder sister go with her to get an American education. Things were quiet after Grandmother left with my second elder sister. I was relieved that I had one less person to prey on me. Mother was always out with her friends. My younger sister and I were pretty much left alone in the house with the maid. Sometimes we got to go with Mother to visit her friends and play with their children while Mother played mahjong with the adults.

One day we were visiting with Mother at her friend's flat whose husband was in America. The place was lively all the time, with men and women coming and going throughout the day, and a game of mahjong always in progress. Tables were crammed with food. The building was in a more fashionable part of Kowloon than ours. Her husband bought it years after my grandfather had bought ours. I could tell my mother's friend was free to do as she wished. Her children ate and played freely. They didn't have to ask permission to do anything. They also dressed more fashionably than we did. She often had big parties with enough food to feed the whole neighborhood.

The woman's youngest daughter was my second elder sister's age. She usually thought of games that I wouldn't dare to imagine on my own. Her mother let her play with soap and water, which I was never allowed to touch at my house unless I was taking a bath. In their home, even I didn't have to ask permission before I ate.

"Margaret, your daughter does not look too healthy," I overheard a friend say to Mother. Mother looked up from her game for a moment and nodded in acknowledgement.

"I know of a very good herbalist. Maybe he can help her," the man continued.

I was still bleeding when I went to the bathroom, but I'd gotten used to it.

"Oh really? Maybe you could take Oi Ling to go see him, if you don't mind," Mother answered, while she studied her mahjong hand.

"Sure I will. She does look gaunt." He waited for Mother to respond, while she played her hand.

Mother said, "You can pick her up after school. She goes to the Catholic school in Shek Gip Mei District." She picked up a mahjong tile and threw it onto the center of the table.

I was surprised that someone took notice of me. I did not know him well. He was dating the older daughter of my mother's friend. He had come to visit our house with my mother's friend on only one occasion to demonstrate his martial art on the roof. That visit had left a deep impression on me. Although he had a small stature, he looked fierce and confident.

The man said he'd pick me up the next day. I felt good that a casual friend of Mother's cared enough to take me to see an herbalist.

When I got out of school the man was waiting in front of the gate. He nodded to me and didn't say a word. I followed him on a long walk up a steep hill. When we reached the top, way down the street I saw a cluster of buildings commonly called "seven layer blocks" painted in the usual dull orange. They were government-built housing for the very poor. I had never been close to one of them. As we got closer, I became more intrigued. It was a different world. The stench from the open sewer was overwhelming. Dirty children ran around without clothes and played with garbage. One boy tried to fish out something in the sewer by dipping a long straw into it. The trash that we threw out in our house was pristine compared to what they played with.

I followed Mother's friend to the second floor. The entire building was composed of slots of cement boxes smaller than our kitchen. No one bothered to close their doors. One could see the interior of the entire box from the hall.

"Come in here." A man gestured for us to step into his tiny room. The two men greeted each other.

"Who is this girl that needs my help? You can call me Doctor Lai," the herbalist said, studying me with his small beady eyes.

"She is the daughter of a friend of mine."

The herbalist was exceptionally ugly. I could tell that his slicked back, jet-black hair was dyed. I knew it was unusual for a man to dye his hair. It made me queasy to look at him. He had a pockmarked face, a very large nose and a wide mouth. His manner of speech was from the street. As Mother would say, it was low class. I didn't really care. I came because Mother told me to. The box was furnished with two rickety chairs and a tiny table placed between them on one side of the front room, and there were piles of cheap dirty kitchen supplies stacked on a table on the other side. I took three steps into the box and sat down on one of the chairs in front of the flimsy interior wall. Behind that board through an opening, I could see a homemade bunk bed set against the outer cement wall. I had never visited a place so stifling. It felt like a place of desperation. During the entire time, I wanted to bolt from my seat and dash home.

The herbalist sent me home with herbs. I carefully followed the instructions. First I had to mix the herbs with three bowls of water in an earthen pot and then boil it down to three quarters of a bowl. I drank the tea when it was cool enough to gulp down while I held my breath. It was extremely bitter.

The following day, I went back to the herbalist with Mother's friend. He checked my pulse and we left with another potion of herbs. The herbalist asked his friend to tell my mother to give me the herbs for a few days to see if they would heal me.

It only took two doses of the herbal infusion to stop my bleeding.

"Mah-mee! There is no more blood!" I called out to Mother after I went to the bathroom.

Mother was amazed.

"Maybe I should go see this herbalist for my headaches," Mother said thoughtfully, then asked, "Do you know how to get there by yourself?"

"Yes, I'll take you, but I have to warn you, it is dirty!" I knew Mother's squeamishness about things like that. She wouldn't even touch the eggs I collected from our chickens if I didn't wash them first.

The following day, I met Mother outside the school. The closer we got to the "seven layer blocks," the slower Mother walked. As we climbed the stairwell leading to the herbalist's tiny cube, I saw Mother's face scrunch up. She was about to vomit.

"I told you," I whispered as we approached his place.

"I am Doctor Lai." The herbalist smiled broadly. His eyes gleamed as soon as he saw Mother. He motioned me to the tiny table and rickety chairs. The entire time he was feeling my pulse I saw him checking Mother out from the corners of his eyes.

Mother and I went home with our herbs. I prepared them for both of us. To my surprise, Mother was very enthusiastic about going back to that dirty place. I found myself going to the herbalist every other day and each time it took longer and longer before we could go home. Eventually, I started to do my homework there on the tiny table while Mother talked to Doctor Lai behind the flimsy board where the bed was. Sometimes I had to wait for hours after I had finished my homework. I started to make friends on the floor, especially with one woman and her daughter. The girl was called "Six Fingers" because of her extra thumb. I often watched her while her mother gossiped with other women on the floor.

"Did you hear about Ah Gum's big row with her sister two days ago? Her sister was doing it with her husband! The creep needs to have his penis chopped off," Six Fingers' mother exclaimed, raising her brows.

"It's her sister's fault! She thinks she is prettier than Ah Gum so she proved it by fucking her husband. And you think Ah Gum's sister is bad? My brother-in-law's sister is doing all three brothers of her husband," her neighbor said, spitting on the floor and rolling her eyes.

I didn't know people so commonly had affairs or that jealousy and hatred ran so rampantly in families. They didn't care how others viewed them. If I dared to say a fraction of what I had heard from them about my family, I would probably be hanged and my corpse whipped after I was dead.

We hadn't needed the herbal infusions for the longest time but Mother still went to see the herbalist everyday. I had stopped accompanying her and seldom saw her at home. Sometimes my youngest sister and I would meet Mother, the herbalist and his friends at fancy tea parlors or well-known restaurants. We would come home after we ate and Mother would stay there or go off with the herbalist. She usually came home after we were fast asleep and she was often gone before the maid got us up to go to school.

I came home from school one afternoon and was surprised to find Mother home. She was talking to one of the relatives who had a farm in the New Territory. I remembered her from when Grandfather was still alive. She came to visit us occasionally with her son and grandchildren. Her other son was married to one of Father's sisters. They always brought us healthy livestock from their farm and fresh oysters. I'd always looked forward to seeing them because that meant a great feast for dinner in the evening.

"Look what I have brought specially for you!" she said to Mother. "I heard that you have arthritis." She reached into a small basket and brought out a black puppy in the palm of her hand. It barely had fur and its eyes were not yet opened.

"He is only seven days old, the perfect age to be prepared with herbs to boost your strength and lessen your pain." She smiled and handed Mother the prize.

"Our bitch had a litter of puppies and I immediately thought of you. Cook it soon so it won't get too big and lose its potency. This is a male and the best for arthritis."

Mother appreciated her thoughtfulness and put the puppy in a towel on the table.

Black shorthaired dogs were prized for boosting one's health when prepared with a special combination of traditional herbs. On occasion, we were invited to a friend's house to share the prize when they slaughtered a dog. I had eaten dog quite a few times but it was very rare to land a seven-day-old personal potion for one's health. Mother was lucky to have such a gift.

My younger sister and I huddled together to play with the puppy while Mother talked to her relative. By the time she left, we loved the puppy.

"Mother, please, please, please, can we keep the puppy?" we begged.

"No, I have to eat it soon before it gets big," Mother said and started to look for a place to put the puppy before he got slaughtered.

"Mother, we want the puppy! We will take very good care of it. We promise!" My younger sister looked to me and we both said, "Please, mother! We promise that we will take care of him. We promise!" My younger sister pestered mother till she gave in.

"All right, you can keep it if you take care of it. He needs to drink milk from a bottle. He doesn't even have teeth yet. Call him Milky," Mother finally said.

"Meel-kiee, we will take good care of you," we chimed.

We fed Milky with a bottle till his teeth came in. His eyes opened in a week's time.

Mother seldom came home. We ran around with Milky in the flat. We covered ourselves with blankets and got on our hands and knees to encourage him to chase us. We had great fun and he became a large, handsome dog with short black hair.

"813096, remember these numbers! This is where you can reach me," Mother instructed one afternoon. I was surprised to find her home instead of the maid.

"I have fired the maid. We don't need any help in the house just for the two of you. You are old enough to help out," Mother said before I had a chance to ask. She continued, "Doctor Lai has moved. I am going to take you there today so you can learn to take the number six bus to get there."

I followed Mother out the door. We walked to the bus stop and waited for the bus on Nathan Road, the main street that ran from one end of Kowloon to the other. It was late in the afternoon. People pushed and shoved from all sides, trying to get in better positions to rush the bus. When the bus arrived, we elbowed our way on. A fraction of unblocked window allowed me to watch the street which slowly become brighter and cleaner as we rode down the boulevard. I was very careful to remember where we got off. It was the ritzy part of Hong Kong, one of the best-known areas in Kowloon. People were better dressed. Everything seemed orderly and pleasing. I couldn't imagine anyone here talking about their families to strangers.

I followed Mother to a brand new exclusive building. There was even a lift for the residences. I was impressed. We got off on the sixth floor and Mother opened the door to one of the apartments with a key. I peeked inside behind her, anxious to see what a greasy man with a low class way of talking would do in a fancy place like this. It was a well-furnished apartment and very spacious, a rare find in Hong Kong especially in this part of town. I wondered how he had become so rich in such a short period of time. He must have truckloads of patients to afford the rent. He emerged from his bedroom as we came in.

"This is where I'll be and you have my number. If you need me, ring me on the telephone. Here's some money to get dinner for you and your sister." Mother handed me a five dollar bill. I took the money and she turned to greet Dr. Lai. She didn't even hear me say goodbye. I left, caught the bus and went home.

I got to the market just before they closed for the afternoon session. I bought a few things and went home to cook for my sister and myself. It was strange to cook for us for real. I used to fool around in the kitchen, but now we had to eat what I cooked. It came out better than I expected and my sister ate without any complaints. I cleaned the dishes. It was getting dark. I played with my sister and Milky for a while and did my homework. I sent my sister to bed late and waited for Mother to come home. The maid was gone, we were at the house all by ourselves and it was getting scary. I couldn't go to Great-grandmother because she would find out about Mother's absence, so I went downstairs and onto the street to see if I could spot Mother walking toward our building. All of the stores were closed for the night. It was dark and I was more scared on the street. I ran upstairs, covered myself with a blanket and sat on a chair to wait for Mother.

When I woke, the sky was getting light. I was still in the chair. I ran to see if Mother was sleeping in one of the beds. Since my father had returned home, I never knew where she slept. I walked through the house looking in the vacant bedrooms, but there was no sign of her. I cried and didn't know what to do. I took a deep breath and started to think about what needed to be done. I had to get my sister ready for school. My school started a little later, so I had time to get her off to school and still get to mine on time. I woke her up, fed her breakfast, and got her into her uniform. Just as I reached the door, Mother walked in. That was the most welcome sight I ever had in my life.

That night, Mother came home while I was having dinner with my younger sister. She tasted the steamed fish I had prepared and she said, "Oi Ling, where did you learn how to cook this? It is good." Mother actually liked something I had done!

"I learned from watching the cook," I said proudly.

"I don't have to worry about you two. You can take care of yourselves," Mother said to us. I was elated that she complimented me.

But after that, Mother came home only once a week to leave enough money for us to buy food. I had two dollars a day to feed the both of us. I realized I did not have enough money to buy the same foods as our cook. Two dollars would not even cover a whole fish. I still had to get vegetables. I compensated by buying vegetables of poorer quality and the small fish that people bought for their cats. We seldom ate meat because it was expensive. I asked my younger sister to wash the dishes so I could wash and iron our uniforms for school. I swept and mopped the floor. I did everything our maid used to do and hoped if I did a good job, Mother would come back and leave us money to buy food. I was so afraid that if I didn't do a good enough job, Mother would be mad at me and never come back. I was eleven years old.

One morning at three, I was awakened by a shuffling noise. Mother had come home with a strange man. They were cooking something in the kitchen that had a strong sickly sweet smell. I was overwhelmed by the odor and saw the man hand Mother a pot of thick, gooey reddish black stuff that looked like tar. Mother gestured for me to come inside her room. She set down the pot and took out a big paper bag full of tiny bone containers.

"Fill these up and make sure you have the lids on tight," she ordered. I stayed up till dawn to fill them and when the job was done, Mother disappeared for days again.

One time, Mother hid some long pipes under the stone bench up on the roof. She telephoned me at home and instructed me to deliver them to the herbalist's apartment. I lugged the heavy pipes onto the bus and found a seat, balancing them between my legs, with their thick bulbous ends sticking up to my chest. I had a paper bag loosely covering them. As I walked into the apartment, the first thing Mother said was: "How stupid can you be?" and slapped my face. I had no idea why I got hit. She said I had not wrapped the pipes properly. A cop might have followed me to the apartment. She never told me exactly what I needed to do. I didn't understand why a cop would follow me. I only knew that in everything I did, I needed to be secretive and not to make Mother mad.

I was doing my homework one evening and was startled by the sound of the doorbell. It was rare to have someone at the door when Mother wasn't home.

"Who is it?" I asked cautiously and sneaked up to the door and tried to peak and see who was on the other side.

"I am a police officer and there was an accident," I heard a man's voice and saw him through the crack of the door. He was in the usual khaki police uniform with long white sleeves, an indication of a traffic policeman. I nervously opened the door and asked, "There was an accident?" hoping it was not Mother.

"Do you know a lady named Wong Oi?" he asked.

"That is my great-grandmother. Was she in an accident?" My face flushed with anxiety and my mouth became dry.

"She was hit by a car and hurt her shoulder. Where are your parents?" he continued.

"Mother is out for an errand. I will tell her when she returns," my well-rehearsed answer for anyone who asked the whereabouts of my mother.

"All right then, I have already written a report on it and just tell your mother I was here." He turned around and walked down the stairs. I rushed to the phone and tried to reach Mother at the herbalist's apartment. I didn't get her until a couple of hours later.

"Mother, Great-grandmother was hit by a car and hurt her shoulder. What should I do?" I almost cried with relief when I spoke to her.

"Such a clumsy old fart. Take her to a bonesetter and see if she needs his attention," Mother said, annoyed.

"How are we going to get there? It is far away," I asked timidly.

"Take a taxi! How stupid can you be," Mother screamed impatiently and hung up.

I took Great-grandmother to the bonesetter every other day for three weeks. He said her bone was broken. In order to set it well she had to take a concoction of herbs with some mountain snails and cockroaches. I went to the market everyday to get the ingredients and came home to boil it down for two hours. I didn't mind the snails. They were big and had pretty shells but I hated the scratchiness of the mountain cockroaches' legs when I had to stick my hand into the paper bag to get them out. They were half the size of my palm. I prepared the infusion and took it downstairs for Great-grandmother. In a month's time, she was completely healed.

A year later, Mother came home in the afternoon. Judging by her face, I knew I'd better stay out of her way. She ordered me to clean the house thoroughly.

The next day, she hired a maid.

"Your grandmother is coming home tomorrow with your aunts. Under no circumstance are you going to tell them anything," Mother said to me with her piercing gaze. I had no idea what she was referring to, but to be on the safe side I would say nothing.

I remembered the last time Grandmother came home for Grandfather's funeral. Though it was sad, everyone was kind and we were all relaxed. But this time, as soon as my two aunts and grandmother stepped into the flat, I felt a dark cloud descend. They all had angry faces and solemn voices. Mother tiptoed around on her best behavior. I knew something was very wrong.

"What is the man's name?" one of my aunts asked me when we were alone.

"What man? I don't know what you are talking about." I was frightened by the anger in her voice.

"The man your mother is sleeping with," she said, and glared at me with disgust.

"What? I don't know what you are talking about." My mouth went dry. She stepped closer, with her face right above me. I backed into a wall. I had severe cramps in my stomach. My heart raced and the pressure on my chest built until it was difficult to breathe. I thought I was going to die but I knew my duty was to keep everything secret to protect Mother.

"Is he the herbalist?" she pressed on.

"I don't know! I really don't know!" I started to cry and got light-headed. I thought I might pass out. My aunt pressed her face within inches of mine. I couldn't move. My back was against the wall. I had nowhere to go. Desperate, I stooped down under her arms and started to run. I ran up to the roof and found the rattan chair. I collapsed. My heart pumped so hard, I felt it in my throat. I cried till my chest and stomach began to relax.

In the evening, I saw Mother and followed her into her room, and waited for the right moment to speak to her.

I watched as she put on her pajamas. When she walked to her vanity table to study herself in the mirror, I approached her, "Mah-mee, my aunt asked me if you are seeing Doctor Lai."

"Did you tell?"

"No, but I'm scared. She pressed me hard," I said in a feeble voice. Tears rolled down my face.

"Good," she said and started to walk away.

"Mah-mee, Doctor Lai is evil. None of this would have happened if not for him," I cried.

"Just don't tell," Mother said and walked out of her room leaving me crying on her bed.

The next day, Mother told us Milky had to go. I knew Grandmother disliked dogs but I didn't think she'd make us give him up. Mother told her that she would take the dog away that very day.

"Oi Ling, come with me," Mother said. I followed her with Milky tied to a rope.

"Where are we taking Meel-kiee mother?" I asked nervously as she was looking to flag down a taxi.

"Doctor Lai will take him. That's where we are going now," Mother said, still looking for a vacant taxi. I was relieved. At least Doctor Lai was good for something. How nice of him to take Milky in when he had nowhere to go.

Mother sneaked out to see the herbalist almost every day, with me in tow. I gladly went because it meant I could see my dog. We would tell Grandmother that we were going to see a movie, I would wait in the living room for Mother to be done, playing with Milky and watching the men smoking the sickly sweet smelling gooey paste in the pipes that I had gotten in trouble over.

One day, Mother took longer than usual. I became anxious about the time, as we were supposed to be home an hour earlier. Finally the herbalist and Mother emerged from the bedroom. I always turned my head when I heard the door crack open.

"Oi Ling, do you want a brother?" Doctor Lai asked me as Mother prepared to leave.

"What do you mean?" I asked, not really understanding the implication.

"I will give your mother a son," he said with a sly smile on his greasy face.

I almost vomited. I rolled my eyes and turned away in repulsion.

When we walked out of the flat, I had a hard time looking at Mother, but she was happy and oblivious. I could no longer deny their affair. My skin felt like it had been bitten by a million ants. My eyes twitched and I was hot all over. Now I had to go home to face my aunts. I had to continue protecting my mother. I wished I had another life.

"Your niece is pregnant by that damn herbalist, the same man who got Bik Ha pregnant," my aunt said to Grandmother after dinner. We were all sitting around the table peeling and eating lychee for dessert.

"That shameless girl, I don't know how her family can live with her shame," Grandmother replied, shaking her head.

"This is your niece's second child. She already has a son fathered by him. She really has no shame," Mother chimed in.

My face began to twitch. I felt sick and tried to swallow the piece of lychee in my mouth.

"All these women are such shameless whores," Mother said self-righteously. I had to leave the table. My eyes were twitching. I was afraid that I would choke. I forced a smile and excused myself. I would be in such trouble with Mother if I gave anything away by reacting adversely.

One day, I went to the herbalist's apartment with Mother and found Milky gone.

"He ran out of the apartment yesterday and never came back," Dr. Lai said to me when I asked him about Milky.

"Oh, no! I have to go look for him." I started to cry. I went down to the street and walked for blocks looking for him, calling for him. But I couldn't find Milky.

When we returned the next day, the herbalist and some men, who usually lay around on the beds in other rooms smoking their long pipes, were eating heartily at the large table. He waved to my mother and said, "Come get your share. Ah Sing landed a dog yesterday and just finished cooking it... and get a bowl for Oi Ling too, since she is here."

Mother walked over to the table with a sweet smile and ladled two bowls full of dog meat and handed one to me. I sat down and ate in silence. I should consider myself lucky to get a share of dog because it was good for my health. I hung around waiting for Mother after I ate and heard one of the men saying, "Lucky day, just as I needed a boost for my health, Dr. Lai offered dog meat today. The black short-haired ones are the best, well worth the money." The other men chuckled and agreed.

I suddenly felt sick. I started to sweat. Mother was just coming out of the room. I looked straight into her eyes and asked, "Did I just eat Meel-kiee?" She just looked away.

⊷⊷

Like the rest of us, Grandmother had converted to Catholicism. One of my aunts was even contemplating becoming a nun. We went to church every Sunday and they were very friendly with a priest whom they knew from America.

One morning, Father Moore came to our house to take Grandmother to see one of his projects. He was tall, with sincere blue eyes and sandy blonde hair. I was very taken by his appearance. He also exuded an air of kindness. Grandmother took me with her to tour the orphanage Father Moore had created for the very poor in Hong Kong. I was impressed by his work and thought he was an extension of God, creating miracles for the impoverished. I admired him and drew great comfort from the moral values being taught by the Catholic Church. Most importantly, I hoped that it could shield me from the chaos of my life.

Grandmother brought out one of my aunt's wedding pictures to show us. My second elder sister was one of her bridesmaids. She was sixteen. I hadn't seen her for four years and was amazed by how good she looked. Mother showed the picture of the wedding to her friends and told them how beautiful my sister had become. I wished I would grow up looking like her, but in my mother's eyes, I never had a chance. I prayed hard every time I went to church with Grandmother. I prayed to God to let me grow up to be as pretty as my second elder sister.

I was tired of being called the ugliest and dumbest one in the family. It didn't matter how hard I tried. From early on I always came in second or third in my class. My mother's response was that I was not good enough to be first. But my younger sister failed almost every subject and Mother never yelled at her. At some point I realized that for me to be considered smart, I had to be clever enough to make another person feel stupid. Mother prized my younger sister's intelligence when she manipulated a situation in her favor. I was never good at that.

"If you were granted three wishes, what would they be?" my aunt asked my younger sister and me while we were on the roof catching the evening breeze.

"My first wish would be to have a hundred more wishes!" my younger sister said immediately.

"You are so smart!" my aunt exclaimed, impressed at my sister's quick wit. She turned to me and asked, "And you? What are your wishes?"

"I only want one wish. I wish to be happy," I said thoughtfully.

"You must be stupid or you are lying! Who doesn't wish for a lot of money? That is the dumbest answer I have ever heard," my aunt jeered. Money had no meaning to me at that time. I didn't know what happiness was either, but I hoped that I would find it one day.

One afternoon, I accompanied Grandmother to a new development near an industrial area. She was to buy a condominium to house my father's children from his mistress.

"Grandmother, why can't they come to live with us?" I asked her while we were looking at one of the units.

"You are going to New York with your mother and sister and they can't come with us," Grandmother explained.

"We are going to America?" I couldn't believe my ears. I remembered how I dreamed about going to America after my aunt brought us to see the American movie, "Goldfinger." The streets were clean and wide. They were lined with palm trees and fancy cars, and everyone was glamorous. The buildings were impressive and the furnishings were luxurious. How I longed for a chance to live in America and escape my pitiful situation. I finally had a chance to go!

The minute I got home, I ran to find Great-grandmother to tell her the good news.

"Great-grandmother! I am going to America!" I shouted to her before I even got to her door.

"You what?" Great-grandmother asked and seemed surprised.

I was astonished that she did not hear me. She was usually very attentive when I talked to her.

"I am going to America," I repeated, still excited. She turned her face away and looked very sad.

"Aren't you happy for me? Isn't it everyone's dream to go to America?" I asked, confused by her reaction.

"I am happy for you. So tell me, when are you leaving?" She seemed so sad, I thought she might be holding back tears, but I was too excited to think about anything besides getting myself ready to go to America.

"Grandmother is taking my younger sister on an airplane in a few weeks and I am leaving with Mother on a big ship two months after that. I have so much to do. I have to go now and I will come talk to you later." I ran out of the apartment without further thought to Great-grandmother. I was so happy to leave this place for "the beautiful country," which is the direct translation of "America" in Chinese. I was beside myself with excitement and anticipation.

My younger sister left with Grandmother and our aunts for New York. Mother and I planned to leave Hong Kong in October.

Four days before sailing, everything in the flat remained the same, as if we would continue to live there indefinitely. I was worried. The next day Mother finally showed up and pushed everything off the furniture onto the floor. A strange man came with her. He walked around the flat and gave Mother a stack of big red hundred dollar bills. She had sold all of the furniture, but there were still all our personal things. The man took the furniture the next day and left the floors piled with clothes, magazines, china and stuff that had accumulated in the flat for years and years. I was distressed. How could we clean the flat up in time to leave the following day? To my amazement, on the day we were scheduled to leave Mother simply left everything as it was and we got into a taxi with just our suitcases. We stopped to pick up the herbalist before heading to the port where the passenger ships docked.

The ship was leaving at midnight. Guests were allowed to board the ship to say goodbye. I was excited to explore the ship but did not dare to venture too far away from Mother. I stood outside our cabin while Mother said goodbye to Dr. Lai.

After a while Mother opened the cabin door and said, "Oi Ling, go sit in the lounge or go up to the deck and don't come back till the ship starts moving." Then she shut the door to the cabin. I heard the lock to the room click and I walked as fast as I could to get away from there. I didn't want to hear or think about what went on in our room. I was nauseated. I saw Mother stuff something into the herbalist's pocket as I had many times before. No doubt this was the money from the sale of our furniture. I was enraged. He was an outsider. He had no right to the proceeds from our family. I had never felt hate before but now I wished the man who caused me so much pain and misery had never existed.

I heard the announcement from the loudspeaker for non-passengers to disembark. I was thankful that I would never have to see that greasy pockmarked face again. I hoped this was the beginning of my journey to a better life. I smiled and went up to the deck to watch the tugboat pull the ship out of the harbor.

I breathed in the cool night air, feeling light and relieved. I stood at the back end of the ship and watched the lights of Hong Kong waver and dim as they grew smaller and smaller. I was happy. I was finally out of the place where I did not want to be. The island of Hong Kong slowly faded away. Suddenly, I felt a heavy blow to my chest and I couldn't breathe, as if someone had knocked the wind out of me with a powerful punch.

"Great-grandmother! Great-grandmother is all by herself!" I had forgotten all about her. I had been so happy to escape my own miseries.

"I am sorry, Great-grandmother, I will come back to get you when I grow up. I promise I will come back to get you," I cried.

—

The Golden Mountain

It did not take long for me to settle into our cabin. In the hold below our deck, immigrants bunked in large rooms of six to eight beds. They usually kept to themselves in the area around their rooms. Mother would have nothing to do with them. She only associated with the vacationing American-born Chinese who also had private cabins. They all spoke English. I sat around listening to gibberish. When I got bored, I went up to the top deck to play a few games of shuffleboard or into the art room to make baskets or potholders. Since I did not speak English, I kept to myself. I was already used to not speaking for days and that was fine with me.

Unlike the passengers from the hold who took their meals in a dining hall with long tables, we ate in an elegant dining room and had our own table and waiter. It resembled the fancy western restaurant Mother once took us to. We had felt intimidated by the numerous knives, forks and spoons on either side of the plate, not knowing what they were all for. Then there were more plates in different sizes and glasses in different shapes. Mother had shown us how we should use them. It was so complicated. I wished I had just one spoon for soup and a pair of chopsticks for everything else.

The menu was in English. Mother didn't bother to translate it for me. She just ordered what she thought I should have. For dinner, I was frequently served a big piece of beef called "steak." The taste wasn't worth the work it took to hold it down with a fork and cut pieces small enough to put into my mouth.

I also had a glass of milk with my dinner every evening. In Hong Kong, it was a luxury item. I heard that Americans drank it every day. They must be rich, I thought, and anxiously anticipated my arrival in New York.

The night before we were due to arrive in San Francisco, the captain made an announcement in English during dinner. I looked to Mother for translation. She told me we were to enter the San Francisco Bay at dawn and would be going under the Golden Gate Bridge. I was excited to witness my entry to the Golden Mountain but Mother told me not to disturb her if I was going to wake up early to go on deck. She said to come back to the cabin to get her when we were ready to disembark.

I woke up before dawn, crept quietly out of bed and slipped out of our cabin and ran up to the top deck. The morning light was just breaking. It was pale and misty. A handful of people were already there sipping coffee. I saw a faint silhouette of the bridge suspended over a vast body of water. I had never seen such a long and magnificent structure. We were going to cross under it, the gateway to the Promised Land. I felt flushed with emotion and possibility. I knew the best I could do if I stayed in Hong Kong was to marry a man of similar class, raise a few children, play games of mahjong and waste my life away. The thought of being something other than an obedient wife and daughter-in-law filled me with excitement. As the ship came close to the bridge, I looked up and saw a stream of cars passing by. Wow, the thought of being able to drive my own car one day was too much to wish for, but if I dared to dream, I could see myself driving in one of them.

We took a train cross-country to New York. I spent most days on the viewing deck in one of the cars in the middle of the train. The roof of the car was made of glass. It curved down to meet the windows, so I had a panoramic view of the country. The size of America awed me. As far as I could see, wide-open golden prairies glowed under a clear blue sky. Once we reached the Rocky Mountains, the train climbed steadily for hours into the snow. I could not have imagined what real snow was like, I had only seen pictures of it. The white powdered evergreens and rocks took my breath away. I looked through the glass ceiling and the mountains went on and up forever. It was majestic. But when I looked down, I started to sweat. The edge seemed less than a foot from the rail. The mountain just dropped off. We must be miles from the ground below, I thought. I quickly shifted my eyes to the rock walls on the other side.

Halfway across country, I grew tired, anxious to see my younger sister and the place I would call home. I stayed away from Mother as much as possible, watching the prairies and farms pass before me. I had nothing to say to her and found it very odd to see her throughout everyday. I had never spent such a long stretch of time with her in my life. I had to watch everything I said and every move I made. She yelled at me if I dared to relax and forgot to sit up straight or if I put my feet up on the seat.

We stood outside the train station in New York City waiting for my uncle to come pick us up. The streets were crowded and grimy. The cars were dirty and noisy. I must have been at the wrong end of town. I was confident where I was going would be like the beautiful place I had seen in the movie.

An extremely old, beat up truck with paint peeling off and rust spots all over it stopped in front of us. A man in heavy work clothes jumped out and walked straight to Mother. He had very dirty hands and desperately needed a haircut. When Mother saw him she smiled and extended her hand. They greeted each other warmly.

"This is Oi Ling? What a big girl you are. Welcome to New York," my uncle turned and said to me. I smiled and wondered if he had left his fancy car at home and had picked us up in his old truck because he came from work. I knew from Mother that he was an owner of a grocery store. Besides, he was the brother of my father. If Father had owned a grocery store, he would have all of the fancy things to show for it.

My uncle loaded our suitcases into the back of his truck. I climbed into the front and was appalled to find the seats covered with litter and dirt. I hastily brushed them away and offered Mother the seat.

It seemed like a long ride to Chinatown. We crawled through heavy traffic. Drivers rudely honked and yelled out from their car windows. Where were the fancy cars with leather seats and beautiful people? I felt claustrophobic being in the truck with Mother sitting so close to me. I was tired of sitting up straight with my hands on my lap, being careful not to crowd my mother or uncle. The noise and smell of the street grew oppressive. Where were the open blue skies with palm trees? Everyone in this city looked gray and mean. I had never seen so many foreigners in one place at the same time. The pale winter light and the grayish brown haze of the city made them look surreal, rushing by with stone faces, bobbing like wooden puppets up and down the streets.

The truck finally came to a stop in front of an old building.

"Mother is waiting for you in her apartment on the second floor," my uncle said to my mother as we got out of the truck.

This was it? I could not believe my eyes or my nose. The narrow street was paved with cobblestones. People milled around and talked in very loud voices. Groups of men hung around in the front of other buildings. They greeted their neighbors by yelling across the street. The nauseating smells from rotting trash under the displays of produce from a nearby store was overwhelming and who knew what was in the gutter. I didn't want to find out and averted my eyes. The building in front of me, the same as all the other buildings in the neighborhood, was old and dirty. Everything was painted either black or dark green.

I followed Mother into the hallway. I walked gingerly, afraid to step on something I might regret. It was dim and narrow. I climbed the steep stairs behind Mother, still holding out hope that Grandmother's apartment would be a pleasant surprise.

"Hey, Irene! You are here!" my younger sister yelled as soon as I walked into the apartment. She jumped up and rushed over to me. I was surprised that she called me by my English name. Grandmother was already busy talking to Mother. I was glad to see my younger sister after such a long journey with Mother. I could finally relax.

"You better learn to live the American way and call me Louise. We don't call each other by our ranks here," she said and pulled on my sleeves, excited to show me around. I had so much to learn. I took a quick glance around the apartment. I felt like a balloon that had all the air let out of it. The entire apartment was about a third the size of our flat in Hong Kong. It was dark. The only windows were the two in the living room that faced the street and one window in the kitchen at the rear of the apartment, which faced the back of another building that was separated from ours only by a small courtyard. My aunt's bedroom was at the end of the kitchen, next to the bathroom. There were two rooms between the living room and the kitchen. It was called a railroad apartment and you had to walk through each room to get to the other side of the apartment. The interior rooms had a bed on one side and a dresser on the other. The space between them was the walkway for people to get to the kitchen from the living room. The rooms were no larger than eight by eight feet. The floors were covered with worn green linoleum and the walls were painted in an unappetizing apple green. There was a large desk in the living room and a home-made cover with tiny white flowers and a checkered pattern draped over a sofa. Grandmother must have made it. A color television, the only thing that was modern in the entire apart-ment, was on the other side of the room right next to the entrance to my grandmother's bedroom. I had only seen black and white television in Hong Kong.

"Hong Kai's mother passed away two weeks ago," Grandmother told Mother as soon as we sat down.

"I stayed in Hong Kong for all those years to wait for her to die. She chose to go after we left. It was her fate that she would-n't have any descendents by her side," Mother said. "She was not destined to have a good ending. Serves her right."

Grandmother nodded and dismissed the topic. I was shocked and felt a heavy pressure on my chest and severe cramps in my stomach. My hands started to sweat. I didn't dare to cry. I had to show my loyalty to Mother and Grandmother. They didn't like Great-grandmother at all. I knew I better not show that I had cared for her. I had promised myself to go back to Hong Kong to get Great-grandmother when I left and now I would never have a chance to make it up to her. I didn't know how to reconcile my feelings toward Great-grand-mother. I felt hopeless. I closed my eyes and felt heat rising from my neck to my face and ears. I could not breathe. I forced myself to leave the room.

Grandmother told me that I could stay in the middle room next to the kitchen. Louise's room was next to mine. Mother was to live with my second elder sister in a small apartment on the fourth floor. I put my suitcase down on the bed and helped Mother carry hers up to her apartment. Her suitcases were very heavy. By the time we reached the fourth floor, I was panting. I noticed a door in the hallway adjacent to the apartment. I found out later on that it was the bathroom that everyone shared on that landing. I followed Mother into her apartment and was surprised to find second elder sister there, sitting on her bed. I had not seen her for five years. The only image I had of her was the photograph that Grandmother had shown us when she came back to Hong Kong. Second elder sister was in her nightgown, but she didn't look beautiful. She looked exactly as she had when we were in Hong Kong. I was a good three inches taller than her now and I thanked God that He didn't grant me my wish to look like her when I grew up. I had just discovered the power and magic of makeup and padded bras. Now I knew I had hope. I too could use makeup to correct my ugly features.

"Second elder sister, good to see you," I said timidly.

"Call her Teresa. I told you that you have to learn the American way," Louise cut in with her bright eyes and a big smile, eager to teach me the new custom.

"Oh, Teresa, is that ok?" I wasn't sure. It was disrespectful to call an elder by her name. I had so much to get used to.

After the long and exhaustive day, I was glad when it was time for bed. I changed into my pajamas and crawled under the covers and thought of Great-grandmother. Tears fell onto the pillow as I started to cry. I was so sorry that she had died alone. I covered my face with the blanket so no one could hear me. Slowly, I drifted off. I was at the entrance of the roof in the building in Hong Kong. It was night. Fierce rain and wind pounded on the window nearby. I stood by the door cloaked in darkness. There was no electric light inside of the room that led to the roof. I was afraid to go out to feed the pigeons and chickens. Panic struck. I remembered that I had forgotten to feed them for months. I was afraid that they were dead. My eyes flew open. I was covered in a cold sweat.

The next day, I met my first elder sister, Virginia. I hadn't seen her in eight years. She took Louise and me out to lunch. I was happy to see her. She was the same height and weight as Mother and had the same hairdo and dressed matronly like her. It was scary. She looked so much like Mother.

"Take your hands out of your pockets and button up your coat! Straighten up your spine! Who are you trying to imitate? The losers that hang around the street corners?" Virginia barked at me as soon as we were on the street. I slipped my hands out of my coat pockets and buttoned up. Not only did she look like Mother, she growled like her too. Thank God she was married and I didn't have to live with her.

Mother enrolled me in the ninth grade at the local junior high school. It was located outside of Chinatown. Louise was in the sixth grade and went to a grammar school in Chinatown. Teresa was already in high school, so I was the only one who was attending this school. I diligently remembered the way when Mother took me there on the first day. It was scary to walk there by myself, not knowing a word of English to ask for directions. I was afraid that I would get lost and be unable to find my way home.

The school building was huge compared to the schools in Hong Kong. Everything had a thick coat of light brown paint on it. It seemed like they had painted the same surface a thousand times. The floors were bare cement. There were iron bars and gates on all the windows and doors to the outside. They were locked when the school bell rang. I had never been locked in a building in my life.

A very tall man with glasses and a mustache spoke to me when I finally found my class room. It was the middle of the term and forty-seven pairs of eyes stared at me when I walked in. I didn't understand what he said, but guessed from his gesture that he had told me to sit down. I quickly took an empty seat in the back. Some of the kids turned around and I smiled shyly. I didn't know what to do. A few minutes later, the class was in session. To my horror, the students started to throw things at each other and talk back to the teacher when he told them to stop. They would have been beaten with a stick and sent home to their parents if they did that in Hong Kong.

Before long, I started to understand the social structure of school. Half of the students were black and Puerto Rican, a handful were Italian, and the rest were Chinese. Within the Chinese group, there was a distinct division between the American-born and the ones from Hong Kong. Frequent fights broke out between groups and they intimidated each other with their numbers.

I wanted to learn English. I purposely stayed away from the Chinese students from Hong Kong. I could tell they spoke terrible English even after they had been here for years. They could get by in Chinatown without speaking a word of English. Since I didn't have regular friends to hang out with I sat in front of the television whenever Grandmother had it on. It didn't matter what program anyone was watching. I glued myself to it to learn English.

I became an easy target for any given group to pick on because I didn't have any backups.

"You immigrant!" an American-born Chinese boy said to me with disdain as he walked past me at lunch. I didn't understand. The other Chinese from Hong Kong turned their heads and shot hateful glances at him.

"Hey, show me your pussy!" a Puerto Rican boy said to me while he sat with a group of his cronies. They all laughed.

"What is a pussy?" I asked Louise when I got home from school.

"Ha ha! Somebody has finally said that word to you." Louise laughed heartily and continued, "Pussy is vagina and don't even think dick is only a boy's name. Dick is penis and frank is a hot dog."

I was mortified. The boys in school were so crude.

"What is an immigrant?" I asked her again.

"What? Someone called you that? He must be an American-born Chinese. It is a bad way of calling people who are fresh off the boat like you. They think they are better. Just stay away from them," Louise advised.

One day during class, a black girl named Beverly sat next to me. She was one of the toughest girls and would fist fight anybody who challenged her. She had never paid any attention to me. I didn't know if she would get angry if I said anything to her. But I always thought she was pretty. I turned to look at her and blurted out, "Beverly, you are pretty."

"Really?" She was so taken aback. She brushed the hair in front of her face with her hand and looked down. Suddenly, she seemed so shy. I saw a little girl sitting in that chair instead of this tough tomboy. She never said a word to me after but every time she saw someone from the black and Puerto Rican group pick on me, she would say, "Quit it! She is nice. Leave her alone."

They listened to her because she was one of their leaders. I was grateful and amazed that I had expressed a moment of truth in my heart and it had given me year-long protection from the toughest group in school.

One evening after dinner, I finished cleaning the dishes and was surprised to see Teresa come to Grandmother's apartment just to spend time with whoever was around. We rarely saw her here except on Sundays when all of our aunts and uncles came for dinner. She glanced around to make sure no adults were in sight. She motioned me to sit on the sofa and proceeded to tell me what was on her mind. "I have a boyfriend, and his name is Robert," she said smugly. "He brings me a yellow rose everyday and leaves it in front of the door to my apartment."

"Oh really? What does Mom say?"

"Who cares? I am in love!" she said. She seemed puzzled by my fear of Mother's reaction.

"And guess what else we do together?" Teresa asked. I knew this game. Whenever she had something I didn't have, she would flaunt it in the most explicit way possible. I remembered when she got a gorgeous gray dress with a pattern of tiny pastel pink, blue and white swallows sent to her from Grandmother in America. I wanted it so badly and told her that I would be more than happy to get it from her when she outgrew it. I always wore her hand-me-downs because of our closeness in size. She pranced around in the dress and then told me that she would rather give it away to a beggar than let me have it. I never got to wear that dress. She cut it up with a pair of scissors when she was done with it.

"What do you do together?" I asked curiously.

"I go to his apartment when nobody is around and we stay in his bed and he puts his penis into my vagina," she said exultantly.

"That is what you do when you have a boyfriend?" I asked and put my hand over my mouth in astonishment.

"You are so dumb." She rolled her eyes. "I am in love!" Teresa finally said with a smirk and left the apartment.

I sat on the sofa and tried to take it all in. I too wanted a boyfriend. If I had to do what Teresa had done to get one, I guessed that was what I needed to do. But that meant having sex before I got married! What would Great-grandmother think? I had heard enough shameful horror stories from her and Grandmother. I swore I would not be the one they would call a whore. Worse yet, what if Mother found out?

Mother had taken a job as a bookkeeper at a butcher shop one block down from our apartment building. I never saw her unless I went to the shop. I was relieved not to have her breathing down my neck. It was bad enough that every time I saw her she would yell at me for my hair being too long or my skirt too short. There was always something wrong with me.

Louise and I were listening to music on Teresa's record player while she was out. I was going through the box of small records they call "45s" when Mother walked in from work.

"It is so hot today. I am going to Uncle Chui's apartment to take a bath," she said from her bedroom while she changed. Louise and I looked at each other and rolled our eyes. Mother thought we would believe it was more convenient for her to walk ten blocks to her co-worker's apartment to bathe than to just go downstairs to Grandmother's apartment. I was so used to her nonsense, I often went along with what she said in order to stay out of trouble. We knew Mother had not come home to sleep for quite some time.

Since Louise and I were living with Grandmother, she provided us with food and shelter. Mother never asked us if we needed anything. We had to find ways to earn money to pay for clothes, lunches at school and spending money. Virginia told us that we could work in her restaurant on weekends. We eagerly accepted her offer.

Every Saturday and Sunday, Louise and I took a bus from Chinatown to the ferry terminal and took the ferry to Staten Island. Then we had to take another bus from the terminal in Staten Island to her restaurant. The travel time was over two hours. After twelve hours of work, Virginia and her husband would drive us back to Chinatown.

Louise stayed in the kitchen to wash the dishes and I waited on tables.

"You should wait on all of the tables, since my customers know that I am the owner. They won't tip me as well," Virginia said to me the first day of work. I was more than happy to work alone and get the customers to tip me more. She showed me a little box in the back of the restaurant where I should deposit all of my tips.

I met her husband for the first time in the early afternoon of our first day. Virginia and Louise were in the dining room cleaning pea pods for him to cook with later. I went into the kitchen to get us some water. I had a glass filled with water in each hand. Virginia's husband grabbed me from behind and started to fondle my breasts. I screamed and almost dropped the glasses. He smiled slyly and walked away. I took a deep breath and walked out to the dining room. I didn't dare tell Virginia. I was afraid that she would get mad and fire me. I had to keep my job. I needed the money.

At the end of the day, I was happy to find over thirty dollars in that box. When we were ready to go home, I went to collect my tips.

"Hey, what happened to the money?" I said, distressed to find the box empty.

"The tips belong to the house. Here's your salary for the day." Virginia handed me a ten-dollar bill. I guessed I didn't know the rules of restaurants. I was grateful to have a job.

I worked there for more than a year. I tried not to go into the kitchen when Virginia's husband was in there alone. Sometimes, it was unavoidable. Without fail, each time we were out of Virginia's sight, he would rush over to either grab my breasts or shove his hand on my crotch. I would hit his hand as hard as I could and he just laughed. I had to put up with him till I learned enough English to get another job.

I was eager to explore the world outside of Chinatown. Most of the Chinese kids from my junior high school went to the local high school a few streets away from Chinatown. Their whole existence was inside a perimeter made of streets with Chinese signs.

I excelled in art. I had a deep need to express how I felt. Due to my lack of competence in English, I was better off pursuing something that I was good at. My art teacher encouraged me to take the entrance exam for the two high schools that specialized in art. I got into both. I chose the one on 57th Street because it was in a modern building uptown in the city. The other one was old and had too much emphasis on the academic side of art. I wanted to produce artwork; I didn't want to study it.

Every month, someone sponsored a dance in one of the rented halls. Homemade posters plastered all the shops in Chinatown announcing the date, time and the place. They hired a live band and set them up in the front of the room, lined the hall with chairs and placed a small table in the back of the room to serve punch. The teenagers would buy tickets to get in. This was the most popular gathering place for local teens and was frequented by the gang members who went there to pick up girls.

There were two prominent gangs in Chinatown, the White Eagles and the Black Eagles. The members of the White Eagles were generally between the ages of seventeen and their mid-twenties and the Black Eagles were between twelve and sixteen. The older group was the muscle for Chinese organized crime. They collected protection fees from local businesses and if anyone refused to pay the gang ruthlessly destroyed the shop. They were also involved in smuggling and distributing heroin. The members got a commission for their handiwork. The Black Eagles were less industrious. They just hung around and got into fights.

A few members were very good at martial arts, so they were the ones the other members went to if they needed someone to represent the gang. Most of the time, they announced the time and the place for the showdown. Sometimes they had over a hundred onlookers watching the fight and cheering them on.

They used brass knuckles and spiked rings to fight their rivals. That changed dramatically a few years later when they started to carry guns.

"Jane and I bought tickets to the dance tonight. Do you want to come with us?" Louise asked me when I came home from school.

"Really? I've always wanted to see what those dances are like. It is so boring just to go to school and work all the time," I said. "Where do I get a ticket?"

"You can pay at the door. We need to do the dishes quickly after dinner. We have to meet Jane at her house," Louise said, rummaging through her dresser for a desirable outfit.

I peeked into the kitchen to see if Grandmother was already preparing dinner. I needed enough time to change and apply my makeup before we headed out.

We picked up Jane at her house and walked to the dance. A large group of teenagers congregated in front of the entrance. Girls were all done up in heavy makeup and teased hair, prancing around in mini skirts and white go-go boots. The boys wore tight shirts, bell bottom pants and long hair while they stood around puffing on cigarettes trying to look cool as they checked out the girls. I felt the excitement in the air. I paid for my ticket and we went into the hall.

The room was dark and the music was so loud, I could feel it pounding in my chest. I had to squint to see who was there. I recognized guys from the gangs. They hovered around groups of girls who giggled, laughed and nudged each other. But I stayed away from these boys. Good girls didn't associate themselves with gang members. I also saw many new faces. I followed Louise and Jane to a corner and stood around, shifting my weight nervously, waiting. The pounding music added to the excitement. Soon, we were asked by different guys to dance.

Louise and I began to go to the dances regularly. One night, I noticed a group of guys in their twenties with short hair, obviously not gang members. There were about six to eight of them who traveled in a pack. Throughout the evening, they took turns asking me to dance. I was attracted to older guys because they were independent and established. They had jobs and took care of themselves. I loved the attention. At the end of the dance, one of them asked for my phone number. He was the one I liked most anyway, so I gave it to him. His name was David.

"How old are you?" David asked on our first date at a restaurant in Chinatown.

"Sixteen," I said, flipping through the menu, too excited to notice what was on it. "I go to the high school of Art and Design on 57th Street."

"You are sixteen?" he asked, taking a good look at me and smiling. The waitress came over to our table to take our order.

"Yeah, I am in tenth grade," I replied, waiting for him to finish ordering for us.

"And how old are you?" I asked.

"I am twenty eight. I'm a director at the Chinese Youth Development Center." He leaned back in his chair with an air of confidence.

I was impressed.

"Do you mind if I call you in a few days? Maybe we can go to see a movie uptown," David said after dinner.

"I'd love to."

"Telephone." Louise handed me the phone one evening after dinner.

"Hello." I hoped it was David.

"Hello, Irene? My name is Tommy." I heard an unfamiliar voice on the receiver. "We met at the dance a week ago. Do you want to go to a night club with me tonight?"

"How did you get my number?" I asked, puzzled.

"David gave it to me. Is it ok?" Tommy said hesitantly. I was surprised that they shared my phone number. But a nightclub uptown! I would never have a chance to go with any tenth graders.

"Sure! I'll meet you at the Canal Street station at nine o'clock." I could hardly contain my excitement.

"Two Singapore Slings!" Tommy yelled to the waiter above the deafening music. Go-go girls in micro mini skirts and skimpy tops danced in cages suspended from the ceiling. The waiter brought two tall, red, frosty glasses with miniature parasols.

"Thank you," I said to Tommy. I smiled and took a long sip of the sweet concoction. He pulled on my arm and led me to the dance floor. Soon, the drink kicked in and made me woozy. We danced and danced. I felt wonderfully free and, at this moment, I didn't have to deal with my life.

The following day, David called and asked if I had a good time with Tommy. I was shocked that they shared so much information with each other.

"I'd like to invite you to my apartment to listen to some music." I was eager to see him. He stood out from his group of friends. He was the best looking and spoke better English than the rest.

"Ok. I have already done my homework. I'll be over soon," I said with my heart pounding. I was glad that he couldn't see me. I blushed profusely.

David gave me directions to his apartment. "I'll be waiting for you," he said.

I had some notion about what might happen from the conversation I had with Teresa. I was very nervous and excited as I climbed the stairs to the fifth floor. I wiped my sweaty hands on my skirt before I knocked on the door to David's apartment.

"Hi, glad you're here," David said, smiling and swinging the door open.

"Hi," I said shyly. I noticed the apartment was very dimly lit. The deep red curtains were drawn and the light through them cast a romantic glow in the living room. Johnny Mathis was playing in the background. I walked in. David offered me a sweet drink. It was some sort of liqueur.

"Come sit down on the sofa," David waved to me from where he'd sat down. I nervously sat next to him. He put his arm around me. I gulped down my drink and sat up rigidly. He caressed my hair, turned my face toward him with his hand and started to kiss me on my lips. I trembled, then a strange feeling came over me. I had never been touched tenderly by anyone before, let alone been kissed. I was overwhelmed by this wonderful sensation. I kissed him back passionately.

David led me into his bedroom and started to undress me. I felt Great-grandmother's disapproving eyes. But I am in love, I told myself. I've never felt so wanted. I closed my eyes as my naked body rubbed against his. Every inch of my body tingled, quivering in response.

I was frightened when he penetrated me. I felt he didn't care. I listened to the lyrics of Johnny Mathis and pretended that each word was uttered to me from David's heart.

Later, when I felt the soreness, it reminded me that David actually liked me enough to have sex with me. Maybe if I pleased him enough, one day, he might marry me so I could fulfill my promise to be a good girl to my great-grandmother.

Tommy called me the following week and asked me to go out to lunch with him. He had something very important to tell me.

I walked into the restaurant and saw Tommy sitting at a small table at the far end of the room. I walked toward him and noticed that he was distressed. I sat down and before I had a chance to speak, he leaned over and said, "David is using you. He is no good. All he wants to do is to sleep with you. Stay away from him."

I was shocked. Who else knew what went on?

"Please marry me. I don't care if David has slept with you. I will still honor you," he said desperately and reached for my hand.

"I love you. Please marry me," he pleaded.

I sat back in my chair, appalled by his knowledge of my relationship with David. I had no interest in him and couldn't help but feel sorry for him for having these feelings for me.

"I am only sixteen. I can't marry anyone and I am still in school," I said, pulling my hand from his and looking away. I wished David was asking me. I would scream in ecstasy. But the sight of Tommy made me nauseous.

He got up from his chair, dropped to his knees and whimpered, "Please marry me. I will honor you."

I was horrified.

"No, I am sorry." I got up and ran out of the restaurant.

I went to see David at his apartment every chance I had. I snuck out after Grandmother went to sleep at eleven o'clock and came home at dawn before she woke up. I averaged about three hours of sleep.

I rarely saw David anywhere except in his apartment to have sex. I waited for him to take me out. He told me that he did not want to be seen with a sixteen-year old girl in Chinatown since he worked in a social agency dealing with youth. I was thankful for any attention he was willing to give me and found myself unable to ask for anything more.

I began to worry about getting pregnant. I had no access to birth control and David refused to use a condom. The doctor I went to in Chinatown knew my family, so I couldn't ask him. I was too afraid that someone would find out that I was having sex before I was married. I learned about the rhythm method. I was very careful and avoided seeing David on the days I ovulated. Any slip up and it would be my death sentence.

Summer came around and I was finally old enough to get a full time job. I was very happy to get $1.65 an hour for thirty hours a week at the development center. The day I got the job, I calculated that I could save enough money to give my mother a hundred-dollar bill for her birthday in August. I wanted to surprise her. I thought doing something extra special would make her happy and she would acknowledge her appreciation of a good daughter. I was excited by the idea and looked forward to work every morning.

The day before my mother's birthday, I traded my twenty-dollar bills for a crisp hundred-dollar bill at the bank. I couldn't wait to see Mother's face when I surprised her the next day.

On her birthday, I rushed home after work. When she walked into her apartment, I greeted her and said, "Happy birthday! Mom, this is for you." I handed her the hundred-dollar bill, anticipating her praise.

"You think I will like you if you give me money? You can't buy me with your stinking money," Mother sneered. She grabbed the bill, stuffed it into her pocket and walked away.

I stared at the floor and did not know what to do.

My period was late. I was extremely anxious. I waited several weeks before going to see the doctor.

After the exam, the doctor sat behind his huge desk flipping the pages on my chart. He looked up at me with his piercing eyes.

"You are sixteen?" The doctor shook his head and then said, "You are pregnant."

The death sentence.

"Your last name is Kai? Are you Leung Hong Kai's grand-daughter? I knew your grandfather well. Does your family know what you are doing? I might have to tell your grandmother about this," he said to me sternly.

"No! I have never heard of him." I got up and left. I thought I was going to die. My chest was pounding and I felt faint. I would never go to any doctor in Chinatown using my real name ever again.

I needed an abortion. I could not face my family. I couldn't face being the laughing stock of the community. I refused to be the one to destroy my family's honor.

I ran to David's apartment building and sat inside by his door.

"What are you doing here?" he asked when he found me leaning against the wall.

"I have something very important to tell you," I said nervously and followed him into the apartment.

"I am pregnant," I whispered. I had a very difficult time saying the words.

"So? That is not my problem," David said nonchalantly.

"You are the father," I said, feeling ill.

"How do I know? You could have been sleeping with a thousand other guys for all I know," he snorted.

"I was a virgin before we met. You are the only one," I cried.

"Every girl tells me that she is a virgin and that she's sixteen. Who cares?" He was getting impatient.

"David, please, just help me find a doctor. I need an abortion. I can't go home if my stomach starts to show. Please," I begged him. "I don't know how to find one."

"I'll see if my buddies know of any doctors. You better have the money to pay for it yourself. It's not my business. I am doing you a favor," he said reluctantly.

A few weeks went by. There was no word from David and I became desperate. I took Chinese herbs rumored to cause miscarriages. But they only made me sick and I vomited for a few days. I tried jumping from the top of the stairs to the ground and landing on my butt. Nothing worked.

It was the end of my first trimester and my grandmother was getting suspicious.

"You look like a woman with child, you are always tired and rounded out on your waist," she said to me one day when I came home from school.

"I am not, Grandmother. Don't worry." I said as calmly as I could.

"You better not be," Grandmother said, looking at me with her penetrating eyes. My skin crawled and I prayed David would call me soon. I couldn't take this much longer.

A few days later, I finally got a call from David. He told me he had found a doctor in Philadelphia and he was doing me a favor to drive me there.

This was the greatest news I'd had in my entire life. Now there was hope for me not to be kicked out of my home. I could have a family still.

David had never been to Philadelphia before. He brought his friend Wilson along and decided that they would do a little sight-seeing after he took me to the doctor.

"Look at her tits! They jiggle like two bowls of Jell-O," David said to Wilson in Mandarin, ogling a young woman crossing the street.

"I'd like to have my hands on them," Wilson replied, also in Mandarin, laughing.

I only spoke Cantonese, a dialect as different in sound as French from English. They knew I didn't speak Mandarin but didn't know I had learned to understand it from watching movies in Hong Kong. I didn't say anything.

It was late at night. Our instructions were to go to a house at ten o'clock and ask for the doctor by his name. We knocked on the door.

"Who's there?" a husky voice asked.

"We are here to see Doctor Jackson," David answered timidly.

The door cracked open, a black woman in a housecoat took a careful look at us and stepped aside to let us in. The house was stuffy. The living room was crowded with women, mostly in their twenties and thirties. I craned my neck to survey the adjacent rooms. They too were packed with women. Some sat on the floor, others stood leaning against the walls.

"It will be a hundred dollars," the woman in the housecoat said to us. I turned to look at her and nervously handed her five twenty-dollar bills. She gave me a little slip of paper with the number ninety-three written on it. The doorbell rang. She quickly walked over to answer the door and let more women in.

I noticed a white couple standing in the far corner of the living room. They huddled together, looking very scared. The rest of the women were black, slender, high-strung and alone. They dressed in low-cut mini dresses or skimpy tops and short-shorts. I knew I was in the company of prostitutes, but I didn't care. I would rather die than go home to face my mother and grandmother. The sooner I got this over with, the better.

A tall, thin woman stood by a door calling out numbers. Every ten to fifteen minutes, a woman would walk out and another one walked in.

"Ninety-three!" she shouted. I quickly walked over to her and handed her my number. She opened the door and gestured for me to go in.

"I am Doctor Jackson. How far along are you?" a towering black man in a white doctor's coat asked me.

"Three months," I said apprehensively. He had a calming presence and I tried to relax.

"I am going to inject a solution into your uterus. This will induce labor. You can expect to get severe cramps in about an hour," he said. He held a very large syringe with a frighteningly long needle.

"Do you have a place to stay?" he asked gently, withdrawing the needle from my vagina.

"No." I felt faint from anxiety.

"For an extra fee, I can arrange for you to stay at my friend's house. In your condition, it's not a good idea to stay in a hotel," the doctor said, almost sounding fatherly.

"Ok, thank you," I said, quickly putting on my panties.

"Talk to Bobbie by the door. She'll tell you where to go," he said, while I headed for the door without looking back.

I paid Bobbie fifty dollars. All of the money I had earned the entire summer was gone. The three of us walked to another house less than a block away. A heavyset black woman in a blue and white polka dot dress let us into her house.

She showed me a small mattress on the floor which was covered with a clear plastic sheet. It was in a room the size of a closet.

"This is where you'll be. When you feel like you have to push, the bathroom is over there," she said and pointed to a small room adjacent to mine. "If you need me, I am just outside your door."

I peered into the tiny bathroom. The floor was covered with dull blue linoleum, dirty and worn.

"Wilson and I are going out. We'll be back in the morning. I am sure you'll be done by then," David said to me. He didn't bother to wait for my reply and walked out with Wilson.

It had been almost an hour since the injection. I wondered when the cramps would start. I sat on the mattress and looked around the windowless room when they hit in a mind-numbing wave. The pain grew increasingly worse and the intervals between cramps became more frequent. I stood up. My shirt was plastered to my body with sweat. I walked around the small room, bending over, trying to divert my attention from the pain. Nothing worked. I started to pant.

"She is really hurting," I heard Wilson say to David. I hadn't heard them come in.

"Forget it, she is just trying to get our attention," David said with a smirk.

"Irene, why don't you lie down?" Wilson came over, and held my arm to guide me to the mattress.

"I can't, it hurts too much," I said, the sweat dripping down my face.

David pulled at Wilson's sleeve and said, "Let's go, she'll be all right. Just get your wallet. We still have to check out this town."

Wilson picked up his jacket and wallet from the chair. He'd forgotten them when they went out before.

When they shut the door, I suddenly had an incredible urge to go to the bathroom. I ran into the bathroom and sat on the toilet. I felt the severe pressure from the baby pushing and the incredible pain from the constant contraction. I didn't know what was happening and started to panic. I nearly passed out.

The woman came in to check on me.

"I'll make you some weak tea with a lot of sugar. It'll give you some energy. Just call me when it is all over, ok baby? You poor thing," she said, looking down at me with her dark glistening eyes. She walked out shaking her head.

The baby was pushing its way through. I bent over, leaning on my thighs, covered in sweat.

It hit the water in the toilet. I got up and looked down into the bowl. It was a boy. I saw his tiny penis. He had perfectly formed arms and legs. I was scared and heart broken but I wasn't pregnant anymore. I could go home.

"I am done," I whispered through the door. The woman came in and fished the fetus out from the toilet with a scrubber and wrapped it with newspapers to be disposed of in the trash. I went back into the small room. I was exhausted. She brought me a cup of sweet tea. I gulped it down and thanked her.

It was near dawn, when I heard David and Wilson come into the room.

"Shhh, she is asleep. Let's be quiet," Wilson said to David.

"Hehe, do you think that slut really swallowed our cum?" David asked Wilson in Mandarin.

"I didn't see her spit it out," Wilson replied gleefully.

I wanted to vomit.

One day after class, Mr. Seymore, my art teacher asked me if I'd like to accompany him to an off Broadway play. It was playing at a dinner theater in Greenwich Village.

Greenwich Village! I'd always wanted to experience the famous village. I was thrilled. I said yes before he had a chance to change his mind.

I asked Mr. Seymore to pick me up on the outskirts of Chinatown. I didn't want anyone who knew my family to see me with a fifty-year old white man.

I stood on the corner of Canal Street near the subway station. I didn't know what to look for. A shiny red Triumph convertible with its top down stopped in front of me. I was surprised to see Mr. Seymore in the driver's seat.

"Hi, Irene! Have you been waiting long?" He grinned.

"Mr. Seymore! What a nice car!" I blurted out, unable to contain my excitement.

"Get in. I'm glad you like it." He reached over to open the door for me. I hopped in and off we went to the village. It was exhilarating to feel the wind blow through my hair. I remembered the cars I used to see in the James Bond movies. I laughed to myself at the thought of riding in a red convertible.

I had no idea what the play was about. I had a hard time understanding the words. However, I enjoyed the wine, the food, the costumes and the set. Mr. Seymore was very attentive. I noticed him sitting back in his chair, staring at me during the performance.

"Do you want to have a cup of coffee at my apartment?" Mr. Seymore asked as we walked toward the car. "I live only a few blocks away."

"I'd love to," I said and smiled. I was intoxicated. The people and the shops in the village were so outlandish. It was a foreign world. I wanted to explore the lifestyles of the people who lived here.

We walked up to a wonderful, old and well-kept building. The entrance was a pair of heavy doors decorated with lead and beveled glass. When Mr. Seymore opened the door to his apartment, I was greeted by a musky scent of incense. The apartment was spacious. The living room was painted in warm ochre. Richly embroidered pillows were strewn across the lush purple velvet sofa. A lamp stood on the corner table, draped with a deep red velvet scarf with long silk fringes. Columns of candles on beautiful glass plates were scattered throughout the room. It was cozy and romantic.

Mr. Seymore lit the candles and went into the kitchen to make coffee. He brought it out and seeing the excitement in my eyes, he said, "You like it?"

"This is beautiful. It is such a nice place to be," I said dreamily. What a far cry from Chinatown!

He put the coffee on the table and sat on a chair.

"You are so beautiful. I am glad you came," he said, staring at me. Wow, this was the first time in my life someone had told me that I was beautiful. I couldn't believe it. The Americans must have a different standard of aesthetics. My mother and grandmother always said that the Americans were silly. I smiled, but dismissed his compliment.

I took the empty cups to the kitchen. I was trained to clean up after myself. Mr. Seymore followed me. While I stood over the sink washing the cups, he came up behind me and started to kiss my neck. I debated whether I should run out of the apartment or turn around and kiss him back. It was wonderful to have someone like me. David thought I was sleeping with a thousand other guys anyway. He was probably fucking some girl right now.

I went to Mr. Seymore's apartment periodically. He always took the time to ask how I was. Sometimes he would make lunch and bring it to school for me but my heart was with David. I still hoped to marry him one day. I firmly believed in marrying the guy I had lost my virginity to. That was the only way to keep my promise to Great-grandmother to be a good and proper girl.

David called me when he grew tired of whomever he was sleeping with.

"Where were you when I called you last night?" David asked on the phone, agitated. I was with Mr. Seymour and didn't think fast enough to answer him immediately. He sensed my hesitation.

"Are you fucking some other guy?" he growled.

"So what if I did? Don't you fuck around?"

He was furious.

"You will regret this," he snarled and hung up.

Teresa planned to go to San Francisco following a break-up with her boyfriend. She told mother that she was depressed and she needed to go to San Francisco with all of her "empty bamboo stick" girlfriends. I never paid much attention to Teresa until I found out that she was leaving with a shitload of money.

"I have never seen you work. Where do you get your money?" I asked while she packed.

"Mom gave me the airfare and enough money to cover my expenses for a month," she said matter-of-factly.

"I never got any money from Mom," I said indignantly.

"She also gives me a weekly allowance," she said, without looking up from her packing.

"Since when?" I asked. My voice became louder.

"Grandma used to give me a weekly allowance before you and Mom came to New York. Mom took over ever since," she said, getting impatient.

"She never gave me an allowance!" I was outraged.

"I asked! You are so stupid! It is your fault for not asking," Teresa scoffed. She threw her last piece of clothing into the suitcase and rolled her eyes to dismiss me.

I always felt Teresa thought that she was better than I could ever be and now she was leaving for San Francisco with all expenses paid, like a princess with her other well-to-do American-born girlfriends. I was never without a job. I worked part-time during school and full-time during the summer. I had to pay for my own food, clothes, fares for the subway to get to and from school, and supplies.

Grandmother decided to remodel the two buildings. We had to move out of our apartments. Mother rented an apartment for us from one of our uncles ten blocks away and ordered Louise and me to paint it before we moved in. She picked out the color and we did it after school and on a weekend.

"Both of you have to take all of our belongings to the new apartment. I have to work," Mother said, after she inspected the paint job. Louise and I looked at each other and nodded.

Everyday after school, Louise and I put as much as we could into two shopping carts and walked to the new apartment. It was on the fifth floor. After two weeks, we were in.

I was talking to Louise in the kitchen when Mother came into the apartment. One look at her face and I knew I better stay out of her way. She came over to me, reached up and slapped my face as hard as she could. I shut my eyes and clenched my jaw. She slapped me until she got tired.

"You whore! You dirty whore!" Mother screamed. "Who is David? You even had an abortion behind my back. How dare you drag dirt into this house?"

Louise slipped quietly to the back of the kitchen.

"Don't you ever be like this whore!" she yelled and turned to face Louise.

I was flabbergasted.

"Get out of my house. I don't ever want to see your sorry face. I don't want any whore living in my house."

The stinging on my face didn't bother me. But my mind was reeling – how had Mother found out about David and my abortion. I didn't tell anyone.

Mother chased me out of the apartment with a broom and threatened to strike if I didn't leave.

I left quietly. Not knowing where to go, I walked aimlessly, my face covered with tears.

After walking for hours, I found myself in front of David's apartment. I knocked reluctantly. He opened the door.

"What are you doing here?" David asked.

"I don't know how my mother found out about us. I just got kicked out of my house." I had trouble getting the words out between sobs.

"I went to your mother's office this morning and told her everything," David said, exultantly.

"What? Why?" I tried to comprehend what he had just said.

"I told you that you would regret fucking around with other guys. Serves you right getting kicked out of your house. Oh, and she told me that you really are sixteen. I'll be. One never knows," he smirked.

"I am sixteen and I have nowhere to go!" I cried.

"You can't come here. Go find yourself another fucker to stay with," he said angrily, pushing me out of the door. I sidestepped him and walked toward the window facing the street. I couldn't face my family. I was now known to be a whore. I climbed out of the window and sat on the sill with both of my legs dangling outside.

"Go ahead and jump! Nobody cares," David yelled from inside. I suddenly felt dizzy and grabbed onto the window frame. I swung my legs back into the apartment. My heart pounded wildly. I felt I was seven years old looking down to the street, thinking I was ready to jump. I couldn't do it. I ran past David to the stairs, wishing I had the courage to die.

I sat on the steps a few floors down from our apartment. I had no idea how much time elapsed. I was numb.

"Irene, come inside the apartment. Mom is gone," Louise whispered, pulling on my sleeve to get up. "Stay here while she is at work and leave before she comes home."

I followed her upstairs mechanically.

Mother was rarely home. She spent most of her time at work or with her lover. Most of the time, I avoided her successfully. When she happened to see me in the apartment, she passed by me as if I wasn't there.

Mother didn't come to my high school graduation. She never even knew what school I had gone to. I applied to college at the School of Visual Arts. The only way out of Chinatown was a college education. In order to pay tuition, I worked full-time during the summer as an assistant to a teacher in a head start program, and part-time on the weekends as a cashier in a Chinese restaurant.

Teresa came back from San Francisco with a new boyfriend, and announced that they were getting married. Her boyfriend worked for a telephone company and was an American-born Chinese whose father owned businesses and properties like our grandfather.

I soon learned Teresa was pregnant. I wondered what would happen to her if he hadn't agreed to marry her. Mother never called Teresa a whore. She gave in to all of Teresa's demands for a proper wedding and spent almost all the money she had on it. I wondered if my only redemption was to marry David. It seemed that to be accepted by my family, I had to be willing to set up a good front. Whatever happened behind it really didn't matter.

I still saw David on and off, even though he was engaged to an American-born woman. I bumped into them once on the streets of Chinatown. She said she hoped I'd find a good man like David and waved her hand to show off her diamond engagement ring. David had told me she had paid for most of it herself because she wanted a good sized diamond and he wasn't willing to spend the money. I smiled.

David winked at me when she wasn't looking. It meant to wait until she left.

I'll be fucking your fiancée in a few minutes you stupid bitch. You are one of many who have come and gone, I said to myself.

A few weeks later, they broke up.

By this time, Wilson was married and had two children. David and I were having dinner with him at the restaurant he and his wife owned.

"Marry Irene already. She is a good girl and she is smart," Wilson said to David.

"She is a dime a dozen. She fucks Americans. I want to marry a virgin who has a college degree," David said, without batting his eyes.

"You bastard!" I snorted, spitting a fish bone onto the plate.

Wilson looked at David, shook his head and said, "I hope you know what you are doing. You are not getting any younger."

Then they went on in Mandarin, happily counting the virgins they had conquered. I was willing to endure this because I still could hear Great-grandmother's whispers, expecting me to bring honor to our family.

The instructors and students at the School of Visual Arts were an incredible mix of people. They made the people in the village look tame. Groups of men wearing flamboyant dresses and heavy makeup milled around, exhibiting themselves with such confidence that I admired them for their courage. I heard the term "drag queen" for the first time. The women ranged from hippies who wore no makeup and clothes that I wouldn't use as dish rags, to ultra-rich princesses who looked like they'd just left beauty pageants. Most men had long hair and looked hip. The school motto was "be creative, anything goes."

The students thrived on being expressive, a direct contrast to my upbringing. They reveled in the shock waves. I loved being in the company of the outcasts. I felt I had found my flock.

I looked forward to school every morning. I began to pay more attention to how I packaged myself. I saved money to get my haircuts in the salons on Fifth Avenue. I learned to allocate my money by buying expensive accessories, custom-made shoes, scouring thrift shops for cheap vintage fur coats, chiffon, silk and velvet tops to go with my skintight pants.

I'd thought being in an art high school was cool, but now I really learned to be creative. Reinventing oneself was a high art form.

"Arms. I'm going to call you Ms. Arms from now on," said Frank, a well-known poet and an instructor at school, running his hand down my thigh after we made love.

"What?" I mumbled.

"You are Venus de Milo with arms," he said, turning his attention to my breasts, kissing them gently. I smiled and dismissed his words. I still believed my mother and David. My mouth was too big, forehead too high, face too flat, thighs too thick and my feet too big. And Americans were too easy to please.

"I never hear you say a word in class. I'd like to know what you're thinking," Frank said, pulling me closer.

"I have nothing to say," I replied, pushing myself out of bed. I got dressed to leave.

"When will I see you again?" Frank asked, still lying in bed.

"I don't know." I headed for the door. I didn't want to establish a meaningful relationship with an American. Having sex was one thing. I didn't know what an American relationship required for marriage. They had queer notions about love. Great-grandmother would want me to have a proper wedding. I was still waiting for David.

Teresa came home from Long Island every weekend with her husband and two children, a three-year-old son and an infant daughter. They usually came early in the afternoon. Her husband would stay for dinner then leave Teresa and their children with us to go drinking with his buddies. Sometimes he didn't return until the wee hours. It was common for Teresa and her children to stay the night at our small apartment.

When Teresa visited with her family, they all waited to be served. I helped Mother cook and Louise did the dishes after dinner. After a while, we grumbled to each other about bending over backwards to serve Teresa's entire family.

"Do you mind helping me clean your children's mess off the table and the floor?" I asked Teresa one day after dinner.

"My wife works hard at home! When she comes here she is on vacation!" her husband yelled.

"I work too! And when am I going to be on vacation?" I shouted back.

"Look at you! You look like a damn prostitute! Your clothes are always a size too small. You should be ashamed of yourself!" he barked.

I turned red, disgusted by his comments and yelled, "Mind your own fucking business! This is my house and you have no right to talk to me that way."

"This is not your house, you bitch! This house belongs to everybody. I have the right to be here and talk to you any way I want to because I am married to your sister."

I tore out of the apartment.

One early morning, I came home from a party. When I opened the door, I found Teresa's husband in a rage. I saw him slap his three-year-old son across the head. The force was so great, the boy hit his head against the wall.

"Stop that! You can't do that in this house," I screamed.

"Stay out of it! I am not done with him," he growled.

Teresa, my mother and Louise huddled in a corner of the room. No one had the nerve to do anything to stop him. I was afraid if I did something to enrage him further, he would do more damage. My heart went out to my nephew. The fright and pain were all too familiar to me.

I wished I could just pick him up and run away with him, away from this insanity. I made a vow to shelter and take good care of him when I became independent.

I went with my friends to a rally in Central Park to demonstrate against the Vietnam War. We cried in the students' lounge the day America bombed Cambodia. When four students were shot at Kent State University, heavy emotions reverberated across the country. We celebrated the legalization of abortion. Militant feminists burned their bras. I marched with my friends down Fifth Avenue on the first Earth Day. The word "Pollution" was a new addition to the American vocabulary, coming into the collective consciousness.

A reporter smuggled a camera into Willowbrook Institution and captured the horrific treatment of the mentally handicapped living there. He organized a day in the park for the residents and asked for volunteers to pair up with them for the day. Stevie Wonder and John Lennon gave a concert that evening to raise funds for a new facility. I went to Central Park to volunteer.

I was paired up with a girl who had Down Syndrome. She hugged me as soon as I walked up to her. I was taken aback. I had been taught to stay away from people who were different and had developed a fear of them. I had to talk myself into touching the short, stubby fingers of her hand. She drooled when she got excited and rocked back and forth, but when I looked into her eyes, I saw a gentle being. Despite our physical differences, she really tried hard to make a connection with me. By the end of the day we were laughing and hugging. I had her sitting on my lap. She taught me an important lesson. If I had the courage to open my heart to encourage love and compassion, wonderful things would follow.

I went to Madison Square Garden by myself for the concert that evening. My heart stirred when John and Yoko came onto the stage. Yoko stood behind John when he sat in front of the keyboard and sang "Imagine."

Tears rolled down my face.

"It is Father's Day this coming Sunday. I want you to buy a pair of cashmere socks for Uncle Chui," Mother said on a rare occasion when both of us were home.

"He is not my father. A pair a cashmere socks costs two weeks of my pay," I said. My stomach churned. The thought of her telling me that I had to use my hard-earned money to celebrate their fucking around disgusted me. She was the one who tossed me out of the house when she found out that I was sleeping with a man. Now, who was the whore? I caught myself, astonished that I dared to talk back to her. I saw the puzzled look on Mother's face. I was surprised she didn't hit me. She stormed out of the room instead.

The next day, I left a gift-wrapped package on her bed for Uncle Chui. At least I'd had the guts to tell her how I felt.

I majored in graphic design. We were given an assignment to bring in a piece of work titled "erotic." I asked all the instructors I knew what erotic meant to them. One guy showed me a photograph of a woman fingering a piece of foam sticking out of the torn fabric. I got it. Erotic was something that stirred one's sexual desire.

I showed up in class the following week with a deep pink velvet box that had a black satin heart sewn to the middle of the front panel. In the center of the heart, there was a verticle slit lined with flesh-pink satin. I put two big balloons filled with very warm water in the box. The pressure of the balloons squeezed the slit tightly together. By the time I was called to present my project, the warm water had caused the satin to sweat. I asked the instructor to slip his hand into the pink satin slit. The class watched as he slid his hand in.

He gasped. He sat down, stared at me and said, "Irene, you are dangerous."

Everyone got out of their seats and pushed around to experience the erotic box.

"Hey Irene, can I please borrow this for tonight?" a male student hollered.

I laughed so hard. The guys hooted and whistled. Women snickered loudly. The instructor watched the chaos in amusement.

On weekends, a few of my uncles and aunts gathered regularly at Grandmother's apartment with their families.

I got off work early one weekend and decided to visit the family at Grandmother's. I was asked to stay for coffee and pastries in the kitchen, while the younger children had milk with their sweets in the living room. I had finally made it to the grown-ups' table. I sat around and listened to their gossip.

"Father Moore is living in Los Angeles and I heard that he is doing well," one of my aunts told Grandmother.

"Since when did Father Moore come to the United States?" I asked curiously.

"He knocked up a sixteen year old girl and got kicked out of the church. He is living with her and their two children now," my uncle jeered.

"He did what? No way!" I couldn't believe it.

I was angry. No one had forced him to be a priest. He should have left the church when the temptations became too great. Now I knew there was nothing sacred about being Catholic. The church sold us the idea of salvation. If we had sinned, all we needed to do was to go to confession. The sinner and priest were hidden from each other and everyone else. All was forgiven by saying a few prayers afterwards. Then we could go home to repeat the same thing over again and again. In turn, we gave money to support them and let them wash our guilt away on our next confession.

Father Moore was the last straw. I swore I'd never set foot in a church again.

I sat in the lounge at school, listening to a group of women discuss the idea of woman's liberation. A fat girl with stringy, greasy hair and clothes I wouldn't want to see in my trash was saying, "I hate men. They create these fucking rules that we have to look beautiful to please them. We should be taken as we are, the way we want to be."

"Yeah, fuck men. They are morons. They make us wear high heels, makeup and dresses that no one can breathe in. We have to sit around batting our eyes and do dumb things," another chimed in. I wondered if they'd be saying the same words if they spent a little time on themselves in the morning. If they saw a fat man with his belly hanging out, dragging his sloppy ass across the room, would they find him attractive?

"I don't know, maybe it's all in the packaging," I interrupted. "I am in graphic design. You couldn't sell an ounce of perfume for two hundred dollars if you just ladle it out of a Mason jar."

"I just won't buy into that bullshit. I won't pay for the fucking packaging," the fat girl said angrily.

"Packaging applies to both men and women. We just have to choose to play the game or not," I said, looking at her belly spilling below her pants.

"It's easy for you to say. You look gorgeous all the time. What if a person was not born sexy and exotic?" the other said to me while the fat one stared at me scornfully.

"Trust me. I wasn't born this way. I work very hard every minute to look my best. It is not just playing the men's rules. I feel good when I look good." I wished they knew what I had to go through to get here. It was no easy task to navigate the American standard of beauty and I still had to go home and face Mother's constant put-downs.

When I walked into my next class, the instructor was already there.

"Irene, I am glad you came. I was afraid it would be a boring class without you," he whispered, eyeing the package I had in my hand. I smiled.

The instructor started the class. Our assignment was a self-portrait. As expected, most of the students brought either drawings or paintings of themselves.

"Hey guys, this is an art school, ok? Anybody can bring in a damn drawing of his face. Van Gogh's portrait was his shoes. Come on. Show me who you are, not what you look like!"

When it was my turn, I put up a photograph of my naked torso, shot from my shoulders down to the top of my legs with my ass turned partially to the front. I'd had a rubber stamp made to look like a stencil on the crates imported from Hong Kong. It said, "Made in Hong Kong." I stamped it on my ass with black ink. I had on a see-through magenta bikini. It was pulled down by my hand to show the stamp.

I spent my entire paycheck on a haircut at the Vidal Sassoon salon on Fifth Avenue. The shag was all the rage at the time and I wanted the best. I had on a skimpy braless top and skintight jeans when Mother called and told me to come pick up a package for her at the store where she worked. I left immediately, not wanting to get in trouble for taking too long.

"Look at your hair! What are you trying to look like? The beggar women who live on the streets? Can't you look decent for once? And look at how you are dressed. You embarrass me.

You look worse than the whores who walk the streets. You just have a face that begs to be hated," Mother blasted as soon as I walked in.

I was numb to all her words by now, but it still bothered me that I could never please her. If only she cared that I did extremely well in school. I said nothing, picked up the package and walked home.

The year was 1971. The sexual revolution was in full swing. Linda Lovelace was a sensation. At this time, I befriended Eddie who majored in film. He was in the process of producing and directing an artsy porno movie. I started to hang out with the crew and cast and to date the male lead. Tom was a very good-looking guy and an exhibitionist. One evening on our way back to his apartment after dinner, he suggested that we stop at a store to pick up something for dessert.

"What would you like to lick off my body?" Tom asked, leading me down an aisle with his arm wrapped around my shoulders.

"Hmmm, ok. Let's see," I said, kissing him and looking for a squeeze bottle of honey.

"Do you have any whipped cream?" he asked the clerk. Picking up a bottle of chocolate syrup, he turned to me and whispered, "I want to have you in chocolate and whipped cream." We laughed. He paid the clerk and we headed for his apartment.

We frequented the X rated theatres, sex shops and peep shows in Times Square. Eddie was one of the pioneers living in Soho. It was still the factory district and was a ghost town at night. The only people going in and out of those cavernous buildings were the hippest people in the city. I was a regular at his parties.

Eddie's loft was huge. He'd set up several stations of warm saké, a keg of beer and wine. Loud music blasted throughout the night. One of the regulars was a model we hired for our work. She danced nude with a bunch of guys and often ended up having sex with them. Joints were passed around. Lines of coke were in constant supply on a glass table in the back. The people here were usually artists, musicians and my friend's cast and crew. No one bothered to ask each other's name or what one did.

As the night went on, most people shed their clothes. Two women and three men had sex on the king size bed in front of a good-sized audience while I had sex on the couch with two men. After a while, I ended up watching them give each other blowjobs.

Mother had stopped seeing her lover. I heard that his wife had arrived with their two sons. He invited us to a fancy dinner at his house to welcome his family to New York. It was sickening to see Mother in front of his family, her phony smiling face in front of his wife after she had fucked her husband for years. I had a difficult time swallowing my food and asked my mother for permission to leave.

David and Mother had become the best of friends. She often made him food and talked to him for hours. She had assumed my life with him short of fucking him. I saw David less and less and was angry with Mother for her betrayal and hypocrisy. Why would she befriend the man whom her daughter the whore, was sleeping with? I distanced myself from them and seldom went home when anyone was around.

"Irene, come over to my apartment. I've been trying to reach you for a week. I smoked grass for the first time the other day. I have some with me. Do you want to try it?" David said on the phone.

"I've smoked for ages and I am busy tonight. I'll see you around." I hung up. It suddenly dawned on me that he was a jerk. Where had I been? What possessed me to stay with this creep for so long? The thought of marrying him made me physically ill.

During my last year at the School of Visual Arts, a select group of graduating students in the graphic design department were asked to show their work in a gallery. People from advertising agencies came to view the work.

On opening night, we were invited to meet the people from the agencies. The gallery was packed. All of the agency people were men.

"Hey, baby. Which piece of work belongs to you?" a man asked me, holding a glass of wine in one hand and sliding his other hand down my back and onto my ass. He pulled me closer and started to kiss my ear. I tried to turn away politely, but another man already had his hand on my ass.

"Come to my office. I'll see what we can do," the man who tried to kiss me said and slipped me a card. I was disgusted by the idea of having to have sex with whoever hired me.

I left early. To party and have fun and be free with my own sexuality was one thing, to have sex to get or keep a job was too degrading.

I grew tired of my reputation in school. It was getting to a point where people did not take my work seriously. I was tired of the constant expectations from guys who thought I would sleep with anyone. I still had the notion that I was a proper girl from a good family. I wanted to be as far away as I possibly could from my mother and David.

I went to the library and compiled a long list of art colleges in Europe. When I got applications back in French, Italian, and Spanish, I narrowed the list to one college in England. I sent out a letter to the Royal College of Art in

London to ask for an application for admission. I knew nothing about the college. All I knew was that I could earn a master's degree after three years of study. I received a thick envelope with all of the requirements. I noticed the queen's seal in gold on the letterhead. The stationary was very proper and snobby. I loved it.

I had to submit a portfolio of at least fifteen pieces of my work. I labored day and night to refine the projects that I had created during the last three years. I didn't have much time to make the deadline. I also noticed that the last phase of the process was a personal interview which was optional for overseas students. I felt it was pivotal for me to be interviewed in person and decided to take my portfolio to London.

I had saved enough money to go to London for three days. I was lucky to get an interview with the professor of the School of Graphic Design during winter break. I thought the interview went well, but I had to wait until April to find out if I got in. It was a long four months.

"I have applied to an art college in London," I told David when I met him for dinner one day.

"You are going to a graduate school? Do you really think you can get in? Don't waste your time," he said condescendingly.

The little confidence I'd had of getting in vanished. I prayed that a miracle would happen so I could get out of this hell of New York and Chinatown.

A thin envelope arrived from the Royal College of Art in April. I opened it with trembling hands. There was only one page to the letter. I was so nervous I couldn't read the words at first, but I could see "congratulations" was the first. I screamed in disbelief. They told me to expect a packet in a few weeks with the information on tuition fees and instructions on how to register and arrange for living quarters as a foreign student. I went to sleep with the letter under my pillow.

Leaving New York was a reality. I lined up a full time and two part time jobs for the summer to finance the coming school year.

I went to Grandmother's.

"I am going to London to pursue my master's degree," I said proudly, sitting on a small stool in front of her while she drank her tea on the sofa. It was unheard of for someone in my family to go abroad for graduate school. I remembered my aunts and uncles complimenting their friends' children on the rare occasions they did so well.

To my surprise, Grandmother sighed and said, "Don't be like your aunt. She is in her thirties and still unmarried. She is too picky." She glanced at me and continued, "And look at your shoes. The heels are at least four inches high. You are a tall girl already, you tower over all the guys and now you try to be smarter than they are. How are you going to get yourself a husband? Stay home and don't get too educated. No Chinese boys will want you."

"I'll get married after I come back from London." I smiled and nodded.

I stopped caring if anybody cared about my future. I rarely saw Mother or David. I couldn't wait to get to work in the morning. Each hour I worked brought me closer to the reality of leaving.

When I stepped out of the airplane in Heathrow Airport, I was elated. I finally wouldn't have to go home to face Mother and her judgments. David was also far behind me. I had the freedom to create a new life.

I took a taxi to the hostel where students from the Royal College resided. The buildings in London were so old, I felt as if I was wandering amid a landscape in a huge museum. Red double-decker buses slowly moved through the streets. I hadn't seen them since Hong Kong. They made the city feel familiar.

I managed to carry my suitcases up a very narrow and steep stairwell to the third floor and looked for room 303. After a walk down a long hallway separated by doors every twenty feet, I found my room. It was the size of a closet. There was a tiny bed, a table, a chair and a freestanding wardrobe in an eight by eight feet space. At least there was a window looking out onto the street. I could call this my home for now and it was precious to me.

I unpacked, excited about starting class on Monday. I put away all of my things. I made the bed and lay down, feeling free, and drifted into a wonderful sleep.

A knock on the door woke me the next morning. I was startled. No one knew I was here. I hadn't contacted the college yet. I rushed to open the door and was stunned to find David standing in front of me.

"How did you get here? Who gave you my address?" I said, shaken.

"Your mother told me and I wanted to talk to you. Let me come in," he said, smiling. I stepped aside to let him in. It felt crowded with two people in the room. He stared into my eyes and said, "You really love me, don't you?"

"It takes you six years to find out?" I said sarcastically.

"Pack up your stuff now and go back to New York with me. Let's get married," he said softly, wrapping his arm around me.

I took a step back, looked into his eyes and said, "No! It's too late. I am staying here."

I could see the bewilderment spread across his face.

"This is your last chance. If I walk out of here, I will never come back again," David warned. He had no clue that I was not the same girl he used to know. For the past three years, I had been exposed to a new world and I no longer had the desire to be a good Chinese wife.

"Goodbye, David," I said. He turned to walk out of the room. I never saw him again except on the streets of

Chinatown when I went home to visit. He remained Mother's best friend.

I had to report to the school of graphic design at nine o'clock in the morning. I expected to get a schedule for classes. I walked into the graphic design department and found it was a large open space of two separate floors with a wall of windows looking out to the Victoria and Albert Museum. Cubicles were set up on each floor. In the center of the first floor, there was an open space set up with a small group of chairs, already filled with students. A young, good-looking guy sat on a stool facing them. I found an empty seat and sat down quickly.

"Welcome to the School of Graphic Design at the Royal College of Art. My name is David Tuhill, one of your tutors," the man on the stool said to us. "You should congratulate yourselves for being here. As you know by now the Royal College is the most prestigious art college in the world. We have an exceptionally large class this year. There are fourteen of you. The two classes ahead of you were eight and ten students to a class. It was difficult for us to go through the process of elimination. There were two hundred and eighty applicants this year, so be very pleased that you are sitting here today."

I didn't know anything about the college until this moment. I felt very good about myself.

"Pssst," a tall English guy next to me whispered to get my attention. I turned to look at him and smiled.

"Do you know why you were chosen for this class?" he asked sincerely. I shook my head and smiled again, waiting for his answer.

"The professor picked you girls to keep us boys happy. He knows we need to be happy to produce good work. None of you are serious about work anyway, just taking up space. All you are good for is as someone's wife after you graduate." He smirked.

"Go fuck yourself." I snorted.

"Oh, a mouth of a sailor! That excites me even more." He grinned.

I rolled my eyes and turned away.

There were no official classes. The college operated on a tutorial system. I was assigned to my own cubicle that included a large desk, a chair and a locked set of drawers with three white walls as an enclosure. The college opened at seven thirty in the morning and closed at ten in the evening. We came and went as we pleased. There were six tutors in the School of Graphic Design and each of them had their expertise in special areas. If we needed their help on a specific project, we could set up a meeting to discuss it with any of them. They would come to our cubicle to give us guidance. There was an army of technicians to execute our projects. The college owned a printing press and it was at our disposal. All we had to do was to get the project approved by a tutor. Then we would write up our orders and send them to the technicians to have it done for us.

Only two official reviews with our professor were given during the school year to chart our progress. I felt like a child in a candy store. I spent most of my time at the college. I only went back to the hostel to sleep.

There were three bars at the college. We could buy beer and liquor during school hours. That was where most of the students hung out. The tutors and professors congregated in the senior common room. The middle common room was for the technicians and the junior common room was for the students. It was very segregated. Unless the students were officially invited by the tutors, we were not allowed to be in the senior common room. The technicians were considered working class. They were never welcomed at the senior or the junior common rooms. The class system was rigid. I frequented the middle common room because I appreciated the work that the technicians did for me and I had befriended quite a few of them. I never saw another student in the middle common room.

I was invited to the senior common room a few times during the school year. The contrast was stark. The waiters who served the professors and their guests wore white coats and black trousers. The tables were covered with white linens. Heavy gauge silverware, fine China and vases of fresh flowers were set neatly on each table. The dessert table was covered with platters of fine cheeses, beautiful cakes and chocolates. The food was of the quality found in very good restaurants. Fine wines were served as well.

The usual fare in the junior common room and the middle common room were french fries that they called chips, eggs, Welsh rarebit (which was like a grilled cheese open face sandwich) and salads. Desserts were anything that was covered with a custard sauce.

I was too excited to care. I had a new culture to explore and unlimited resources to discover and experiment with. I did not fall into any cliques, which I noticed all around me early on. There were many different schools within the Royal College of Art, the school of film, photography, fashion design, furniture design, jewelry design, glass, ceramics, sculpture, textile design, industrial design, environmental design, painting, graphic design, illustration and print making, all scattered in different buildings around the main college. David Hockney graduated from the School of Painting a few years before I got into the college. Henry Moore and Barbara Hepworth were from the sculpture school. Ossie Clark and Zandra Rhodes were from the School of Fashion Design. And finally, Ridley Scott was from the School of Graphic Design. I was thoroughly impressed.

The college had provided me a great environment to express myself without restraints. I was treated as an artist and an adult.

Everything I said and felt was valid. The women's movement was in high gear at this time; there were frequent and heated discussions about the repression we had endured and how we could further the revolution to achieve an equal standing with men. I became increasingly interested in expressing my perspective by celebrating my femininity and sexuality. Assignments were given to us from different tutors. We picked and chose the ones we wanted to work on. We also proposed our own projects. If a tutor approved our proposals and gave us the go ahead, it was considered part of the work for review with the professor.

I spent nearly nine months on a set of six etchings titled "Eight Lines." Each print showed a close-up of a different sexual position drawn with only eight lines to evoke the subtle balance between our physical, emotional and spiritual selves.

During one of the showings of my work, I encountered angry and bitter women. They were furious at me for perpetuating the myth that women should be feminine. But, surely, I thought, men needed to be educated to see us as female human beings who had the same rights and power and that we were also different. We had to have the strength and courage to take full responsibility for our own actions and not to play the role of the victim. I was grateful for the militant feminists who raised hell until we became so conscious of repression and inequality that we found ways to reverse the attitudes.

During a meeting with one of our tutors, he gave us a project titled, "Is there God after all?" Almost the whole class signed up for this project. Most of the students were interested in expressing their feeling about God. Judging from their conversations, their opinions of God were based on their religion. Given my attitude towards organized religion at that time, I was determined to show our tutor this was a dumb project and should not be taken seriously. He had scheduled a meeting in a month to critique our work.

I went to the sculpture school. I was friendly with some of the students and the technicians. I asked them for the materials and made a figurine out of clay. In the front, it looked like Jesus standing with his hands clasped for praying. But in the back, I had his hair resting on his shoulders, so the standing figure looked like a penis. I made a mold and cast it in plaster. I wanted it white for purity and I sanded it down so it was very smooth. Everyone in the sculpture school gasped when they saw the dildo. They couldn't believe that I was actually presenting it in class.

The day of the presentation, I purposely waited to be last. We had to display our work on the table in the middle of the room. Everyone sat around and discussed the success or failure of the particular project. One student brought in a beautiful case with a hand polished wooden base that held a dandelion inside. He spent a month fitting the glass and putting more than twenty layers of wax on the base, hand polishing it to a glass-like finish. He said nothing he could do would come close to the perfection of the dandelion that God had created.

I got up and put the Jesus dildo on the table, turned and looked into my tutor's eyes and said, "Sit on it. This is what I think of your project. I made this especially for you."

He turned beet red and said, " I am very flattered that you have spent so much time to make this just for me." He started to laugh. Most of the students laughed hysterically but a few of them were very angry. They said it was a sacrilege for me to do something so vulgar with the image of Jesus.

My second year at the college, I moved into a flat with a girl I met in the painting school. Her last name was Wurm and she was from L.A. Her openness compared to most of my colleagues was refreshing. I called her "Wurmie." We went to the Friday dances at the college weekly. Her uniform was a knit dress of colorful flowers on a black background and black boots. Mine was skin-tight jeans with pink satin patches and skimpy tops with silver blue platform boots.

We spent hours talking and laughing into the night about men and family, drinking pots of tea while huddling close to the heat, trying to keep warm.

"What the hell is that?" I asked Wurmie one evening when we were in the kitchen preparing dinner. I saw a sickly green paste in a bowl.

"That's guacamole!"

"Molie? Whatever that is, it looks sick!" I pretended to gag.

"Kai! Don't tell me you have never eaten guacamole. It's mashed avocado!"

"I'm from New York. We eat avocados but not that awful looking stuff!" I said, making a face.

"Try it. We eat this all the time." Wurmie handed me a spoon.

"Hey, it's not bad," I said sampling it. "It's funny that people laugh at me for eating pig fallopian tubes and I think mashed avocados are weird." We laughed.

I was introduced to Dolly by two of her Asians friends from the School of Textile Design. She was from Malaysia. She had legs any girl would kill for. She looked exactly like a six foot tall Asian Marlene Dietrich. I could see all the guys drool when she walked by. She had applied to the Royal College as Donald and came to school as Dolly when the first term began. She was the most beautiful transvestite I had ever seen.

Dolly and I became good friends. She liked the fact that we totally confused people wherever we went. They knew that one of us was odd and always tried to figure out if I was a transvestite or if she was straight. It was hilarious. We had great fun.

She lived in a very nice flat in an upscale neighborhood. It was furnished with beautiful antiques and colorful silk cushions strewn everywhere. One day I asked her how she could afford to live in such luxury.

"You can make a lot of money, Irene, because you are capable of having full sex with my clients," Dolly lowered her voice and looked at me coyly. "Most of my clients are Arabs. I see them at the hotels in Mayfair. A few of them are princes. If you want, I can make arrangements for you to meet them. You'll be rolling in money before you know it," she said sincerely. I liked the idea of having a nice flat with beautiful things and a ton of money to burn, but the whispers from my great-grandmother had never gone away. I must be a proper girl from a good family, which was the promise I made to her.

"Thanks Dolly, it is so nice of you to offer. I know you don't tell people this lightly. I really appreciate your trust in me. I think I better stick to getting my school done first before I think about money," I said warmly.

In the beginning, her friends were on guard when they saw me. Dolly told them that I was really ok for being a straight girl and that I was her good friend. They started to relax and accepted me into their circle. Most of them worked in clubs as exotic dancers. I learned from them how to dress and use makeup daringly, to accentuate every one of my assets.

Dolly took large doses of female hormones to lessen her facial hair and soften her voice. She had her breasts enlarged but she kept her wilted penis.

Eventually, she left for Paris and I never heard from her again.

I traveled around Europe on school breaks. I was invited to stay with my friends' families in Berlin and Zurich. I hopped over to Paris and Amsterdam for weekends. My American friends and I loved to hang out at the Louvre when we had extra money.

Every summer, I went back to New York to work and earn enough money for the next school year. Three years went by fast. I was ready to graduate.

"Irene, I have a request for an instructor from Penn State University. You deserve to get a teaching job and go back to the

United States. You don't belong in the rat race here. I am going to send you to Penn State, ok?" the head of the Graphic Design Department said to me one afternoon. "I haven't posted it for the other students yet. I think you should take it."

I was delighted and grateful for his special treatment and thanked him for watching out for me.

"You are an artist. You should be doing your art and not have to worry about making ends meet. Teaching is perfect for you. When you get rich and famous one day just send me invitations to your openings, ok?" He laughed and gave me a big hug.

It was a frantic time at the end of the school year. Everyone scattered to secure a job or go home. Just as I was ready to go back to the United States, I got a call from Mother. She told me Grandmother had passed away in her sleep. I was sad, but didn't think too much about it. I went straight to Pennsylvania from London and didn't make it to her funeral in New York.

Penn State University was a foreign country to me. Everyone there lived and breathed football. I didn't even know what a quarterback was. State College was a small town in nowhere, Pennsylvania. I had never experienced the culture of a state university or a small town before. I was a fish out of water. I had adapted easily everywhere else, but I had only been to big cities. I felt I was on a gigantic farm with a huge herd of blue-legged, plaid-bodied creatures. They all came from small towns across Pennsylvania and had similar attitudes. A few students thought I was the coolest person they had ever met, but most of them saw me as a foreign species from a strange planet and were afraid of me.

I had heard the term "redneck" and had a remote understanding of what it meant but finding myself in the midst of redneck country was frightening. I had forgotten that I was Asian. In Europe, I was classified simply as an American. When I was outside of Chinatown in New York, I was just unique. No one ever had made me feel that I was "Asian."

It was near the end of the Vietnam War. I was having a drink with a student at a bar one evening. A man walked by and said, "Go back to Vietnam," just loud enough for me to hear. My skin crawled.

It was no better inside the college. I was the only female faculty member in the art department and was treated as a novelty item at best and a plaything at worst.

One morning when I went into my office, I found a piece of paper slipped under the door. It said, "Bonjour, Irene" on a drawing of a naked man balancing a champagne glass full of wine with bubbles on his erect penis. It was signed by a married tenured faculty member in the art department who had been eyeing me and following me around.

There were male students older than I was in my classes. Some of them dropped hints that they'd like to go to bed with me. I felt like I was being hunted.

It was the birthday of the head of graphic design department. I walked past his office, stuck my head in and said, "Happy Birthday!"

"Where is my birthday cake, woman? I expect you to bring it to me in your birthday suit. Now show me your ass," he half-joked.

I grew increasingly unhappy. Most of the students were not very interested in the subject I was teaching. They just wanted to get through college as soon as they could. Everyday I went to class, I felt I was going fishing, hoping to catch a student's attention. I felt disconnected. I drove to New York City every weekend just to get away, but I hated going home, too.

Out of frustration one day, I sat for a long time in my apartment at Penn State and stared into space. I rediscovered the place of serenity I'd found as a little girl sitting on the rattan chair on the roof. I started to meditate and began to see my life clearly. It was important for me to have a job, but I realized Penn State was no different than the environment I tried to avoid when I was graduating from the School of Visual Arts. I would be damned if I would give in to the degradations from the men around me just to keep a job. But I was an instructor at a university. This was supposed to be a respectable job. I thought one of the pay offs from working so hard to get a higher education would be to escape these degradations. I thought I would be at the dawn of a new age.

I had been away from my family for four years. I had enough time and distance to realize what my mother had done to me was wrong. I had observed and learned from my peers that my childhood was extremely unusual. I never told anyone about my past because I thought it was the way everybody grew up. I decided to have a talk with Mother on a weekend visit to New York.

"Why did you leave us all by ourselves when we were in Hong Kong? I was only eleven. You came home only once a week just to throw some money on the bed and leave. I was so scared," I said to Mother, my eyes glued on her while she sat at the table drinking her tea.

"I never left you alone. What gave you that idea?" Mother said, turning away.

My chest felt like it had been crushed with a ton of rocks.

"Don't tell me that it never happened!" I yelled. How could she say that! I needed acknowledgement.

"You have a good imagination. Our family are known to have a few crazy ones," she said calmly.

"Don't tell me that I am crazy. Don't tell me that it didn't happen," I sobbed.

Mother stood up and shouted, "It never happened."

She walked out of the room.

Memories of my childhood became fuzzy. I was not sure if anything I remembered actually happened. I was so conditioned to take my mother's words as the way of life. If I didn't believe her, my link to my family would be severed. I could not refute her words. If I did, she would disown me without thinking twice and I couldn't bear that.

At the end of the school year, I didn't want to stay at Penn State and didn't want to go back to New York. I wanted to go as far away as I could from my past. I quit my job and decided to move to California.

"Why do you want to go to California? You don't know anybody there," Mother asked when I told her that I was driving out to Los Angeles in a few days.

"When people have nothing better to do, they go to California. That's what I am doing."

I took only one suitcase and my artwork. I left New York for good.

THE AMERICAN DREAM

❧

California was different. People seemed more friendly and relaxed. At the end of October it was still warm and sunny. For the first time I wasn't anxious about my future. I rented a room in a house right on the beach in Malibu.

Before I left London, a woman who ran a gallery where I'd exhibited gave me the name and address of an art collector to contact in Los Angeles. Tired of the illusion of a proper job, I was ready to put serious effort into developing my career as an artist.

I found Jim's number and called him. He offered to pick me up and take me to dinner that night. I changed into a shimmery, dusty pink leotard with thin shoulder straps, which showed off the red rose tattoo on my shoulder. I pulled on a pair of skintight white jeans with the legs rolled up to just below my knees and a great pair of red and white striped Italian high heel sandals. A little blush and lipstick quickly dabbed on completed my usual evening attire.

I waited for him in front of the house. Before long, a red Mercedes convertible pulled up beside me. A very well groomed man in his late fifties with graying hair hopped out of the car.

"Are you Irene? Hi, I'm Jim," he said, extending his hand.

"Hi, Jim, nice to meet you." I shook his hand. He opened the door to the car, gestured me to get in and whisked me off to an exclusive club in Beverly Hills.

Judging by how the staff greeted him, I knew he must be a regular. I glanced around the room. Flower arrangements shaped into exotic sculptures were placed in strategic areas. Special lighting made everyone appear ten years younger. As we walked to the dining area, the heels of my sandals sank into the thick velvety carpet. Most of the women lounging in the bar were much older than I and were decked in expensive outfits. Expertly applied makeup smoothed and highlighted their best features. They checked me out from the corners of their eyes. We were all on display for each other and for the men.

Jim ordered the food and wine for both of us. Before the food arrived, he leaned over and asked, "Do you like cocaine?"

I thought he said "Do you like cooking?" I turned to him and said, "I love cooking!"

He laughed and quickly slipped me a bag of white powder and a two-dollar bill and said, "Take as much as you want and flush the money down the toilet when you're done." He winked.

I was surprised by the cocaine but I got up and headed to the ladies' room. I used a card to push the powder into a few lines on the toilet paper holder, rolled up the two-dollar bill and snorted. I was amazed at how much money I was holding. There was at least an ounce of cocaine in the plastic bag. After I finished, I promptly threw the bill into the water and pushed the lever. I watched the curled green piece of paper swirl in the bowl and disappear down its gurgling throat into the sewer. I thought how cool it was to actually flush money down the toilet.

I glided back to the table.

"What did you do with the money?" Jim asked, before I sat down.

"I flushed it," I whispered.

"I love it!" Jim chuckled with satisfaction.

We lost interest in the food. Jim led me to the dance floor. A large number of women circulated the bar, hoping to be picked up. A handful of well-dressed men laughed and slapped each other on the back while they studied the women. I cringed. Wherever we lived, women waited to be spoken to.

Jim and I danced until three in the morning and then he took me back to his house.

We drove into the driveway of an old Spanish mansion. The entrance floor was intricately laid with different colors of marble. An antique European crystal chandelier hung in the center of the ceiling next to a grand staircase. Before following Jim upstairs, I peeked into a large, sparsely furnished room adjacent to the entrance. It was the gallery in which Jim displayed his fine collection of modern art.

His bedroom was simple but exquisitely furnished. My entire flat in London could have easily fit into it. The custom-made bed was almost as big as two king-sized beds and it was covered in fine snow-white Italian cotton. Antique Persian rugs lay on the smooth parquet floor. A few photographs by Mapplethorpe were elegantly hung on the walls.

The next morning, I was startled by a knock on the bedroom door.

"Come in," Jim said. I was surprised that he let someone into the room while we were still naked in bed. I pulled the sheet close to my chin and watched the smiling maid set a white breakfast tray on our bed. A single pink rose in a small crystal vase was placed amidst the silverware and a plate filled with fine pastries. She poured us coffee from a silver pot and set down a basket with a variety of newspapers next to the tray.

As he dressed, Jim told me he was an attorney and that I could read about the case he and his firm were working on in the newspaper.

After he left for his office, I walked out to the balcony of his bedroom. To my right and left were numerous smaller balconies off each room on the second floor. Below was a formal court-yard filled with wonderful plants and a beautiful water fountain in the center. The scent of exotic flowers sweetened the air.

I went downstairs and walked past the kitchen. It was large and well equipped. It reminded me of a kitchen in a fine restau-rant. Two servants sorted and ironed a pile of clothes in the laundry area. They smiled as I walked past them into the din-ing room. Two beautiful brocade tablecloths covered the long dining table with silver candleholders at each end. Adorning the middle of the table was an exotic flower arrangement in a crystal vase, surrounded by bowls of persimmons and pome-granates. On the walls, formal oil portraits of dignified men conveyed a lineage of wealth and prestige.

I walked out through a pair of old beveled glass doors into paradise. Old vines and exotic flowers draped down from the trellis over my head. Water cascaded down the wonderful old hand-painted Spanish tiles of the fountain. I closed my eyes to soak in the perfumed air and the melodic sound of water. I felt happy and content. Everything seemed to grow quiet around me. I opened my eyes and looked up, a beam of sunlight shone through the vines onto my face. The colors of the vines and flowers and fountain became more vivid. The sound of the water and the chirps of birds became distinct. I bowed my head, suddenly conscious of the vastness of the universe. I felt com-pletely insignificant. I felt a surge of energy enter the top of my head and sweep through my body, into my heart. I felt loved, warm and humble. I was aware of seeing the world through my eyes, as I had when three years old. "Why am I in me and not in you?" I had asked my mother.

I saw Jim the following week to show him my work.

"I want you to meet my friend Ken. He owns a gallery on Melrose," he said after viewing two sets of my etchings. "Come to my office tomorrow. I'll set up a meeting for you."

"Thank you, Jim. I'll see you tomorrow." I said goodbye and left, excited.

His office was in one of the more prestigious buildings in Century City. The law firm occupied an entire floor. I walked into the reception area and was greeted by a woman in her late twenties who looked like she had just popped out of a fashion magazine.

"Are you here to see Jim? He is expecting you," she said before I had a chance to ask a question. She smiled and led me through a pair of heavy, etched, art deco glass doors to a corridor.

"His office is the last one at the end." She pointed toward the deep recesses of the suite.

"Thank you," I said, and walked down the wide, seemingly endless hallway. Original prints by Andy Warhol and Roy Lichtenstein covered the walls. An army of attorneys worked in offices along the corridor. Like bees in a hive, I thought. I reached the office at the end. The heavy mahogany doors were left ajar.

I was about to knock, when Jim called out, "Irene, come on in."

I walked into the office. Jim sat behind a huge desk in an oversized leather chair.

"Meet my friend Ken," Jim said, waving his hand toward the man who sat opposite him. "And this is my artist friend, Irene." Jim turned to me and smiled.

Ken stood up and greeted me warmly. We shook hands.

"Jim tells me you are quite a good artist," Ken said, taking his seat and checking me out as if I were a piece of merchandise. "He's asked me to show you the ropes of the business."

I glanced at Jim appreciatively.

"Before I get you into the gallery to show your work, you have to court the clients. You should start making the rounds at the parties so they get to know who you are. I am sure Jim is prepared to get you into the circuit," Ken said frankly. He turned to look at Jim and smiled knowingly.

"I'm throwing a party next week and you are both invited," Jim said, leaning back on his chair.

After Ken left, Jim motioned me to come closer. He opened a desk drawer and took out a small silver box. I leaned closer to see what it was. He put his arm around my waist, pulled me onto his lap and opened the box. He scooped out a tiny spoonful of coke and snorted it. He offered the next scoop to me.

We took a few more turns then I stood up abruptly and said, "I better go. See you next week."

Jim slapped my ass and winked. I felt uncomfortable by how I was being treated, yet excited to see what might come of this.

When I arrived at the party, Jim was standing by the door welcoming guests.

His house had been transformed into an art universe. The lighting in the gallery was a piece of art in itself. A woman in a formal black dress sat in the center of the room playing a harp. A soft white light cast a halo over her head. The artwork surrounded her, each piece washed in a dim yellow glow. The muted light over the paintings made the room look dreamy and surreal.

Earlier, Jim had asked me to decorate a cake with one of my drawings from the series of six etchings entitled Eight Lines. I had a two by three foot sheet cake specially ordered to accommodate it. I drew the image with pink icing on pure white frosting. It was displayed by the entrance to the courtyard on a special table draped with fresh greens and flowers.

A troupe of performing artists floated in and out of the rooms and the courtyard. Cocktails and wine flowed. Silver boxes of cocaine were passed around like sugar bowls at a tea party. Everywhere I turned I was either passed a joint or a scoop of coke.

Two hours into the party, practically everyone was stoned. As word passed that I had done the drawing on the cake, I became a main topic of conversation. Several men approached me to talk and started to touch me. I began to feel like prey. I left them and walked into another room. An Italian man followed closely behind. I walked quickly into another room. He followed. I started to run. He chased me from room to room. I ran into the courtyard, hoping to lose him.

"Hey, why are you running away from me? Aren't I good enough for you?" he called.

He caught me near the fountain. He grabbed me by my arm and pressed his lips to my face. I tried to twist away.

"Stop!" I screamed, looking around for someone to come to my rescue. There were plenty of people milling about, but they were too stoned to react. A handful gathered to watch and started to laugh.

"Fuck me! Baby, come on, you'll like it!" he said, holding me tight, forcing me onto the ground. He pulled down my panties. I shoved him off with my arms and legs and ran out of the house. I never went back.

I'd learned to come back to a place of peace when I was tired of running. I sat for hours each morning on the deck facing the ocean. I needed to be still, to see what was coming next.

It became routine for me to take long walks on the beach after meditation. Most of the houses along the coast had large windows facing the ocean. One, just a few houses down from mine, I found particularly fascinating. Instead of oversized windows, the entire wall was made of glass. Inside, a group of five-foot tall exotic animals made of sisal stood near a large cactus. Ebony carvings and masks from Africa decorated the interior walls of the room. The furniture was made of deep earth-toned fabrics, enhanced with strokes of vibrant color. I imagined a magic passageway to exotic lands.

One exceptionally warm night, I stretched out on the lounge chair gazing at the sky, immersed in the wonderful and familiar feeling of being connected with the stars and the moon. A halo surrounded the moon and a bright star flickered close to it.

It must be a sign, the union of the sun and the moon. Is it time to consider marriage? I wondered. I am twenty-six, an old maid by Chinese standards.

My great grandmother's voice grew loud in my mind, as if she sensed I was at a crossroad. I considered my family and my life. All of my sisters were married and two of them already had children. The world was a brutal place for a woman to try to make it on her own. I did want to have children someday. I was tired of the battles I had to fight to claim my own ground. After years of trying to be independent in the western world, the structure of the traditional culture began to seem appealing. If I played by the rules, I would at least know where I stood.

Three days later, while I watched a magnificent sunset from the deck, a beautiful Old English Sheepdog trotted by. Two men strolled several yards behind him, talking and laughing. Their easy demeanor caught my attention. One of them had a bright smile. His eyes sparkled. As I watched him, our eyes made contact. My heart quickened. The phone rang. I reluctantly ran into the house. After the call, I went back out to the deck hoping to catch a glimpse of the men and the sheepdog, but they were gone.

The next morning, while having tea on the deck, I thought of the sheepdog and the man. I leaned over to set down my cup and nearly fell off the chair when I saw the dog running down the beach with the man walking a distance behind it.

"You've got a call, Irene," my roommate yelled from the house. "Not Again!" I thought. I rushed inside to answer the phone. I quickly returned to the deck and looked up and down the beach, waiting for them to walk by again. They never showed up.

That evening, I sat on the lounge chair hoping. It was rare to see the same person on the beach unless they lived close by. I recognized most of the neighbors and he was not one of them. I looked down the beach. To my amazement, the sheepdog was running toward my house and, as before, the man strolled behind. I was determined to meet him. I jumped down from the deck to the sand and walked toward them.

The thunderous sound of the waves pounding the surf made me nervous. It sounded like the rolling drumbeats before a person was introduced in front of an audience. As we approached each other, I felt anxious and shy. I hadn't felt this way since I left Chinatown.

"Hi, my name is Bob. Are you the girl who lives in Mr. Dehorst's house?" the man asked with a friendly smile. I had to squint to see his features against the bright setting sun. Everything was golden, as if I had been cast into a land of magic.

"Yes, I live there with Deanna," I said softly. "My name is Irene."

"Do you want to come up to my house and smoke some opium? I just came back from Hawaii. I travel a lot," he said casually.

"Yeah, I'd love to," I said. I would do anything to get to know him. Besides, I'd never tried opium. It was the drug of choice for the Chinese. I wanted to experience the allure that had put China to sleep until the Opium War with the British.

"We're standing right in front of my house," Bob said and turned toward the deck stairs. I followed him and looked up. My heart pounded wildly. It was the house with the African motifs. Was this an omen? Only days ago, I'd contemplated the idea of marriage. I took a deep breath and continued to walk up the steps.

I sat on the sofa and waited for Bob. He came out of the bedroom with a wooden cigar box in his hand. He sat down next to me and opened it. I was amazed at the assortment of drugs inside. He took out a small pipe, loaded it with opium and lit it. He passed the pipe to me and I inhaled deeply. I leaned back, stretched my legs out on an ottoman and started to float away. Everything in the room became alive with vivid colors. My eyes caressed every item in the room. I felt like a snake slithering slowly over rocks. I enjoyed the sensual pleasure of the visual feast. I immersed myself in the decadence of being in the moment. I understood its hold on the Chinese.

One evening, Bob decided to show me what he did for a living. I followed him to his garage where he parked his yellow Mercedes convertible. He opened the trunk and stood back to reveal a beautiful assortment of antique beads from Africa. The rich patinas on the worn surfaces of amber, silver, coral, brass and glass beads were dazzling. It was like viewing a pirate's treasure chest. I tried to imagine what the beads meant to the people who had worn them and the stories behind them. Bob told me he traveled to Africa, handpicked each strand of beads and sold them to jewelry designers and retail stores around L.A. and in Hawaii.

In the two months since I'd met Bob we'd become inseparable. I rarely went home. In our third month, Bob asked me to bring my stuff over so I wouldn't have to pay rent on an empty room.

"We should get on with our lives," I said to Bob one afternoon, while we lounged around on the deck. "Either we get married or I should leave. I don't want to just be stuck in the zone of frozen time and waste my life away."

"After my divorce three years ago I swore I wouldn't get married again," he said with a frown. "All the girls want is my money."

"What money?" I looked at him, surprised. "All you have is the stuff in the trunk of your car. Is that a big deal?"

"That's a lot of money to me. My parents never gave me a penny. I had to borrow money to start my business. This is all I have and I am not letting any girl take that away from me," he said. He sat up to make his point.

"Do you really think everyone just wants to rob you? Your parents put you through law school," I reminded him. "That's a lot of money. Besides, I think you have a very interesting business. We can build on it."

"I don't trust anybody," he insisted.

"Bob, you have to open your heart and see the other person's intention. Not everyone is out to get you," I said, reaching out to him and squeezing his hand.

Two weeks later, Bob and I got married in a tiny chapel in Santa Monica. Bob's friend from the beach was our witness. It was just the three of us. The pastor stepped on a button under the small table to start the wedding music as he began the brief service. I laughed through the entire ceremony, which only lasted twenty minutes. It reminded me of a Las Vegas quickie wedding chapel. Bob and I wore white Guatemalan shirts with blue thunderbird designs on the pockets and white yoga pants.

I was the first in our family to marry a Caucasian. If my grandmother had been living, she would have disowned me. But at least I was married. I hoped Great-grandmother was pleased.

Bob had an insatiable appetite for getting high. We immersed ourselves in a wonderland of drugs, living from high to high. Cocaine kept us up for days and then we took Quaaludes to sleep. Days blended into nights, sometimes, we remembered to eat. The world outside of our house became increasingly remote. A large mirror we used to chop and line up our coke was the only item of meaning to me. Everything else was inconsequential.

After several months, I noticed a lifeless, old woman staring back at me from the mirror while I snorted up a line of coke. I had aged ten to fifteen years. My skin was dry. I had dark circles and wrinkles around my dull eyes. My hair looked like straw and fell off in handfuls. I was terrified. The sound of the waves and the sweet smell of sea air were not enough to hold me in our downward spiral. I became increasingly paranoid, induced by the endless use of cocaine. I demanded that we extract ourselves from Malibu and focus on our future. I threatened to leave if we didn't change our lives.

Bob agreed. He decided that we should leave the country to go on a buying trip so we could not get hold of any drugs. We packed up everything in the house and found an apartment in Santa Monica. A few days later, we left for Africa and Europe.

On our way to Ethiopia, we stopped in Kenya to see Bob's boyhood friend who taught at the American International School in Nairobi. He had been there for many years and had become friendly with a few young men from the Maasai tribe, a nomadic people. He introduced us to them and asked them to take us to their families. We rented a red compact Toyota with two spare tires and drove over two hundred miles out into the wild. Bob and I sat in front, two men sat in the back and the third man rode in the open trunk. The car bounced wildly on the dirt road. We screamed and laughed all the way to our destination.

As I stepped out of the car, I looked around for a village. We were in the middle of nowhere. The red earth stretched from one horizon line to the other as far as I could see. The sky was a brilliant blue. A few baobab trees stood far in the distance. I had never seen such vastness in my life. When everyone was still I only heard the wind blowing and my heart beating. We followed the men into the high veldt grass. Suddenly, their bomah lifted from the landscape like a mirage.

Women and children ran out to greet us from the bomah, a cluster of cow-dung huts surrounded by a chest-high fence of twigs to keep the goats and cows safe at night from wild animals. The men were out with their cattle and wouldn't be back until dusk. A group of children gathered around me to touch and fondle my long, straight hair.

Outsiders were rarely allowed in their camp. They were afraid of the little boxes the westerners aimed and clicked at them with a flash of bright light. They believed cameras took away their souls and captured them inside.

The earlobes of both men and women stretched down past their shoulders. Their earrings were made of leather and beadwork. Teenagers wore various sizes of wooden disks in their earlobes to slowly stretch them out. Their idea of beauty was to have the longest earlobes possible.

We were invited to meet and have tea with the matriarch of the camp. The entrance to her hut was draped with a piece of leather. I followed Bob in. When the flap fell into place behind me, I found myself in the dark. The only light source was a glowing ember in the middle of the dirt floor and a small smoke hole at the top of the domed hut. I froze. I couldn't see and was afraid I'd fall on someone. I inched forward slowly and sat down. I heard muffled giggles and then everyone burst out in good-natured laughter at my awkwardness. I learned later that they had never been exposed to artificial light and could see in almost total blackness.

A woman handed me a gourd that had been cut in half to make a bowl. I took a sip of the warm liquid in it. It was sweet and strong, a strange mixture of goat's milk, sugar and tea.

At first, I was put off by the pungent odor of the cow dung and animals that roamed freely in and out of the hut. But soon I got used to the smell and the animals running around as if they were one of us.

After tea, Bob and I walked and talked with the two young men who had brought us to the bomah. They both spoke some English.

"Do you see the bird on the branch?" one of them pointed to a tree about fifty feet from where we stood.

"Where?" I asked, straining to see it.

He took a step back and threw a stick in the direction he pointed. The stick was smooth, about a foot and a half long with a round ball at one end made from the root and trunk of a small tree. I heard a loud thud. He ran toward the tree and picked a large bird off the ground. I shook my head in disbelief. I hadn't been able to see his target and he hit it with such accuracy.

"This will be part of your meal tonight." He smiled and carried the bird by its feet as we started back to the bomah.

After dinner, we gathered outside the huts under the moonlight. The women and children sat in a circle around an older man. The rest of the men sat on the outer edge of the circle. The elder began to tell a story. Everyone seemed entranced by his narration. I had no idea what he said, but I sensed that he was passing down the stories of his people's lineage and history to their descendants.

After a while, a short man came in from the outside and everyone grouped around him delighted to see him. He was a singer who traveled from one bomah to another to entertain the tribe. He was fed and given shelter for his service. After warm greetings, he started to sing. His voice was smooth and rhythmic. I could almost hear the stories in his songs. Everybody got up to their feet and started to dance. About fifty people jumped as high as they could with their arms raised and clapped their hands loudly. The silver light of the moon highlighted the strong features of each dancer. The beat of the song went faster and the pitch got higher and the dancers jumped faster and faster. Laughter rang out everywhere. Their eyes half closed, each dancer was completely rapt in the rhythm of sound and their bodies. I too was enraptured. I leapt up and jumped as high as I could over and over, feeling completely free and unattached.

Someone offered me his bed. I was grateful to sleep inside. I had already heard the cries of the busy wild animals that roamed at night. I went into the hut and found a piece of cowhide shaped to the form of his body. This was his bed. The goats were already inside, making themselves at home. The bed was much more comfortable than I expected. I smiled and went to sleep with the animals huddling nearby.

A week passed. I didn't care what time or day it was. Nothing mattered but what was happening at the moment. I wasn't concerned that I wore the same clothes and hadn't taken a shower. We walked five miles for water. I generally stayed in the bomah with the women and children while Bob went with the men to tend to the cattle. Sometimes, they were gracious enough to let me tag along with them to gather wild honey.

I became aware that I could see and hear much more than I ever had before. I realized the over-stimulation of the cities and drugs had deadened my senses. For the first time, I learned how to live just to be alive.

Bob and I arrived in Addis Ababa, Ethiopia and checked into the Hilton. It was a profound change from Kenya. The main street was the only paved road, herds of sheep and people made up most of the traffic. Grimy, run down buildings flanked the thoroughfare. Families in tattered clothes hung out on the side of the storefronts. It was a drastic contrast to the glittering hotel frequented by well-dressed westerners just a few blocks away.

Although the living conditions in Ethiopia were extremely poor, the people were gentle and reserved. Almost everyone had luminous, soulful eyes. I could see how the queen of Sheba so easily seduced King Solomon with her beauty and wisdom. But I also sensed fear in the general public and noticed people whispering in twos or threes on the streets.

We were invited to dinner at the house of a business associate, Asefa. He was a wealthy man by Ethiopian standards. He owned a car, an old beat up Volkswagen Beetle, which he'd bought on the black market. The only vehicles on the road that looked halfway decent were dusty government-owned cars.

Asefa picked us up at the Hilton. We met him around the corner from the hotel and drove through back streets so people wouldn't see him dealing privately with foreigners. A few of his relatives had been executed because they were suspected of having ties to the opposition force, which was battling the government. One day, the police had shown up, lined them up on the street and shot them.

We arrived in Asefa's compound, a group of houses built with cement blocks that had metal roofs and dirt floors.

Asefa supported an army of relatives. Groups of them milled around inside the compound. They smiled and bowed to us when we passed. I followed Bob and Asefa into the main house. The furnishings were bare and old. It reminded me of a Goodwill furniture department, but to Ethiopians, this was luxury. There was even a running toilet, the ultimate symbol of status.

"Please sit down," Asefa said to us warmly and summoned his wife to make the famed Ethiopian coffee for us. She carried in a small burning stove and a pot of boiling water. A daughter brought a tray of cups, a beautiful container that held the green coffee beans, a large copper disk and a whisk. I was fascinated by all the paraphernalia used to prepare the coffee. Asefa's wife sat in front of us. She put the copper disk on top of the hot stove and dispensed the green coffee beans on it and stirred them around with the whisk. Soon, the beans started to turn brown and a wonderful aroma filled the room. She transferred the beans into a bowl and crushed them with a wooden stick. The ground coffee was then poured into the pot of hot water and steeped for a few minutes. She poured the dark amber liquid into the small cups a quarter filled with sugar and offered the coffee to the men first and then to me. After we were served, she disappeared into the other room.

Dinner was served in another room. I was pleased to see that at least the women were allowed to join us. To honor their guests, they slaughtered a goat. Bob told me the slaughtering of goats was reserved for important occasions. I sat next to Asefa's wife, who hardly lifted her eyes and always looked away to avoid direct eye contact with us.

There were platters and baskets full of highly spiced food. We each had a plate in front of us but no utensils. Asefa tore a piece of flat, gray, steamed bread from a basket and scooped some goat meat out of a platter with it. He walked over to Bob, holding the bread and meat with both hands and put the food into Bob's mouth with a big smile. This was the custom to honor guests. Then he came over to me and gently pushed the food into my mouth.

We only went to the hotel to sleep. Bob spent most of his time bargaining with Asefa at his stall in the marketplace or in his house. Workers brought in sacks and piles of merchandise throughout the day. When I wasn't picking out beads with Bob, he would tell me to walk around the marketplace to search for new finds. The market was a huge low-lying building with a tin roof. Inside it were rows of no more than ten by ten stalls cramped with traditional cotton embroideries, baskets, antiques, utensils and imported second hand clothes. After ten days of intense bargaining and choosing merchandise, I was exhausted.

We hopped over to Sana'a in Yemen by crossing the Red Sea. As I stepped out of the airport, I felt transported. Everything was the color of sand. Tall rock buildings built into steep hills, some with domed tops were packed closely together. I walked through narrow alleyways, my feet sinking deep into the pale sand. I peeked through a dark doorway into a cavernous room where a donkey with blinders pulled a giant stone mill grinding wheat. I was mesmerized that night by the fourth century landscape set against the blue-black sky dotted with thousands of stars. I took a deep breath. I was in a dream world, as if I had entered the stories of "One Thousand and One Arabian Nights."

Long black robes covered the women from head to toe. They wore masks of the same color with two small eyeholes so they could peer out into the world. These mysterious figures in black floated in and out of the dark archways and alleys. The men strolled through town with their shoulders back and chests thrust forward. Their swords prominently hung from the sashes that bound their flowing robes.

Bob went from dealer to dealer transacting business. I worked alongside him, carrying our money in a large shoulder bag and picking out beads. As I went through the merchandise, I noticed that the men rarely spoke to me and would deal only with Bob. Obviously, they tolerated me, as they did other foreign women who bared their flesh, only to get the foreign currency that they so fiercely coveted. Nonetheless, when they looked at me, I felt their hatred.

"The men are creepy here. They hate me and pretend that I don't exist," I told Bob in our hotel room one evening.

"Don't be ridiculous. They treat me fine. You are so oversensitive," he said, busy going through the merchandise we'd bought that day.

"You are not a woman. I can just feel their vibes. The way they look at me makes my skin crawl," I insisted, fidgeting with the hem of my shirt.

"Pay attention to me and forget about other, less important things. Who cares anyway? Go get yourself ready for dinner. I am hungry," he said impatiently. I went into the bathroom and got changed for dinner and was quiet for the rest of the evening. Slowly I was learning not to discuss my feelings with Bob. He wasn't interested, just like my mother when I was a little girl. I started to keep to myself. At the end of each day, Bob was only interested in reviewing our merchandise and transactions. We'd discuss the profit margin on each item. He would tell me to count them and box them up. I only spoke to him when it was necessary. I began to pay more attention to the fascinating new cultures around me and found it more exciting.

We were in Yemen for ten days. I hadn't spoken to, or even been close enough to a woman to have eye contact. I felt increasingly oppressed by the Arabian culture. I would be better off as a dog in Yemen than as a woman. A dog could at least walk down the street freely, whereas a woman walking down the street must hide her flesh and any sign of expression. By the end of our stay in Yemen I could hardly breathe and was desperate to get out.

Morocco was colorful and eclectic, a mix of European, Arabic and African culture. We drove from Casablanca to Marrakech. The buildings were Moorish in design and decorated with colorful tile work. The rooflines resembled mosques. Most people spoke Arabic and French and the businessmen generally spoke some English.

The souk was cramped with little stalls of antiques, spices and perfumes. I watched a snake charmer at the entrance of the marketplace, fascinated by how his flute controlled the huge cobra rising from a basket. A man in an ornate red and gold costume carried a large leather bag decorated with hundreds of foreign coins and a water bag made of animal skin. A few tin cups hung from his belt. He tried to sell me a cup of water. A group of children surrounded me to sell me candies. I was overwhelmed by the barrage of people trying to make a transaction, but at the same time, I found it very exotic.

Bob and I were invited to have dinner with Hadj, one of the wealthier businessmen. From the outside, the façade of his house looked just like a tall stone wall with a massive wooden gate. Each panel of the entry gate measured at least eighteen feet high and ten feet wide and was elaborately carved. A small door, about four feet high and three feet wide, was cut into one panel of the gate.

A servant greeted us holding the small door open. We stooped down to get through the opening. When I straightened up, I found myself looking at a palace. The courtyard was covered with hand-painted tiles in hundreds of colors and geometric shapes. A tiled water fountain accentuated one end of the yard. The house was three stories high. Balconies on each floor looked down into the courtyard. Hand-painted doors and wooden windows with intricate carvings embellished the ground floor.

A servant led us to a grand staircase, inlaid with more tiles and railings made of wonderful ironwork. We went up to the second floor and into a room the size of a ballroom. The walls were covered with yellow tiles painted delicately with blue and green geometric designs. The ceilings were made of carved wooden panels. Benches built around the four walls were covered with silk and wool pillows and cushions. In the center of the room, a large copper platter placed on a wooden stand served as a table.

Hadj was already seated on the floor with his three sons surrounded by more pillows. He gestured for us to join him. I was the only woman in the room. I knew he had a wife, three sons and four daughters. I wondered where the women were. After a few pleasantries, one of the sons went out to inform the servant that he wanted dinner served.

One by one, the daughters and the wife came into the room with big platters of food. They set them down on the big copper tray, then turned around and left. Hadj did not even acknowledge them. He only nodded to his wife to show her that he approved.

I was amazed at the labor that went into the food. Every dish was fit for a banquet. For dessert, we each had a crystal goblet full of perfect kernels of pomegranate seeds, shimmering like rubies under the light from the ceiling. There were six of us. It must have taken one of the daughters hours to fill the glasses.

We spent the next ten days at the souk buying merchandise. I was tired. I couldn't wait to get home.

Several days after our return to California, we sat at a table cataloguing the merchandise. Bob looked up and said, "Let's start loading up my truck. We have to sell what we bought."

I dropped my hands and looked at him with disbelief. "I am tired," I protested. "Maybe we should rest for a week or two before we start planning our sales trip."

"I spent a lot of money. I want to make it back and more. There is no time to rest. Sell, sell, sell," Bob said, raising his voice.

"Start packing," he ordered. We hadn't even completely unpacked from our buying trip.

We were on the road for two months. We went from client to client, ranging from jewelry designers to small stores to galleries. Since I didn't know the business and was eager to learn, I followed instructions and cooperated with Bob. This road trip became the blueprint for our future.

"I'm tired of buying merchandise for others," Bob said while he added up the checks. "I want to manufacture my own product and wholesale it to the stores so I can keep all of the profit. I saw a nice product in Hawaii the last time I was there. No one's doing it on the mainland."

He stopped punching numbers on the calculator and went on, "I'm going to take you to Hawaii. You can learn the business. We can come back to California and make a killing."

"What is it?" I asked, curious. I thought it might be good to change the pace. I was still exhausted from our selling trip. Hawaii sounded like a nice break.

Bob, encouraged by my interest, put his arm around my shoulder and said, "They are beautifully carved candles. I'll get the plane tickets right away. You'll love it."

Hawaii would not be the change of pace I'd imagined. As soon as we arrived, Bob began checking out all of the hand-carved candle stalls and inquiring about learning the business. We walked around the marketplace and talked to people from morning to evening until we found someone who was willing to teach us for a handsome price. I learned the intricacies of candle making in a week, going to the candle store early in the morning, and returning to the hotel late at night. Bob didn't want me to waste any time because time spent meant money wasted.

As soon as we returned from Hawaii, I rented a warehouse in Santa Monica. I had the equipment made, built the workbenches myself and had the place running in less than two weeks.

Now we had to market the candles. Bob decided that we needed to find representatives for our candles in different showrooms across the nation. He sent me off to different gift shows in various states. He stayed home while I traveled with ten to twenty boxes of candles and beads to do three to five day shows in San Francisco, Dallas, Atlanta and Minneapolis. I took orders from customers who owned shops and galleries, and squeezed out time to walk through the wholesale marts to find wholesalers to take our candles. I found representatives for the candles in all fifty states.

One day after working ten hours at the factory, I came home, sat down and realized that I had become a robot. I had fallen into the habit of taking orders from Bob without question. I was repeating the pattern of the little girl who was so willing to please and so afraid to show her emotions.

How did this happen? I'd been married for just over a year. In the beginning, I found Bob's business intriguing. The excitement of learning something new and traveling to exotic places overshadowed my suspicion of his antiquated view of women. I hadn't known him well enough before I plunged into his world.

I worked ten to twelve hours at the factory, coming home to cook and serve dinner, clean dishes and do laundry while Bob watched television.

One evening after dinner, as I cleared the dishes from the table, I said to Bob, "Why don't you help me do the dishes so I can vacuum the floor?"

"That's your job. I am done. I worked all day at the factory," he said, sitting on the sofa with his legs stretched out. He turned the volume of the TV higher.

"I worked all day too. Why is this my job and not yours?" I said, raising my voice and dropping the dishes in the sink. They crashed loudly.

Bob sat up and yelled, "Housework is a woman's job!"

"Is working in a factory twelve hours a day a woman's job too?" I screamed, turning to face him, my hands on my hips.

"This is the twentieth century. Women want equal rights so you better fucking make fifty percent of the household income to become equal." He stood up, so he could talk down at me. I backed off.

"I can't take this anymore. I am tired. It is too hard for me to keep working my ass off," I said to Bob after dinner, while clearing the table. "I want a divorce," I muttered, not daring to look at him.

"You think I am going to let you go that easily? You promised you would stand behind me." He walked over to me, held my shoulders tightly with his hands and stared straight into my eyes and said, "Now keep your promise!"

I turned away. Those words weighed heavily on me. He knew how important an oath was to me. I dropped the matter.

During this time, my mother visited us for the first time. She was pleased to see that we owned a business that had a good possibility of growing into something prosperous.

One evening while Bob attended to business at the factory, I confided in Mother about my marriage.

"I want a divorce. I am very unhappy. Being married to Bob didn't turn out the way I thought it would," I said, looking out into the backyard, not knowing how Mother would react.

"You had your fun and you're not getting any younger. You have chosen your own husband, much better off than I was. Once you have married a chicken, you follow the chicken. When you marry a dog, you follow the dog. You have played the field enough. This is what marriage is about. Stick to it and learn to be a good wife," Mother advised.

I heard Great-grandmother and Grandmother all speaking with one voice through her. I heard them say that this was what marriage was about — to accept and to endure — as had all of the women in my family. I had never seen an ideal relationship and had better learn from the women of my lineage to become a good, dutiful wife. I must forget about everything I had experienced before I was married. The idea of having a family was too important to abandon. It didn't matter whom I had chosen to be my husband. It was my attitude that needed to change. I must be willing to make it work.

Overnight I made the decision to survive by reverting to a good Chinese girl.

Slowly, I slipped into a routine that I didn't even question. In order to keep my marriage, I had to learn to endure. Bob took advantage of my change of heart. He began to time my trips to the grocery store.

"You have been gone for over an hour. Where else have you been?" he asked suspiciously.

"I asked the butcher to cut the steaks to the size I wanted. He took forever," I said, unloading the groceries. Bob came over to fish the receipt out of the bag and took my checkbook from my purse to see if the amount of the check and the receipt matched.

"I need to buy a pair of shoes for work. Maybe I'll go this afternoon," I said, not paying much attention to him.

"Do you need them?" Bob asked looking up from the checkbook, "How many pairs of shoes do you need?"

"The pair I'm wearing has holes in them!" I said, exasperated.

"You can stretch it out for a few more weeks. I'll go get them with you," Bob said without missing a beat.

One afternoon, I walked home from a nearby store. I saw my neighbor Christina watering her flowers in front of her house, ten houses away from ours. I stopped to say hello.

"Irene! Come here!" Bob yelled from the front of our house.

"Gosh, your husband is calling you home again. You better go. I'll talk to you later," Christina said, averting her eyes, as if she didn't want any part of it. Most of my neighbors knew the routine. Bob either called me home by telephone or yelled down the street, usually within ten minutes.

I got pregnant.

"We can't afford to have a child now," Bob said when I told him.

"I never have enough time to do everything I need to get done. Maybe it's not a very good idea," I responded without much thought. But then I stopped and pondered our situation. We were not poor by any means. We had bought a house in a good neighborhood, owned a business, and had two cars and a healthy income. Bob would always feel deprived. I was twenty-nine and felt my biological clock ticking. If I didn't have the child now, when would it be the right time? If I was going to devote myself to marriage, I wanted a family.

"I want to have this child, Bob. Maybe we should think it over," I said.

A few days later, Bob wavered. I took the opportunity to call both of our parents to tell them about my pregnancy so Bob couldn't back out.

I worked till the day I gave birth to my daughter. Labor started at midnight and Mae was born at 4:15 in the morning. When she was two days old, I was back at work with her in a stroller by my side.

Late one night, I sat in a rocking chair in our bedroom breast-feeding Mae. As soon as Bob walked in, I knew it was trouble.

"When are you coming to bed?" he asked irritated, "You never pay any attention to me anymore. All you care about is the baby. I want you to pay some attention to me." He threw the comforter to one side of the bed and sat down grumpily.

"Don't speak so loud, I want Mae to go to sleep. I only have four hours before she wakes up again. I am exhausted." I looked away, trying to control my exasperation.

Bob was furious, he stepped in front of me and put his hands on his hips and yelled, "It's all your fault! If you didn't insist on having a child, I wouldn't be feeling left out."

"You are too loud and upsetting the baby. Good night Bob," I said, dismissing him.

"I hate this!" He went back to bed, yanked the cover over him and went grudgingly to sleep.

"My brother is in the hospital," Bob said, putting down the phone. We had just come home from work.

"He overdosed on heroin. Someone found him unconscious in his apartment. We better go and see what we can do for him." It didn't come as a surprise to me. Since I married into this family Jack was always involved in something dubious.

We went to see him in the hospital. He had fallen over onto his back and lay there with his leg folded under him for hours before he was found. He lost the use of his right leg due to the damage done to his sciatic nerve from the fall and was in constant pain. He was due to leave the hospital in two days and he had nowhere to go.

"You can come home with us. Irene can take care of you," Bob said to Jack, turning to look at me.

I saw Jack lying in the hospital bed. Judging by the way he looked, he needed a great deal of care. I had serious doubt that I could handle caring for an infant, an invalid and operate a business at the same time.

"I don't know if I can do it," I answered, almost inaudibly.

"Blood is thicker than water. You have to do it," Bob said with finality.

I had no idea what it took to take care of a heroin addict during withdrawal. He was depressed and demanding.

"Go talk to Jack, he needs cheering up," Bob said to me, when I finished doing the dishes.

"I am tired. I want to sit down," I said feebly, wishing I had another life.

"Go sit down in his room and talk to him!"

I stood up and walked to Jack's room. I was too tired to fight.

I brought food into his room daily and he would talk to me for hours about how he hated his mother. I also had to prepare his bath and help him get in and out of the tub.

Jack was back on heroin. His former wife, a nude dancer at a strip club, delivered his fix to him at our house. She floated in and out of the house as if we weren't there. Jack took the liberty of covering all of the windows in our entire house with aluminum foil.

"I'd like to take the foil down from the windows if you don't mind," I said timidly one evening while delivering Jack's dinner to his room.

"The light bothers my eyes! Leave it alone!" Jack growled, glaring at me with hatred. I left the room quickly.

"Bob, I want to get rid of the foil on the windows. Jack won't let me and he's being belligerent," I said that evening, hoping to get some support.

"Leave him alone, what harm does the foil do?" Bob said impatiently. I was silent for the rest of the night.

Jack no longer saw me as his caregiver. Instead, I had become his servant. I tiptoed around him and Bob. Mae was only six months old. The combination of the lack of sleep and exhaustion from work was wearing me down.

I felt hopeless, unable to change the situation. I couldn't see an end in sight.

Standing in line at a supermarket, I suddenly felt severe pressure on my chest and intense cramps in my stomach. I couldn't breathe. I held onto the shopping cart as tightly as I could, gasping for air. My heart beat so fast and hard, I felt it in my throat. I'm having a heart attack, I thought. I looked around me, bewildered—the aisle was closing in. I became frightened of the shoppers behind me. What if they do something irrational, like start a killing spree? I thought. I prayed the line would move faster. I got dizzy, my knuckles turned white from my grip on the shopping cart. My mouth went dry. I desperately needed to go to the bathroom. Sweat poured down my face. I finally paid for the groceries and ran to my car. I threw the bags in the trunk, got in and locked all the doors. I was panting. I forced myself to make the five-minute drive home.

By the time I got home, I'd calmed down somewhat and told Bob what happened. He said it was psychological and that I should be able to control it. But over the next few months, my symptoms worsened. I became immobilized by fear. At least two to three times a day, I struggled through episodes of dizziness, heart pounding and gasping for air.

I was afraid of open spaces. I needed to be enclosed in a house or a car, where I felt safe. It was essential for me to see familiar faces, like my daughter or Bob. Strangers frightened me. Even when friends came to visit, I locked myself in the bedroom and refused to be seen. I sometimes tried, but I could only hold a conversation for a little more than two minutes before they transformed into strangers who might harm me. Bob grew exasperated with my inability to cope.

We were friendly with a psychiatrist who lived across the street. He stopped by one evening, took one look at me and said, "Irene, you don't look too good."

He leaned forward in his chair, concerned. "What is happening?"

"I am afraid to go outside. Sometimes I think I'm going to have a heart attack," I said, averting my eyes.

"It is all in her head. All she has to do is to stop thinking about it," Bob said, annoyed.

"She needs help, Bob. This is serious," our neighbor said sternly.

"She doesn't look sick to me." Bob turned to me and forced a smile.

"I'm going to make an emergency appointment for her to see my colleague. She has to see her immediately." He stayed until Bob nodded in agreement.

I got an appointment to see the doctor the next day. I walked into her office, feeling fairly calm. The room exuded an air of serenity. The colors were muted, the furnishings simple and sturdy. The doctor greeted me and asked a few simple questions. She reminded me of a sensible aunt, firm and direct.

"Tell me about your father," she said, nodding her head, encouraging me.

I stared at her. I had never spoken about my father to anyone. I stuttered and started to sweat profusely. "H-h-he d-d-died," I stammered. I could not breathe and gasped for air. After struggling for ten minutes, I finally said it, my voice barely audible, "He died of a heroin overdose."

I had betrayed my father. I'd told our secret to a stranger. Now someone outside knew about our shame. I could see the disapproving look on Great-grandmother's face. A good girl would never divulge anything to anybody about her household. I sat on the couch withdrawn, like a convict on death row.

"It is all right, you are not there anymore. But your brother-in-law must leave your house immediately," she said soothingly, leaning back in her big leather chair.

"He is not leaving. My husband will be so angry with me. I have no way of asking him to leave," I cried, overwhelmed with fear.

"It's ok. I will talk to your husband," she reassured me. She gazed at me compassionately, as if to feed me with her strength.

I listened while she called Bob on the telephone. "Your brother must leave the house today or your wife will have to be admitted into a hospital." She paused. "You have no choice. Either he leaves or your wife will be hospitalized. He has to be gone the latest by tomorrow," she said firmly and hung up the phone.

She turned to me. "You come to see me tomorrow. I want to see you daily until you feel better."

I thanked her, relieved to know something was being done to change the course of the life I felt so trapped in.

As soon as I got home, Bob came down on me.

"How dare you force my brother out of my house? I will never let you forget this for the rest of your life," he shouted. "You are separating my family. You bitch!"

I was so frightened. I ran into the bedroom and curled up in the bed.

He chased me into the room and hollered, "Get it out of your head, you idiot. Get yourself together and get some work done."

I closed my eyes and felt myself falling, falling into a black abyss and there was no way out.

Jack left the house the next day and Bob refused to let me go back to the psychiatrist. She had told me to breathe into a brown paper bag when I hyperventilated, explaining that I became dizzy when I breathed so fast that I took in too much oxygen. I began to carry a brown paper bag with me at all times.

But my symptoms only worsened.

I often felt my father standing behind me, leaning over to whisper into my ear.

"Bah-ba, please, please go away," I would cry, pleading for Father to leave. "I know I shouldn't have told anybody about you, but please go away. I won't tell anymore."

Several times a day, especially when alone, from the corners of my eyes, I saw shadows moving. I would turn quickly and ask, "Who's there? What do you want?" Sometimes, I would scream for them to go away and leave me alone. I was terrified that someone would come into the house, sever my spine with a big knife and take my daughter away.

I hated being crippled by my condition and was determined to climb out of this black bottomless pit. When I held my daughter, I knew I had to get myself together to take care of her. I had no confidence in Bob raising her if anything happened to me.

I started a routine for myself. Every time I became confused after an anxiety attack, I would turn on the "Kohn Concert" by Keith Jarrett. The familiar music was my cue to return to the present. I would find Mae and force myself to engage with her in some way. This act seemed to pull me out of my delusion. I was willing myself to stop the spiral into the abyss for her.

One afternoon, as I sat with Mae watching "Sesame Street," a toddler on the show ate a chocolate cookie and smeared the chocolate all over her face. I stared in horror as the girl morphed into a monster. I averted my eyes and looked at my daughter. I held her hand while she laughed at the girl on television being messy. I reminded myself to feel the warmth of her hand and pinched myself to feel the pain so I knew I was not hallucinating. I kept telling myself to focus on Mae, my reference for reality.

During my recovery, Bob decided to concentrate on the import business and sold the candle factory. He felt he had to work too hard for the amount of money we made. He observed that the designers who used our beads to make earrings and necklaces to sell to retail stores were doing well.

"Irene, you are an artist. Why don't you design a line of ready to wear jewelry so we can sell them with our beads? I'll make double the profit." I could hear the calculator clicking in his head. This was the first time he had ever referred to me as an artist. It was a bittersweet acknowledgement.

"You want me to make up some samples and hire people to make them up like the other designers do?" I asked, curious. It had been over a year since my first anxiety attack. I was feeling more stable and thought I could take part in the business as long as I didn't have to travel too far. It might be a good idea to use my skills to create a nice line of jewelry.

"Yes, make up some samples. I'll test the market and see if we can sell them. We'll go from there," he said, pleased that I could work again.

Bob sold everything I made to one client.

"Irene, you need to start making more of those earrings and necklaces." He proudly showed me the empty case.

"I thought I was going to make samples and we'd hire people to assemble them." I couldn't imagine continually whipping out dozens of earrings and necklaces.

"Why should we pay someone to do it when you can do it yourself? Just start making them in your spare time," he said impatiently, slamming the case shut.

"What spare time?" I looked around at our merchandise. "I have to pack your orders, take care of Mae and the house."

"Just do it," he said curtly.

Every day after dinner, Bob sat in front of the television. It was his time off. I would finish washing the dishes and sit down to make earrings and necklaces. On a good evening, I made over a hundred pairs of earrings and dozens of necklaces. I couldn't make them fast enough for Bob to sell them. I didn't know if it was a blessing or a curse. I was constantly under pressure to make more. Before long, still psychologically fragile, I reached the point of burning out.

During a visit from Dickie, a high school friend of Bob's, we touched on the subject of burnout. He was a counselor for one of the synagogues in Los Angeles. He suggested to Bob that I needed some time alone to pursue my own interests before I flipped back into my dark days. Bob was open to the idea. I was getting better and he wanted to make sure I didn't have a relapse.

I told them that I would like to start painting again. Bob agreed to hire a contractor to convert the garage into a studio.

He supposed that if he gave me two hours of painting time, I'd be obligated to produce the amount of jewelry he wanted.

I was ecstatic to see the workers installing the two skylights and drywalling the garage, just as I'd requested. A wall blocked off a five-foot deep space for storage, the rest of the area was my studio. I went out to shop for paints, brushes, stretcher bars and canvas. I had not been so happy since I married. I watched them put in the finishing touches with great anticipation. I prepared myself to start sketching for my first painting in almost six years.

As I watched the carpenter put in the last details, Bob drove up in a red Porsche.

"This is my little car. I always wanted a Porsche." He grinned.

"Great, Bob. You look good in it," I said, waving to him and smiling.

When I came home from shopping the next day, I pulled my car up to our driveway. Bob was standing in front of the garage holding a chainsaw. I rolled down the window and asked, "What are you doing with that?"

"My Porsche needs a garage. I don't want to leave it in the driveway. You have just lost your studio," Bob said matter-of-factly.

"I what?" I screamed in disbelief. I jumped out of the car and rushed into the garage.

He had just finished sawing through the bottom portion of my studio wall. The drywall had already been ripped off the garage door.

"What did you do to my studio?" I choked back my tears.

"You've just lost it," he repeated, and went to return the chainsaw to our neighbor.

I stood in front of the garage, stunned. It felt as if the blade had just cut off my soul. A piece of me died with the studio. In order to survive, I dared not hope. I had to cover myself with another thick blanket of denial and withdrawal. My motto became: just do what I am told.

Bob decided that we should remodel our house. I worked with the contractor to design the interior and oversaw the process. Bob was so impressed with my work that he decided to purchase a run down house and put me to work renovating it. He then sold the house for a considerable profit. This became my side business, in addition to traveling with him, buying and selling our merchandise and making earrings and necklaces.

As our business grew, we started to get into high-end collectibles. I made necklaces that sold for from two to seven thousand dollars alongside the museum quality wearable art. We were known in the business as the importers with the best merchandise. I became a cash-generating machine.

We bought two more houses in the same neighborhood to produce rental income. As our economic level went steadily up, Bob wanted to climb to newer heights.

My son was conceived in London during a buying trip. We had decided to have another child so Mae wouldn't be alone when both of us were gone.

My mother lived in Michigan with Louise. She called me every so often to complain about her isolation living in a small town. I encouraged her to come to Los Angeles. At least she would be in a city and could go to Chinatown.

She began to stay with us for three months during the winter. Eventually, she lived with us most of the year and went back to Michigan for short visits.

Bob's parents came to visit from Palm Springs.

"Go peel the apples and cut them in bite-size pieces and offer them to your in-laws," Mother ordered, staring at me with one of her "do it right now" looks.

"If they want an apple, they can get it themselves. They are Americans. I am not in China," I said, and started to walk out of the kitchen.

"You do as you are told. I want them to see how well I trained you. We are from a proper family." She stepped in front of me and shoved the bowl of apples at me.

I nearly gagged on her words. When had she done anything that reflected training from a proper family? But as always, I pouted and did exactly what she told me to, like a good girl should. I took the apples and started peeling.

Bob felt it was time for us to elevate our status by living in a grand house.

"I saw a house for sale in Cheviot Hills for a million dollars. I want you to take a look at it," he said when he came home from a walk.

"It must be a fixer-upper for that price," I said, not paying too much attention.

"I like the location and the outside a lot. When I was a child only the rich kids lived in Cheviot Hills," he went on.

We went to see the house the next day. It was a disaster. The Spanish house was originally built in the 1920s and was used as a speakeasy. The previous owner had destroyed it by remodeling with a mish mash of French, Spanish and American styles. The master bathroom was filled with dark brown fixtures, and the tiny kitchen was left the way it was from the 20s. I was told that they ran out of money in the middle of their remodeling. However, I could see the potential of the original house. I was excited by the prospect of turning this back into a glorious Spanish mansion.

Bob decided this would be our dream house and it would be my job to remodel it. This was the area in which I'd have total freedom to use my creativity.

We bought the house. I hired a contractor and went to work. I fell in love with Malibu tiles after seeing an exhibition of them in a museum. The factory that produced them had been in business for only three years before a fire destroyed the entire building in the 1920s. They were the most beautiful, magnificently colored tiles I had ever seen. I tracked down a craftsman who could reproduce them. The geometric and organic art nouveau designs were hand-screened and colored. Some of them had as many as twenty-two colors in one tile.

I worked with the craftsman to create color schemes for the kitchen, five bathrooms, a guesthouse, three fireplaces, two water fountains, the swimming pool and the outdoor dining area. I had the front door custom made in Santa Fe, New Mexico. An artist with vast knowledge of eighteenth-century Mexican wrought-iron design made the ironwork for the railings and window treatments.

I handpicked each slab of green slate for the water fountain behind the swimming pool. I wanted a specific green tint for the water in the pool and worked with a builder who custom-blended the color of the plaster to create the green that I wanted.

Bob went to Morocco to pick out some furniture. We then flew to New Mexico for a couple of days to have sofas and chairs made from antique rugs I had picked out. The head and footboard of our bed were made from a pair of eighteenth century doors from India. The tables in the kitchen and dining room were antique doors from Morocco topped with glass. Our house had the feel of the Moorish and Spanish of the Old World, with all the modern conveniences.

Our children went to the best private schools and we had a full time housekeeper, gardener and pool man. We owned a van, a Volvo station wagon, a Porsche, a very successful business and four houses. It was the American dream.

The Awakening

We lived in luxury but our daily routine was always the same. I worked twelve hours a day; taking care of the household, whipping out necklaces and running the business when Bob was away on buying trips. Moving into this grand house actually had created more responsibilities and stress for me. Mother became more demanding. I think she felt she had to demonstrate her well-to-do status by telling the servants what to do. The housekeeper became her chauffer.

"You better tell Mae to leave Sam alone," Mother insisted one evening. "She constantly bosses him around. And I am sick of it!" She stared at me, as if expecting immediate action.

I was busy in the kitchen slicing vegetables for dinner. I listened to the kids fighting upstairs. Screaming, shoving and throwing things were daily occurrences. I was too exhausted to deal with the dynamic between the three of them. Mother made matters worse by singling out Mae as the sole aggressor. Sam took full advantage of her favoritism.

"Ouch! Ouch... Mae is hitting me!" Sam cried.

I listened to their thrashings upstairs.

"He took the remote from me and threw it at the TV. Somebody has to teach him a lesson!" Mae yelled downstairs.

"See? I told you. Go punish her for hitting her brother," Mother said with contempt. But I knew Sam shared the respon-

303

sibility. Although only in the second grade, he was sent to the principal's office daily for fighting and temper tantrums.

"Is dinner ready yet? I'm hungry!" Bob yelled from the den, oblivious to the barrage of screams upstairs. "You better get it ready soon. You have to take Sam to his baseball practice at seven."

I looked at my mother and slammed the lid on the pot and said, "I'll deal with them later. I need to finish cooking dinner so Sam won't be late."

Buying time, that was what I was good at. I never had the energy or the right frame of mind to deal with anything. I was lucky if I had time to think.

When dinner was ready, I pushed the button on the intercom and called the family to the table.

I served the food and sat down without saying a word. My children knew better than to engage in any exchange with me if they didn't want to get yelled at. They ate in silence and scuttled upstairs as soon as they finished.

I saw my children briefly for breakfast before school, and again in the afternoon when they came home. As soon as they entered the house, they raced upstairs to do homework, play video games or watch television. They came downstairs when they heard my voice on the intercom calling them to dinner. After we ate, they retraced their steps upstairs. I didn't see them again until the next morning, when the routine began again.

Both of my children were full of rage but they knew not to come to me. I was too busy making money, keeping up the illusion of a successful family. I ignored their cries for help. Their anguish tortured me, but I could do nothing for them. Pushing through one more day was challenging enough.

Mae had been severely depressed for years. She was an insomniac and could not go to restaurants or other places with crowds. If she did, she would get sick and throw up. I didn't feel I could do anything to help her.

Bob and I were called into Sam's school on a regular basis to confer with the principal and his teachers on his behavior.

"Sam gets angry easily. Other kids usually take a while before they go into a rage, but Sam goes from the first floor to the tenth floor in a second," Abbey, his primary teacher, said during one of those meetings. Bob and I sat quietly as we did every time we were called in.

"I don't understand. Sam's greatest defenders are his teachers. He is a handful for any one of them but they really like him," Joel, the principal, said. He shook his head.

"He is a good student and has a kind heart. He just needs to work on his temper," Abbey explained.

"We have gone through this so many times. I don't know what to say," Joel said, leaning back in his chair, resigned.

"Can you recommend a therapist you trust to help Sam?" I blurted out. My routine at these meetings was silence. Everyone was surprised.

Bob looked at me. Joel and Abbey looked at each other. They couldn't believe what had come out of my mouth.

"Of course!" Joel sat up, raised his brow and said, "I'll go get a list right now."

As he walked toward the door, I saw Abbey and Joel exchange relieved glances.

At least now I could get Sam some help. It was out of the question to ask Bob.

I'd known for a long time that if I wanted to help my children with their problems, I needed to take a close look at their emotional needs. But to do so, I would have to examine my own life and that would obliterate the mechanisms I had engineered to survive. My whole world would collapse and I would become completely lost. For a long time, I wasn't ready to take that risk. Now, at least, I could get someone else to help Sam.

Our family went to an annual party thrown by one of Bob's long time friends, Robert. He lived in an exclusive area in Santa Monica on a cliff overlooking the Pacific Ocean. The houses on his street were all architectural gems. One could watch spectacular sunsets over the Pacific Ocean from his backyard. Robert's guests included attorneys, dentists like himself, owners of successful businesses, television personalities, starlets, and an agent for football stars. Many of them had gone to high school with Bob.

The women sat in small groups and gossiped. Their children scattered in the well-manicured yard played with each other. I sat with Ellen and three other women under the shade of a magnificent maple tree.

"How are your kids?" I asked her casually.

"Oh, they're ok," she said, turning to the wife of another dentist standing by the pool and raising her voice. "But the big news is, we traded in our Mercedes station wagon for a van with leather seats. It's the big thing now, you know, to do the van thing."

She made sure she had an audience and continued, "Remember the boutique I always go to in Beverly Hills? I went in there last week, hoping to get something to spice up my life. I was sipping my latte and getting bored of watching the models parading around with their new inventory." She rolled her eyes. "But thank God, the sales girl convinced me to get this blue dress with the sterling silver belt. I bought it and wore it that evening. Guess what? Earl walked into the house and noticed me. Really. He noticed me!"

How pathetic, I thought.

On my way to get a drink, I strolled past several groups of men huddled together talking about financial and sexual conquests, reminiscent of high school boys' bragging contests.

"I just got out of the hospital for hepatitis. What a drag that is," I overheard Earl, Ellen's husband say with a smirk. "You never know what these bitches have, even when they pretend that they are not whores."

"Every time I'm out of town, I rent a Jaguar," he said, smiling, looking around to see who else was listening. "Without fail, I always find a chick more than willing to go to dinner and come back to the hotel room with me. It's a guarantee."

The men laughed and slapped his shoulders.

"Too bad I don't travel with my business," a dentist from the small group poked his finger at Earl's chest and laughed. "My wife knows where I am all the time. But at least I don't have hepatitis."

That's a consolation, I thought.

I sat by the pool and realized that people are not important in this world. I was dumbfounded and sickened by the realization that to us what was more important than anything else was to show the world we were successful. Our lives and our children were a mess. Most of the women at the party either openly acknowledged that their husbands had affairs or that they were girlfriends of newly divorced men at least twenty years their senior. The middle-aged women held onto their lifestyles despite their unhappiness, while the younger group concentrated on capturing the financially well-established men who treated them like trash.

These parties seemed to pump the very blood that kept the wealthy alive. Men and women found comfort in sharing their miseries as well as displaying their continued success. To the outside world, we embodied the American dream. We lived in this beautiful perfumed package, but when you opened it, there was an overwhelming smell of sewer, the stench of people rotting away.

For years, I had lived this dream. Bob's friends and acquaintances often viewed us as an ideal couple. A few women actually asked me for advice about creating a successful marriage.

⁂

The children and I wanted a pet. Bob had told me that the best pet he'd ever had was a Mynah bird. I found a bird breeder and bought a baby macaw, another very intelligent bird. He was a hybrid, half green-wing and half blue and gold. It was not fully feathered, and needed to be fed with a syringe. I named him Merlin, perhaps to bring some magic or strength into my life.

The bird became my primary focus and we soon bonded. I started to smile more often. As Merlin became full-grown, he had intense blue feathers on his wings, green and blue on his head and back and a bright orange chest. He treated me as his mother. Every morning, as soon as he saw me, he would say, "Hi Merlin, Merlin! Walnut... Merlin, walnut." He flapped his wings and bobbed his head up and down. Between words, he made the same squeaky kissing sound that I used. I'd make the kissing sound back and give him a walnut in the shell. After he ate his nut, he would climb onto my shoulder and kiss me by sticking out his tongue. Then we sat down and shared a breakfast of fruit before work.

While I strung necklaces, he would play with beads, pushing them around the table with his beak or picking them out of one glass jar and dropping them onto the table or placing them in a different jar. His company made the tedious work more tolerable.

"You pay more attention to that bird than to me. He has become your new baby," Bob said to me one day while Merlin cooed on my lap. "You can make him do anything, but he doesn't come to me like he goes to you. I hate that damn bird."

I looked down and said nothing.

A few months passed. Bob began to harangue me daily about Merlin.

"I can't stand his loud squawk and the sight of him on you all the time," he yelled, walking toward the table where I was making earrings. Merlin was standing on my shoulder, grooming my hair.

"How about me? Why don't you spend as much time with me as you spend with that fucking bird? I want him out of this house!" he shouted.

"You can't be serious! You are not going to make me get rid of the bird," I said, looking up into his angry eyes. Merlin started to squawk loudly.

Bob took another step closer. He towered over me and growled, "You bought it and now you better get rid of it!"

"I am not going to let the bird go," I protested and tried to calm Merlin down. He had puffed up his feathers, ready to bite.

Bob stopped for a moment, taken aback.

"Sell it, find someone who wants it. Give it away. I don't care, I can't stand it anymore," he fumed.

"No, you can't make me do that. I love this bird."

That only made Bob angrier. He stepped in front of me and looked straight into my eyes and said, "I give you one week to find someone to take the bird. If a week passes and the bird is still here, I will just let him go free in the backyard."

I was horrified. Merlin would never survive outdoors.

"Please, Bob, please let me keep the bird," I pleaded, tears welling up in my eyes.

"No! I hate that damn bird," he shouted. I felt his screams vibrating in my bones.

"He won't survive on his own. What if I can't find someone to take him in a week? Please don't make me do this," I begged.

"It's up to you to decide if this fucking bird lives or dies," he said with finality.

I desperately called around and asked everyone I saw the following week to help me find a home for Merlin. I cried whenever I held him on my lap.

On the seventh and final day, I found someone willing to take him. He came with a borrowed truck to take the cage with the bird. When the man started to load the cage onto his truck, I said goodbye to Merlin and began to sob.

Bob rushed out from the house and said to the man, "Hey, I changed my mind. I don't want to give my bird away. We are going to keep it."

Drained from a week's crying and desperation, I could not look at Merlin. I knew Bob would use the bird for leverage to get what he wanted. He would make me go through the hoops again and again. From that day on, I never touched Merlin and he began to withdraw, plucking out his feathers wherever he could reach them. I fed him his food and water, but averted my eyes from his. He perched in a corner with his eyes half closed. He didn't speak. When he made any sound, he just squawked. Every day, I quietly swept up his feathers from the floor.

I felt hopeless. I often felt the desire to escape from the daily chaos. I longed for a regular spot in the house for meditation, as I'd had on the roof with the oversized rattan chair — a place that might provide some solace as my life spun out of control. I asked Bob if I could move one of our comfortable living room chairs into our bedroom. He said no.

We went to another party. The host usually hired entertainers like Tarot card readers, palmists or handwriting analysts to enliven the crowd. This time, he hired a hypnotist. As the guests streamed in, we talked in small groups catching up on gossip.

"Any volunteers?" the hypnotist broke in. We all turned toward him at the back of the living room where a small area had been cleared. A tall wiry man in his late thirties, with a friendly voice, he appeared to be warm and trustworthy. I immediately raised my hand, desperate for any means to explore my life. I was rotting in my gilded cage, hungry for meaning and wondering if there was another way. As I had at the meeting at Sam's school, I found small opportunities to help myself.

He called me forward. I heard the buzz of interest as I walked through the party but I didn't meet anyone's eyes. I stood in front of Carl.

"Please sit down," he said and motioned me to sit on the sofa. He asked everyone to be quiet.

"Please close your eyes and relax. Just pay attention to what I am saying," he said, standing a few feet in front of me.

I smiled and closed my eyes.

"You are letting go of everything and falling into a deep, deep sleep. Follow my voice and go deeper," Carl began. Soon, I sensed myself growing heavy, as if I might fall asleep. I vaguely heard him speaking. Unable to make out the words, I absorbed his soothing voice. I felt safe, as if I were gently floating in a warm pool.

His voice suddenly cleared.

"Where are you now? And what do you see? What are you doing?"

I couldn't open my eyes, but I became aware that I was staring out the window of my parents' room at a clear blue sky. Mother sat on her bed wearing yellow seersucker pajamas with big pink plastic buttons and prints of tiny lavender flowers and green leaves. I lay on her lap, sucking on her breast. I looked up and saw her face, framed with soft curls. She gazed straight ahead, and then glanced down at me. I felt a bone chilling coldness when our eyes met. I shuddered.

I heard myself say, "I am sucking on my mother's breast." Tears rolled down my face.

"Ah, feel the warmth and relish the love from your mother. Stay there and be content," Carl said.

I started to sob, my heart wrenched with such pain. I understood for the first time: it was useless to try to please her. I never had a chance.

I meditated wherever I could find quiet corners of the house when Bob was busy and the children were away at school. I continued to fight for my own spot. It became my one cause. Finally, I wore Bob down and he allowed me a five by seven foot space in an alcove off our bedroom. I bought a Japanese bamboo screen to provide some privacy and moved in the living room chair. It had taken a full year, but I had achieved my goal.

I started to meditate daily and found refuge from my life. After months of regular meditation, the noise of the world became silenced by an inner stillness and I began to see my life clearly.

Each evening, exhausted from working all day, I collapsed in bed. On top of the physical exhaustion, I was emotionally drained. Was this the price I must pay for sustaining the façade of success for society and my family?

I had everything money could buy but I only talked to my children via intercom. I hardly had any physical contact with them. My son had been seeing a psychiatrist since he was seven years old and my daughter had been in and out of severe depression for years. I was twenty pounds overweight and had constant headaches and backaches. We had an army of doctors and psychiatrists to ameliorate the symptoms, but the situation just got progressively worse.

While I meditated, a recent event began to float in: I was stomping away from my children, dismissing them gruffly, while Bob demanded I make more necklaces. I screamed at them all and walked into the kitchen pretending to prepare dinner. I banged pots and pans around to demonstrate my discontent. While I watched this event unfold, I was stunned by the way I treated my children. I had accepted the condition of my life without question, occasionally mustering up some feeble form of protest through displays of anger and frustration, as had generations of women in my family before.

I needed to talk to Bob.

One evening when I felt Bob might be receptive, I ventured to speak my mind. "We have enough money to last for the rest of our lives. I don't want to spend all of my time making more money. I want to live a meaningful life, maybe spend better quality time with our children," I began quietly.

"You think we have enough money? Who are you kidding? We have bills to pay," Bob responded in disbelief.

"All we need is one house to live in. We can sell the other three houses and have more than enough money to pay this house off and still have tons of money to live on," I said, hoping to convince him we were not just scraping by.

"What are you talking about? You think I want to give up what we have?" His voice darkened in annoyance.

"I am not asking you to give up what you have, just consolidate and live a more meaningful life instead of just being a slave to the almighty dollar. I have been a slave long enough. I know we had to struggle to get to where we are. We have done that and we don't need to do that anymore." I sat up straighter, as if I needed more substance to uphold my position.

"I want to buy a summer house in Morocco. I want to add to what we have. I want more, not less," he went on, and turned on the TV to dismiss me. I knew if I pressed on, I would be pushing him into a meaningless fight. I walked out of the room so he could watch his television in peace.

"Your daughter has a sharp tongue," Mother said in disgust, startling me from a quiet moment in the backyard.

"She constantly bosses her brother around. I told her to stop and she had the guts to talk back to me. Next time she does that, I will slap her face," she continued. I looked at her and wondered what gave me the endurance to tolerate her invasion into my space for forty-three years.

I gathered myself and stood up, looked straight into her eyes and said, "They are my children. You do not have the right to hit them. You had your time with me. The rule is that you can't hit my children. You cannot set foot in my house if you don't abide by my rules. If you don't think you can do that, you can't return here after you go to Michigan next week."

I watched as shock spread over her face.

"We'll see. Maybe I won't come back," she said haughtily.

I knew she expected me to soften my tone and beg her to come back but I never took my eyes off of her and said, "It is your choice, you know the rules now."

She stood there for a moment, not knowing what to do next and then walked away.

Mother left for Michigan the following week. Bob had also gone on a buying trip to Africa.

While the kids were in school, I lit a candle and incense, a daily ritual since I began meditating regularly. I sat in my chair, crossed my legs, straightened my spine and closed my eyes. The familiar scent of the incense brought me quickly into a space of stillness. Slowly, I lost the sense of my body and surroundings. The images that congested and cluttered my life slipped from consciousness until my mind felt unburdened and clear.

It was apparent that Bob did not share my desire to live a more meaningful, conscious life. If Bob had not been my husband, or my mother had not been my mother, would I have put up with their behavior? I had become an obedient daughter and wife, as my cultural heritage demanded. But my mother and husband had grossly abused their familial roles. I knew that to live, I had to wrench myself from the bonds of the life I had created and accepted. That meant I had to ask for a divorce and discard everything with which I was familiar. I had nothing beyond the world Bob had allowed me. I had no support. I knew no one and had nowhere to go.

I walked around the house. I had everything money could buy, but nothing of real meaning except for my children and I was failing them miserably. I had little faith in my ability to support them on my own. During the week, I lay in bed for hours, overcome by incredible fear.

Do I just think about it for the rest of my life? Or do I take action and force myself to walk through the flames? What does it take to do that? I asked myself again and again. I knew I had to commit myself completely to do it. If I didn't survive, at least I would have tried. If I made it, the fire would have purified me. I sensed a potential strength in myself I had not acknowledged in years. The next day, I picked up divorce papers from a paralegal.

Bob came home from his buying trip. After the children went to sleep, I approached him and said, "Bob, I want a divorce."

"What? Why do you want a divorce? Come on, everything is fine. What do you want?" he asked, glancing up at me and back to the images flashing on the television.

"I am very unhappy. I don't want to continue to live this way. I want a divorce." I stared at him resolutely until he looked up again. I knew he had never seen me in such a calm state. He switched off the TV.

"Tell me what you want and I'll see if I can make you happy," Bob said, smiling, bargaining.

"I have been telling you for years. You've never listened. I can't go on like this anymore. I want out," I insisted.

His lips curled in anger.

"Fine, get the fuck out of my sight. Take the car and never show your face again." He threw the key to the station wagon at me.

"Go on. Leave!" he ordered.

"I want a divorce, Bob, not your permission to let me out of this house."

"You can take the car and leave. The children and every-thing else stay. You are not going to steal my money. Nothing, nothing belongs to you," he shouted.

"Do you want me to settle this with an attorney then? It will cost you more money than working it out with me." I handed him the court paper for the divorce. Until that moment, I don't believe he took me seriously.

"Ok, if this is what you want, this is it." He walked out of the room.

This room, this house was my art. I looked at the antique Afghan rug I had found in Santa Fe and remembered the process I had gone through to have it made into a sofa. I had created every element in the room from my own palette: the hand-carved chairs upholstered to my specifications, the place-ment of the window to frame the garden. This was the only world I knew, but everything was associated with Bob. The minute I acknowledged our separation, I felt like a stranger among my own things.

Then fear and bewilderment struck. The future I had long con-templated, but been unable to imagine, had arrived. I had to face the unknown with my children alone and for real. For too long I had held onto a rope attached to a horrible situation. But the mere act of holding on to a rope tied to something had made me feel safe and secure. Now that rope was frayed and unwinding. The free fall I was soon to experience terrified me. If I was not willing to retain what my rope was tied to, I must be courageous enough to risk the fall into the fire below. I felt the sweat drip down my face and chest.

"Why are you getting a divorce?" Mother was surprised when I called to let her know. "Things are going so well."

"They have not been well for a long time," I said quietly.

"You have everything most people can only dream of. You are throwing all that away? You better think this over."

"I want to live a more meaningful life," I explained.

"What kind of talk is this? A meaningful life? You must be having an affair. Are you having an affair?" she asked, alarmed.

"No, I am not," I said, increasingly irritated by her response. "I don't have to have an affair to get a divorce."

"Don't fool me, I know. You'll be stupid to throw all you have away for a stinking affair. It won't even last, trust me, I know how it is." I listened to her voice rise in volume and self-righteousness.

"It is not like that! I really just want to live a life of my own choosing," I protested.

"You chose your own husband, and how about the children? You can't be selfish to do what you want and let them suffer." I had hoped she would at least attempt to understand.

"The way things are, the children are suffering greatly. I never have time for them. I am trying to straighten out my life and take better care of them," I said patiently, knowing how pointless my explanations would seem to her.

"I'll talk to you later, Mom. I am getting a divorce and I wanted to let you know before you heard it from someone else." I quickly said goodbye and hung up the phone.

The tension in the house became unbearable. Bob began to squirrel away our collection of antique beads and artifacts. He told family, friends and acquaintances how I had screwed him. Soon he had rallied support from all of his friends and family, isolating me more and more. He tried to turn the children against me, telling them I had stolen money, and, like my mother had said, that I'd been having an affair. I did little to counter his accusations, except to tell them they were lies. They were left confused, unsure who to believe. As in the past, Bob was methodically trying to push me over the edge. But I was stronger now, determined to carve out a life of my own.

One day, I came home from picking up the children from school. I noticed a strand of valuable beads was missing from our display in the living room. I quickly went upstairs to check on our collection of rare antique beads hidden in our walk-in closet. I was stunned to find a third of the collection was missing. I slipped out of the house and drove to another house we rented out but kept the garage for storage. The place was filled with commercial beads, baskets and carvings. I rummaged through the room and couldn't find anything. I sat down and wondered where Bob could have hidden such a large amount of beads. I looked up at the loft where he stored old junk from the house. I pulled over a ladder and climbed up to see if I would find anything. There they were! Five shopping bags full of rare beads sat in plain sight. I hauled them into my car and went home.

"Where are the beads that were missing from our collection?" I woke Bob up from his nap.

"What are you talking about?" he asked groggily.

"At least a third of our collection was missing. What did you do with them?" I stood next to his bed, staring at him.

"I don't know what you are talking about. You sure have a way of making something out of nothing," he said without looking at me, still in bed.

"Don't fuck with me, Bob. I found them in the storage and they are locked in my car and I have all the keys," I said angrily. He bolted up and said, "You what?"

"Leave this house immediately before I call the police!" I ordered.

"It's all your fault! You started the divorce and made me feel like a scared rabbit. I need to feel secure by putting things aside for my future," he said, raising his voice, standing up with his hands on his hips.

"Leave this house now!" I demanded.

"This is my house and you can't make me leave!" he screamed and took a few steps closer.

I was afraid he might strike me and retreated into my bedroom. I locked the door and said, "You have stolen from our common property. I have the evidence in my car. I am calling the police if you don't leave right now."

I called Louise one evening, soon after she had learned of our separation.

"Don't expect me to take sides. I like Bob, so you are on your own," she said nonchalantly. "I know a few couples who are divorced and I am still talking to all parties. Bob is my friend."

I was speechless. After a long pause, I said, "I am not asking you to do anything. I just called to see how you are. I won't bother you with the details of my life."

I had hoped that my youngest sister, whom I had virtually raised, would lend me some emotional support, but loyalty was not the greatest asset in my family. I focused on the children's daily routines, taking them to school and other activities, to keep some sense of normalcy in their lives. I vowed not to sink to Bob's war tactics. Instead, I virtually stopped talking to everyone who knew me.

Before Bob moved out of the house, Dickie and his wife Nina stopped by. She pulled me aside and whispered, "Irene, are you nuts? Do you know how many women would kill to be in your position? What are you thinking? You have everything most woman only dream of."

"A woman can't live on money alone," I said sardonically. "Those women, they can have it all. I don't want it. I will be glad when I am free of the gilded cage."

She looked at me quizzically and said quietly, "Maybe Bob is right. You have gone a bit crazy."

A few months after my divorce, Louise called.

"Mom is in the hospital," she said. "She came into my room this morning and asked to be taken to the hospital. She collapsed before I had a chance to get her into the car. The doctors said she had a heart attack."

I heard some sniffling and coughing as she composed herself.

"She is in a coma," she managed to say.

"What is her chance of survival?" I asked cautiously.

"She's on a ventilator. It doesn't look good," she started to cry.

"I'm going to make arrangements to come. I'll be there as soon as I can."

Teresa and her husband had already visited and left for Louise's restaurant. Virginia had seen Mom and returned home. I went straight to the hospital from the airport, grateful that I would be the only one there.

I walked into the room. I was shocked to see Mother's condition. She looked helpless lying there with a large tube snaking from the ventilator into her mouth, forcing oxygen into her lungs. Intravenous tubes wound down from a metal pole into her arms. I took in the slow drip of the liquid. The once almighty Mother seemed so weak and small. Her gray hair reminded me of all the years that had elapsed since I had been the little girl who had tried her best to please her mother to no avail. I was a grown woman and I was still her child. I felt safe in her presence for the first time.

I took Mother's hand and held it with both of mine. I whispered into her ear, "Mah-me, I am here." I searched her face for minute movements of facial muscles that might indicate she was trying to communicate with me but her face was flat and calm. I closed my eyes and listened to the humming of the machines in the room and to her breathing.

A warm sensation washed over me. It was as if her life flashed before me. I realized that she had done her best. She had been unable to love and nurture her children because she could not function as a mature woman. She was forever that little girl who had never recovered from the devastation caused by her own mother's abandonment. Since birth, her mother had catered to her every whim and then suddenly married her off to a stranger and a world she had never known, before disappearing into China. Nurtured by American society, she found herself ill-equipped to deal with the confinement of the Chinese culture or the aggression from the men around her. She had lived her life precariously, her actions determined by raw emotions without contemplating the consequences. She had been a wild mare in a glass house. I now understood that whatever damage she had done was not intentional. I just happened to be one of the innocent bodies in her tempestuous path. I squeezed her hand and nodded. I whispered in her ear, "Mom, I understand and I love you."

Her face seemed to soften. I stood by her bed and cried my heart out. It was as if my tears were washing away forty-four years of pain and resentment. I felt grateful. I had finally found my way to forgive her and to love her.

Late in the afternoon, after all of us had said goodbye to Mother, her doctor asked our permission to take her off the ventilator and told us to prepare for her passing. The nurse removed all of the tubes and waved us into the room. We rushed in, anticipating Mother's sudden death. Louise cried, holding onto Teresa's arm. I walked over to take Mother's hand in mine. To everyone's surprise, she began to breathe on her own. The doctor and nurse quickly checked her vital signs. All were good. She looked peaceful, as if she were in a deep sleep.

We stayed in the hospital for most of the night. The nurse finally told us to go home and come back the next day to talk to her doctor. She assured us that she would call immediately if anything changed.

The next day, we had a conference with Mother's doctor. He was surprised that she was doing so well. He said her condition was stable. It was possible that she would stay in a coma indefinitely. It would be wise for us to consider transferring her to a nursing home to reduce the cost of her care. He advised us to wait until the next day. If her condition remained the same we should consider filing paperwork for the transfer.

We stayed in Mother's room to chat for a while. Lightheartedness replaced the apprehension we'd felt at the prospect of Mother's death. We joked and gossiped as if she were conscious and watching us.

"Did you see the receptionist's face when we were out there talking to her all at once?" Louise said while straightening mother's sheets.

"Ha ha, yeah, that was funny. She probably has never seen so many Chinese in one place," I said and we all laughed.

We turned to look at Mother. She appeared to be so at peace. We grew quiet.

Teresa leaned forward and said softly, "We are all we have. We should start taking better care of each other." For the first time, I felt included. "Togetherness" was a new concept in this family for me.

Louise nodded in agreement. I felt their closeness. Maybe now, I thought, I have a chance to let my guard down. This might be a new bond between us. I glanced at Mother lying so still in her bed, her face wan but calm. We sat close together, my sisters and I, at the foot of Mother's bed. There was nothing else in the room, three sisters and their mother, a family together. The barriers we had built between us for so many years felt frail, as though the slightest word could blow them away. I dared to hope that my sisters would finally accept me, that our differences and our history would diminish and finally disappear into the closeness I now felt between us.

Late that evening we went back to Louise's house. We would visit Mom together the next day.

At five in the morning, the phone rang. It was the nurse at the hospital. Mother's blood pressure had dropped dangerously low. Her breathing was labored.

We rushed to the hospital.

The door to Mother's room was open. We could hear the grating of her breath from the hallway. In her room, we held each other for a few moments, as Mother fought for air. Teresa and Louise took turns saying goodbye to her. I was the last to hold her hand. I bent close to her ear and whispered, "I love you." I kissed her forehead. When I stood up and watched Mother struggle to inhale, I realized it was my forty-fourth birthday. It was as if she had waited for my birthday to give me the most precious gift: the freedom to live my own life. I closed my eyes and silently thanked her. She exhaled her last breath. Gone with Mother was the role of the punching bag. I straightened up and breathed deeply. I felt free and light. The weight of my family's judgments had lifted, gone with her forever.

TRANSFORMATION

A year passed. I was ready to make changes. I devised an exercise routine consisting of yoga, chi-qong, stretching, strengthening and aerobics. If I were serious about changing, I'd have to exercise before the kids got up in the morning. So I crawled out of the warm bed at five and hopped on the NordicTrack. After just half an hour, I was gasping for air, and sweat dripped down my face and chest. I stretched. Bones and ligaments creaked in protest. I moved on to weights. I could barely move my arms after curling five pounds for two sets of tens. I dreaded dragging my body through the torture again the next morning but within weeks, the pain diminished. I began to move smoothly and confidently.

I abandoned the supermarkets and bought from local organic farmers to support sustainable farming. I also started a compost bin and recycled everything. I bought in bulk when possible to reduce packaging and bagged groceries with my own cloth bags.

I decided to sell our expensive house and had a huge garage sale. What I didn't sell, I gave away.

I rented a three-bedroom apartment in a nearby neighborhood. I moved while Mae and Sam visited Bob. I picked them up and drove to the apartment. I opened the door. Mae and Sam exchanged glances.

"Wow! Mom, this is it?" Mae said, looking at the sparse living room. There was only a sofa, a chair, a coffee table and the NordicTrack. They stood silently, and then rushed in to see their rooms. They each had a bed, a chair and a table. Nothing else. The entire apartment was painted white.

I smiled and said, "By the way, we have four white plates and cups, four sets of silverware and four glasses. So you guys can take turns having one friend come over at a time."

It was an enormous adjustment for us to live in close quarters and in a modest lifestyle. We all rolled up our sleeves and learned how to take care of ourselves without the help of a housekeeper.

Mae had to earn her allowance by washing the dishes and taking the trash downstairs to the trash bin. I taught them how to do their laundry. Every weekend, they took turns taking the laundry downstairs to use the coin-operated machine. I cleaned the bathroom and the kitchen. They cleaned their own rooms.

"Mom! It's almost nine o'clock and I haven't showered yet. Mae's in the bathroom!" Sam yelled from his room.

I knocked on the bathroom door and said, "Mae, Sam needs to shower. It's almost his bedtime."

"Geez, I'm just finishing. I forgot he has to use the same bathroom."

"Make sure you dry the floor and keep the fan on."

"Ok! Ok! Gosh, I know!" Mae grumbled.

Sam stood by the bathroom door holding his pajamas, waiting to shower for the first time in his life. They never had to consider others' needs before they moved into this apartment, but they were learning fast.

Sam did his homework at the kitchen table while I cooked dinner.

"How was your day in school?" I asked casually.

"We went on a field trip to the locomotive museum and was I scared! Adrian and I got separated from the group and we were lost for over half an hour," he said, looking up from his workbook.

My heart began to race.

"But we had a lot of fun while the teachers looked for us." He chuckled.

I suddenly realized I'd never had a conversation with Sam about day-to-day goings on in school. I'd lived a separate life from my children. I had a lot of work to do to reconcile with them. They turned out to be my best teachers.

"Don't leave your glass in the sink. Clean up after yourself immediately," I scolded Mae one evening.

"I'll clean it later," Mae yelled from the living room.

"Do it now!"

"You left your glass in the sink yesterday! Why can't I do the same?"

I was speechless. Her behavior reflected my own. If I wanted my children to not be lazy, I'd better not be. It was natural for them to look to me as their role model. I needed to earn their respect. I needed to allow them the freedom to explore and only step in to offer guidance if I saw danger. It was a delicate balance. They kept me on my toes and I became a much stronger and better person under their forever-watchful eyes.

One evening after dinner, I went into my bedroom to meditate. I walked over to my nightstand, lit the candle and incense. Before I settled in my chair, I heard laughter coming from the living room. Mae and Sam were playing a game they made up. Instead of the thrashing and screaming of anger and frustration of the past, they were laughing and squealing in delight. Tears streamed down my face. It was the most wonderful sound.

"Mom, Ashland is your kind of place. You'll really like it. Plenty of hippies still run around there. They eat health food and recycle everything," Mae exclaimed, when she came home from a field trip with her class to Ashland, Oregon for the Shakespearean Festival.

"Really? You think I am still a hippie at heart?" I half joked and smiled.

"You and your spiritual leanings, eating health food, meditating and caring for the environment and stuff. It sure sounds like the people from the sixties to me. I read it in my history book," she teased.

"Am I that old? You can read about people like me in the history books?" I sat down next to her, pleased that she was in a good mood.

"Ha ha, Mom you are old!" she laughed. "I am serious though, you really should check it out! If you don't want to stay in L.A. when I go to college, that is the place you should go. I know you. You'll like it."

"We'll see," I said half-heartedly.

During the last weeks of her junior year in high school, I traveled all over the country with Mae to look for her ideal college. We decided to take a road trip during the summer and drive up the California and Oregon coast to Portland to visit Reed College.

It was my first time traveling with the children by myself. I had forgotten what it was like to be free to travel at my own pace rather than by Bob's intense selling schedules. We took our time exploring the coast.

We walked along the coast at Big Sur. We stood at the edge of a cliff and watched the water sparkle against the intense blue, cloudless sky. We listened to the slap of waves against the rocky coast. For once, I felt unburdened, like a mother bird leading her two young offspring to fly over the cliff into freedom, leaving the crumbling nest behind.

Mae said, "Mom, I am glad you are driving us up to Portland. This is so beautiful."

"Yes, isn't it? I am so glad that I have decided to drive too." I breathed in the clean, crisp air and let out a deep sigh. I had held my breath for twenty years, how wonderful it was to breathe again.

The Monterey Bay Aquarium was known for its shark exhibit. We walked beside the tank's forty-foot tall glass wall. Sharks glided past behind the glass. Sam excitedly told us the names of the various sharks, which he'd learned from his books at home. I was amazed at the size of the great whites. They moved so gracefully and powerfully, true examples of how nature had perfected the form and function of every living thing.

We spent most of our morning looking at the exhibits. On our way out, Sam pulled us toward a large shallow pool filled with tide pool animals such as sea urchins, sea cucumbers and sea slugs. Children were allowed to pick them up to examine them like a petting zoo. Sam picked up a spiky sea urchin and tried to poke Mae with its spines. She screamed and started to run. Sam shook the water off the sea urchin to get her wet. They ran and shrieked in glee.

We drove along the Redwood Forest. I parked the car and we hiked into the Redwoods. The trail was soft and spongy with layers of mulch from fallen leaves. The smell was musty. Thousands of insects whirred around us in the forest.

"Mom! Look at all the centipedes! Let's get out of here!" Sam said nervously, grabbing my arm. I looked down and saw hundreds of centipedes scuttling over and under the leaves. The ground seemed to be moving. I stood still, took a deep breath and then laughed at what city dwellers we were.

"It's ok, this is their home. Let's see how they live," I said, encouraging him to walk further. He turned around. On a tree trunk a few inches from his face, a yellow slug the size of a small banana seemed to stare at him.

"Ahhh! A banana slug! Yuck! Mom, let's get out of here!" he screamed.

I managed to laugh, convincing myself not to be nervous and said, "Take a closer look. It is actually quite beautiful. Look how it moves. It is so cool."

He gathered his courage and stepped closer to take a better look. "Hey, it is much bigger than I thought they were. The picture of them I saw in my book didn't do them justice. The yellow is much brighter in real life."

I, too, started to relax.

We ventured deeper into the forest. The only human sounds we heard were our footsteps. We walked in silence. I went ahead and came across an enormous redwood. Its majestic presence humbled me. I felt my insignificance. My size and age were only a blip in comparison. How could we ever fathom cutting it down for our use? I bowed my head and reminded myself I was just passing through.

The next day, we had lunch in Crescent City, a few miles from Oregon. As soon as we crossed the state line, the colors changed dramatically. The ocean was gray-green instead of the pristine blue of California. The shore was rocky and void of sand. The waves were much more forceful and the light was defused. The California coast was pretty. The Oregon coast was rugged.

At noon we arrived in Portland and decided to have lunch before going to the Chinese exhibit at the Portland Art Museum.

We had a mediocre lunch in Chinatown. It was like the

pseudo-Chinese food from a hundred years ago, when the Chinese immigrants first opened restaurants in America and tried to get by with only American ingredients. We hoped the exhibit at the museum fared better than the food.

As soon as we walked into the main room of the museum, my antennae stood up. I spotted a Ming Dynasty throne chair in the center of the room. Our eyes grew bright as lanterns. This was the first time China had let these artifacts leave the country. We came across the burial cloak for a princess. It was made of two-inch squares of jade sewn together with pure gold wires. We marveled at the workmanship of countless pieces of rare porcelain and eating utensils used in the palace during the Ming Dynasty. We walked into a special area where the life-size and life-like terracotta figures of four soldiers and a horse from Xian stood at attention as if still guarding their emperor's tomb. I was awed by the fine artistic skills from the many nameless artists who had created their crafts thousands of years ago. I suddenly yearned to take my children back to Hong Kong to visit the graves of my great grandparents, my grandfather and my father – for them to experience some connection to their heritage.

The next day, we took a tour at Reed College. We spent half a day on the campus. Of all the schools we'd visited, Mae seemed to like Reed best.

We took a detour to Crater Lake before heading into Ashland. It was ninety-five degrees outside and the air conditioning was running on maximum. When we looked through the car windows at the lake, we couldn't believe our eyes. There was a snow bank several feet high on the roadside by the lake.

"Mom, please stop the car so we can play in the snow!" Sam shrieked.

"You're only wearing T-shirts, shorts and sandals."

"Pleeeeeeeeze, Mom. We have never seen snow before! Please let us play in it," Mae begged.

I pulled the car over. The car doors flew open and out rolled Mae and Sam into the snow. Sam dove down to pack a snowball and threw it at Mae. She squealed and ran. Sam was making another snowball while Mae snuck behind him and kicked snow on him. He screamed. I sat in the car and watched with pleasure. After they had enough of the snow, they ran back to the car all red from the cold but grinning.

Ashland was a quaint little town. The population of seventeen thousand would not fill half a stadium in L.A. Mae was anxious to show me all the places she had been.

"Come in here! I want you to see this cool bead store I told you about," She called out to me from inside a small shop. I went in and looked around.

"Oh my God! Mae, I have completely forgotten about Sam!" My heart raced.

Sam sauntered into the store, smiling. "I like it here! I feel safe walking down the street."

I was shocked. I had forgotten to hold Sam's hand. I'd only been out of L.A. for ten days. How wonderful to find myself not fearful for my children's safety. I realized a small town like this was very conducive to raising children, especially in my situation. I needed the support of a small community. I decided to check out the schools the next day.

I was surprised to find the public school system very progressive. I was impressed by the teachers' commitment to education and to the children they taught. I went back to the hotel to talk to my children.

"I want to go to Reed next fall. Are you moving out of L.A. once I go to college?" Mae said to me before I had a chance to say anything.

"Mom, can we move here if you are moving out of L.A.?" Sam asked before I answered his sister.

Mae winked at him and said, "Let's make a deal, Mom. If I get accepted to Reed for early decision, you move here. Then we'll be only five hours apart."

I saw four dancing eyes beaming at me and I said, "Ok, you guys got a deal."

"A letter from Reed, Mae! Come out here and open it," I called to her.

"Let me see!" Mae screamed, running into the living room.

She tore open the envelope. A puff of shiny confetti shaped like stars, moons, palm trees, cows and sailboats fluttered from the envelope across the table and onto the floor.

"I'm in! I'm in!" Mae cried.

We jumped and screamed. I was proud of her for doing so well. For me, it was my passport to leave Los Angeles.

I started to make plans and did more research on the middle school in Ashland.

Bob was furious. He hired a judge, an attorney, a psychologist, and his accountant to build a case to bar me from taking Sam to Oregon. I had to get permission from the judge.

The hearing date was on my forty-seventh birthday. I arrived at Bob's attorney's office at eight thirty in the morning. The attorneys from both sides argued all day. I sat in another room waiting, occasionally having a few words with my attorney. The judge interviewed both children. When Sam came out of the room, he was visibly upset. I wasn't allowed to talk to him in private. Bob's attorney had already accused me of coaching Sam what to say in front of the judge.

At 7:00 pm, my lawyer informed me that I was granted permission to leave California with Sam. Bob tried, unsuccessfully, to make me pay the legal fee of twenty thousand dollars. That was my best birthday present.

Since it was a Friday, Bob took the children for the weekend. I went to dinner alone at my favorite organic restaurant in Santa Monica. I felt light and happy.

The following month, I drove up to Ashland while Mae and Sam spent the summer with Bob. I rented a house and ordered three beds to be delivered on the last day of July, our arrival date. Once again, I tossed out everything. I planned to move to Oregon with only our personal belongings. I did not want to bring along anything of my past.

I shipped boxes of our clothes to the new address and packed our station wagon the day before Mae and Sam came home from Bob's. The next morning, I waited in front of our apartment building for them to show up. As soon as I saw them hop out of Bob's car, I waved them over to the car. I opened the doors.

"Get in!" I said.

They looked at the packed car and got in. I slammed their doors shut. I got into the driver's seat, locked the doors, backed the station wagon out of the driveway and we were off to Oregon. No one said a word.

The moment I saw the sign for Interstate 5 north, I took a deep breath. I felt like Dorothy in the Wizard of Oz. I was on my yellow brick road. But unlike Dorothy, I knew in my heart that I was the wizard behind the curtain.

After two weeks of unpacking and acquiring the necessary furniture, I drove Mae up to Portland. It was exhilarating for both of us to start a new life. She was nervous. There were so many things for her to get used to. She had traveled to Africa, Europe, Australia and New Zealand. Nevertheless, this was the first time she would be away from home for an extended period. I assured her that I was only a phone call away. I would be there if she needed me.

It was hard to say goodbye.

A week later, Sam started middle school. It was an enormous adjustment for him. We knew no one and he had to fit into a foreign environment. The private school he'd gone to in L.A. had only twenty students in his group and every student had his own tailor-made curriculum. The school itself was a large house that had a homey feel to it. There were only twelve students in his sixth grade graduating class.

The middle school hallways were larger than any of the classrooms in his old school. It was intimidating. Sam was not happy. I knew I needed to give him time to adjust. I didn't pressure him about schoolwork. The most important emphasis now was on his social skills. He could catch up on academics later.

"Do you want me to sign you up for baseball?" I asked Sam after school one day.

"No!" he cried out.

"But you were an all-star player last year. Don't you want to play again?" He was a good athlete. He'd played football, baseball and basketball since he was four.

"I don't want to join any teams. I am sick of it," Sam spat, walking away.

"Why Sam?" I asked soothingly, moving closer to him.

"I can't stand the jock attitude. The school has strong cliques and I don't want to belong to any of them."

"I can understand that. But," I persisted, "if you don't want to play team sports, I want you to choose an activity to stay active." I felt the tension dissipate.

"Ok, since I did kickboxing when I was six, I'll take karate."

I thought that was a good choice. It would help boost his confidence.

"Great, I'll look around in Ashland for a dojo," I said, happy that Sam had agreed.

We settled on one that was ok and Sam began training twice a week.

I got a call from the agent whom I had rented the house from. He asked if I was settling in ok since he knew I was from Los Angeles and didn't know anyone in Ashland. He went on to tell me that his fiancée was Korean. She met a group of Asian women once a month for a potluck lunch and invited me to join them. I thanked him but declined. I had never joined any groups and had no desire to start now.

He called again the following two months and I kept telling him no. On the third month, his fiancée called and told me that she was coming to pick me up in two hours. I finally relented and scrambled to find something to cook to take to the potluck. I whipped up some pasta and pesto sauce and thought that would be a nice dish since it would sit well for hours.

Yoon Jae whisked me off to a house on a hill. She opened the door and I stepped in. There were Asian women everywhere, standing in groups, sitting on sofas around the coffee table and on chairs in front of a wood fire. I had never seen so many Asian women gathered in a house besides my own home in Hong Kong. I was surprised to find a community of Asians in a town the size of Ashland. I walked over to a large table where everyone had put their plates of food. I cringed. The dozen dishes they'd brought were authentic ethnic foods from their countries. One in particular stood out from the rest. On a white platter were brown triangles of baked tofu topped with a spread of cream-colored tahini, meticulously placed with a spray of bamboo leaves and a red geranium on the side. It was a feast for the eyes as well as for the palate. I wished I could hide my bowl of pasta under the table. I later found out that it was from Etsuko, a macrobiotic cooking teacher and caterer, well known in Ashland.

Most of the women were Japanese. A few were Korean and two were from Taiwan. All were married to Caucasians except Sachi. She was retired, had been in Ashland since the early seventies and knew everyone.

The group that I had avoided for months turned out to be very warm and friendly. I stayed for hours after lunch and was intrigued by the Japanese culture. This was the first time I had an opportunity to be close to the people from that country. I was eager to learn more.

I went to the potluck gathering monthly.

One evening, I was having dinner with Sam at a Chinese restaurant we frequented. The owner sat at our table to chat with us.

"Why are you still renting? We just bought a house on the edge of town," Jade said. She had come to Ashland with her husband from Hong Kong seven years ago.

"I don't know if I want to stay here after my son graduates from high school," I said, serving Sam some noodles.

Jade poured me more tea. "Buy a house now and sell it when you are ready to leave. You'll get more than your money back in six years. Why pay rent?"

"You've got a point there but I don't want to bother. I just got rid of everything in L.A." But the idea intrigued me.

The next day, I thought more about what Jade had said to me. I looked in the real estate section of the newspaper and called around to make appointments to see the houses that were on the market.

In two weeks, I saw over thirty houses and settled on one under construction on the south side of town.

Moving into the new house was symbolic, another step toward myself. I vigorously adhered to my meditation and exercise routine. I had shed old emotions and habits. Now I needed to add to my clean slate. I painted a seven-foot mural of a white iris on the eighteen-foot wall in my living room.

I took Ikebana, the classical flower arrangement with Sachi and her class. She was an established sensei. I learned

Macrobiotic cooking from Etsuko and followed her to an organic farm almost weekly during the summer to learn more about organic farming. I planted an organic vegetable garden in the back of the house and tended dozens of roses in the front. Occasionally, I was invited to the symphony or a party. My life started to take on a new shape.

One day, waiting for a shop to open in Medford, a town fifteen miles north of Ashland, I walked along the small storefronts of the strip mall and stumbled upon a karate dojo. On the front window, I read an article about the eighth degree black belt sensei of traditional style karate. I was impressed by his philosophy. I decided to take Sam to sit in on one of the classes.

The next day, we observed a young instructor conducting his class. I was awe-struck by his precise movements. His stances were solid. Each move was intensely powerful, yet full of grace. Like a symphony — a rush of clear notes from the piano and followed by the thunderous drums. He was one of sensei's devout students. I later found out that the young instructor was a three-time world champion. By the end of the class, the excitement in Sam's eyes mirrored my own.

"Mom, can I sign up? I want to start training here tomorrow. This dojo makes the one that I'm going to seem like a baby-sitting service," he said, pulling on my sleeve for an immediate answer. I had to collect myself for a moment. I had not been so impressed and moved by anything for a very long time. The instructor embodied the direct translation of karate, "the empty hand way," uniting the spirit, the mind and the body.

"We'll both sign up and start training tomorrow. I want to train with you," I said. Sam's face lit up.

"Wow, Mom, I never would dream of training with you. This is so cool."

By far, I was the oldest student in the dojo. During the first few weeks of training, every muscle in my body hurt. I soaked in an Epsom salt solution for hours every night until the tension and ache melted away. To walk, I had to wrap my knees with ace bandages for support. The pain inspired me to continue training in karate. To achieve the balance that I sought, I needed to strengthen my physical body to align with my spiritual self.

We started to train four times a week. After six months time, I could finally walk without the ace bandages. My body had significantly changed. I developed muscles in my arms and shoulders. My waist slimmed down and my legs grew stronger and more muscular. I felt myself walking with more confidence, in a sort of glide across the floor. Besides the physical changes, there was a shift in my meditation. I felt more solid and grounded. It was much easier to enter the space of stillness. For the first time, I felt that I had found my base. Instead of reacting to my circumstance, I was able to come from the center and expand into the world.

One day while on the floor practicing the movements of a kata, a formal exercise, I stood in front of the mirror moving my hands to mimic the way Sensei had taught me. I repeated the movements more than thirty times and they were still nowhere near where I wanted them to be. I fixed my eyes on the image of my hands in the mirror — everything else just melted away. I soon became aware of the intense concentration it took to induce memories into my body, to train it to move in a purposeful way. It was meditation in motion. My mind became more and more still. In order to make that one perfect move, I had to practice until it came naturally. When a master executes his one perfect move, he flows in a state of grace. That was what I needed and wanted to apply to my life. Now that I had unlearned what was forced upon me by my culture and the world, I had to practice aligning myself physically and spiritually until it came naturally to me.

Every day, I tried to apply the concept of the master to my life. When I learned a new idea, developed a new belief, I practiced until it became part of my body and mind. The ideas and opinions of others no longer easily swayed me. I did not watch television. My children had convinced me to "get with it" by learning to use a computer. I stayed in touch with the world by getting my information from the Internet, on my own terms. I seldom engaged in mindless discussions with the few people I saw. I was extremely selective. I didn't do many things. But whatever I did, I tried to do it well. I did not own many things but everything I owned was of the best quality. I created an environment that was nurturing and supportive for me. I lived simply.

It had been three years since we moved to Ashland. I fell into a routine: take care of Sam, practice karate and meditate. Occasionally, I visited with my Asian friends. I felt strong and established. It was a clean and satisfying life, but I started to feel something was lacking, and I wondered if I was ready to take on a relationship. How would I begin? The only experience I had was dysfunctional. The thought of a relationship gave me the jitters and besides, Ashland was very thin on eligible men.

Summer came. Mae came home for her break.

"Mom, I think it's time for you to get a life of your own. You are a hermit. Find yourself a boyfriend and get on with it," she teased.

"What do you mean? Should I stand outside on the street corner and hang a sign around my neck saying that I'm available?" I laughed.

"I met my boyfriend online. You use a computer! It is fun!"

"Are you kidding? How do I know if they are what they say they are? They are just words on the screen," I said, rolling my eyes.

"You are so dull. Nobody can rape you through the computer screen. You can turn it off, or block them out. Gosh, just have some fun. You used to be on the front line and lived on the edge, remember? Are you getting that old? Where is that cool bitch?" It was her turn to roll her eyes.

"I can hardly type. I feel funny talking to a person on the computer, like the first time leaving a message on an answering machine," I said timidly.

"Mom, you are hopeless. Come on! Give it a try so I can say to my friends that my mom is cool. She is hip to get online," she laughed.

"Whatever," I dismissed the conversation and went back to cooking dinner.

A few months went by and I diligently stuck to my routines but the nagging urge to make some change in my life grew stronger. I finally convinced myself I had to address the issue. How was I to meet a person and have a decent connection? A man was not going to fall out of the sky and land in my living room. I needed to put myself out into the world to see what would happen.

One morning after meditation, I walked over to my computer and compiled a short description of myself: I was an artist and a vegetarian. I meditated and actively trained in karate seeking to balance my physical and spiritual selves. I posted it in the personals. It took less than twenty minutes.

The next day I had more than twenty responses from all over the country. The respondents were diverse. Their professions supposedly ranged from medical doctor, attorney, clothing manufacturer, to professor at a university. There were so many lonely people out there. They had no real interest in what I had written about myself. Instead they bragged about their own accomplishments. A forest ranger from Montana actually said that he was going to take the next plane to Oregon to meet me. He was ready to take a Chinese wife.

I deleted my profile from the personals. It was up for less than twenty-four hours.

However, one short email consisting of only three sentences caught my attention. It said: "Bravo, to find balance in your life. My name is David. I also am a vegetarian."

I wrote back and asked more about him.

We corresponded sporadically for a few weeks. Sometimes I sent him an email and there would be no response for a few days. Just as I thought he had lost interest, an email appeared.

One evening, as I was reading a news story online, an instant message came from David. I was surprised and didn't know what to do to respond. I watched the box anxiously as I tried to figure out how to write him back. What if he got tired of waiting? It took a few minutes. I wondered if he was still there when I responded. When he replied, I was relieved. We talked, typing responses back and forth. We both noted the full moon outside. David told me that when he used to live in the Santa Cruz Mountains he would hike to the top of the mountain in the full moon and blow on his conch shell. Wild animals responded with howls. I was enthralled by the image. In that instant, he captured my heart.

After I wrote good night, I walked into my bedroom. The silver light from the full moon illuminated my bed and floor. I stood in the midst of it, breathing in the magic moment. I lay in bed under the light. I could think only of David.

I got up and wrote him this email:

When I went to sleep, the silver light of the full moon shone into my bedroom. I left my drapes open and lay in bed thinking of you... Your thoughts and how fortunate it is for me to have met you. It is so very rare to have someone who recognizes and sees me for who I am. Though we have never met physically, you know me so well. It is such a blessing. As I was falling asleep, the thought of you brought me the

*beginning of my dreams... dreams of lavender and silver
light... and the sound of the conch shell...*
    Irene

I waited nervously for his response. I'd never had the
courage to express myself in words but he told me he loved my
words and began to address me as his Silver Lady. I sent him
another email a week later:

*Under the glow of the moonlight... Accompanied by a
thousand stars. I look into your eyes... The familiar sensation floods my body with excitement... Something I have felt
from the ancient past, many life times ago... The connection
I thought was long lost comes rushing back... "It's you, welcome back," I whisper in your ear... We embrace under the
silver light... Surrounded by singing angels and heavenly
glow... Lavender dream... A gift from the angels.*
    Your Silver Lady

I couldn't wait to get on the computer to talk with him
each evening. I began to see the world differently. I walked
out to the rose garden, into the pale blue light. A mist of soft
rain kissed my face. The scent of damp roses wafted around
me. I felt a deep sense of contentment. I closed my eyes. My
heart stirred. A lost desire from a distant past rushed into my
consciousness — a dream of sharing my life with someone I
was hopelessly in love with. I opened my eyes and saw the
roses I had picked out and planted. If I dared to dream, I
could create it. I smiled and thought of David. I wondered:
could I be in love?

As we talked online one evening, I asked him to tell me more
about his daily activities. Without hesitation, he told me that he
was married. I was devastated. My magic world crumbled.

David sensed my disappointment and told me that he had difficulties with his marriage. He had been struggling with the idea of dissolving it for years. He told me about his need to get back into meditation and follow his spiritual path, a part of himself that he had neglected for too long. It was refreshing for him to find support from someone who was on a similar path.

But I was not so sure I was willing to continue our communication. I was torn. I thought I'd found love, but now I saw there was no future in this relationship. Yet I had never known the magic that we had created for each other. I wouldn't and couldn't deny how drawn I was to him.

We began to talk more intimately about our past, our children, our current situations, his marriage, his desire and difficulty in getting back into meditation. We did so with such openness, honesty, and understanding, that we became deeply bonded. After weeks of communicating through emails and instant messages, we decided to talk on the phone. I was nervous. When the phone rang, I jumped.

"Hello, Irene? Is this you? The real you?"

I heard an upbeat and young voice on the phone. The person I knew so well through written words was suddenly real and alive. I blushed like a little girl talking for the first time to a boy she'd had a crush on for a long time.

"David, hi, this is Irene. The real me. Your silver lady," I said shyly.

"Wow! This is amazing!" we both said at once. After a couple hours talking, I was awed at our ease with each other. We abandoned the computers. It took too long for us to type out the words. We talked daily on the phone instead.

David was very established in the world. He had a respectable job and lived in an upscale neighborhood. He was deeply rooted in the Bay Area with family and friends of many years. Like my past, he had everything he wanted in the material world. He was very comfortable, but discontentment gnawed at him. He needed to find ways to fill the spiritual void in his life. I knew too well what he was going through. Every day, we shared our ideas of how to bring more awareness into our lives. My evolution from the person I was before my divorce to who I was now profoundly affected David.

I made plans to see my friend Wurmie from the Royal College. I hadn't seen her for nearly twenty years.

"I am coming down to Berkeley to visit my friend from college in a few weeks. I wonder if we should meet," I asked David one evening.

"You are? This is incredible. I can't imagine seeing you in person."

"After all this time writing and talking I don't know how this will work out," I said nervously.

"This will change everything, but I am very excited," David said enthusiastically.

"We should meet at my friend's house in Berkeley. Is that ok with you?" I asked. After all, he was just a voice on the phone.

"We absolutely have to do what feels comfortable for you. I'll meet you at your friend's house when you get here," he insisted. That touched me deeply.

After we got off the phone, I called Wurmie right away.

When I told her I was meeting a man I had met on the Internet at her house, she yelled, "You what? Kai, what are you thinking? Haven't you heard enough horror stories about these people who met online? You are crazier than I remembered."

"Hey, Wurmie! We are supposed to be on the cutting edge. Are you getting that old? Not everyone online is a mass murderer, you know," I teased.

"I am conservative. That's what my children tell me all the time now," she said reluctantly.

"Ok, just tell me what I can do to make you feel at ease."

"I have to be here with my husband when he arrives and if we think he's ok after we meet him, then we'll let you go with him. How's that?"

"Yes, Mother! I am forty-nine years old. I think I can take care of myself pretty well now," I said half jokingly. But I was glad that she had at least agreed to let me meet David at her house. After I got off the phone, the reality of meeting David in person kicked in. I blushed the first time I talked to him. What was I going to do when we met face to face?

David was on his way. I was nervous and excited. I checked myself in the mirror. I saw a strong and muscular woman. My long black flowing hair fell down my back. I wondered what my grandmother would think of this. No Chinese woman older than thirty would have loose long hair. What a risqué thing to do, and I was meeting a man I had met on the Internet. She must be rolling her eyes in her grave. I smiled and walked back into the living room.

The doorbell rang. Wurmie opened the door. I turned to face the man in the doorway. Our eyes met. His eyes gleamed. Electricity coursed through my entire body.

He walked over to me, shook my hand and said, "Here you are. I am David."

I was speechless. I tried to collect myself. I smiled, not wanting to let go of his hand. After a few minutes of pleasant exchange with Wurmie and her husband, we knew without saying anything to each other that we needed to get out of her house.

As soon as we stepped outside, I felt something so familiar when he touched me with his gaze, as if I had been with him all of my life.

"I have an idea where we should go," David said while opening the door of his car for me.

I was at a loss for words.

We walked into a colorful old hotel. A lady showed us to our room. A wood fire warmed the sitting area. We closed the door behind us and walked over to the overstuffed sofa. Before we had a chance to sit down, David took my hands and pulled me close. I looked into his eyes. Electricity rushed through my body again. I reached up and kissed his lips. He responded with the same intensity I felt.

We soaked in the jacuzzi tub staring at each other; bewildered by the incredible depth of passion we had for each other.

We sat in front of the fire in silence. I felt that I could reach into his soul. Tears rolled down my face. I finally had found someone who spoke the same language as I did. I curled up beside him on the couch. He wrapped his arms around me. I felt so safe, a place that I had never known. I closed my eyes and took a deep breath, wishing this moment would never end.

I broke the news to my sisters. I told Louise that I had met the most wonderful man. She was happy for me. Virginia was not interested. As usual, she acted as if I hadn't said a word, talking on about her own life when I told her about David.

When I spoke to Teresa on the phone and told her about meeting David in California, she casually replied, "Oh yeah?"

"He lives in San Francisco. I am so happy."

"He lives in San Francisco? He sees gorgeous women every day. What's so special about you?"

I changed the subject.

I didn't tell any of them that David was married. The fact that I was "the other woman" did not sit well with our family history. Since my great grandmother, all females in our family were proper wives. Concubines and mistresses were the whores.

After our time together in Berkeley, not a moment went by that David was not on my mind. That I didn't have the freedom to contact him at his home and had to wait for him to call me, combined with the fact that I had no idea when I could see him in person again, made me question my position. I had worked hard for five and half years to strengthen myself and swore that I would not put myself in a compromising position once I got into a relationship. What was I doing? Was I that desperate for someone's attention? Was our relationship morally wrong? Not too long ago, women in China were drowned when they were caught having affairs with married men. I had heard enough stories from my own family referring to the whores who had committed adultery. On the other hand, David was the most thoughtful, loving and wonderful man I had ever met. We were honest, open and respectful to each other. But I cringed at the idea of waiting on the side for David to be available. I did not want to be someone's mistress forever. I cried for days thinking about ending the relationship.

I couldn't stop myself from talking to or seeing him. Instead, we started to meditate at the same time every morning, he in San Francisco and I in Ashland. He started to work out to strengthen his body and I continued to train in karate.

I resolved to take each day as it came and enjoy our time together but in the back of my mind, I resented that my life was controlled by the schedule of his married life.

One late morning, we walked on the beach. The sun was brilliant. The deep blue water reflected the sunlight like millions of stars shimmering across the sea to the horizon. White puffy clouds dotted the sky. The wind blew strong. We walked on the water's edge. I held David's hand and stopped to face the sea. I stretched out my arms, lifted my face up to the sun and felt the wind blow through me – as though my body was just a frame. It was blowing my past away. I could almost feel the heaviness blown out from my body. All that was left was an empty shell. I felt so clean, so light. I turned to look at David.

He pulled me toward him and kissed me. I felt his love filling my clean and empty body. Gone were the contaminations of my past. I had worked hard to dislodge the false boundaries and the rigid rules my culture had imposed on my life. Now I took one more step to recognize that it was my own responsibility to nurture, appreciate and honor love when I found it.

I went home and called my sisters. David is married, I told them. I didn't care what they had to say. I focused on seeing our relationship more clearly, what it meant to me outside of the dictates of society. I was humbled by the fact that I was extremely fortunate to have found such a love. I was grateful for each moment David and I had together. I'd had unrealistic ideas of the ideal relationship. I thought it should be free of problems and complications, like Cinderella. Once her foot fit into that perfect glass slipper, she would live happily ever after. I now learned to appreciate what I had. Through David, I realized that an ideal relationship was to be able to support each other in working through weaknesses, to encourage each other to be more of who we are. To have the patience to listen to each other's fears and difficulties. And most of all, to be each other's biggest fan.

No matter what we went through during the day, especially through trying times, the moment we heard each other's voice, we were cast into a space of tranquility. Like a pool of refreshing, clean, and sweet water, we submerged ourselves in each other and were transformed. I felt I could do anything with David by my side.

After spending three wonderful days with David, I came back to Ashland and received a call from Louise.

"Virginia is in the hospital. She just had a stroke," she said bleakly.

"Oh God. What is her condition?" I said, shocked. I felt like I had just landed on a bed of rocks after flying so high.

"She has lost the use of her right arm and leg and her speech is slurred." Her voice was almost inaudible.

"Give me her number at the hospital. I just hope her condition is stabilized and she's not getting worse."

I called Virginia.

I talked to her daily on the phone and called Teresa and Louise to confer with them. I had kept a cordial distance from them since my divorce but now we were faced with real issues. I tried to work out what needed to be done for Virginia realistically. I was surprised and frustrated by our conversations. I realized that I had not dealt with my sisters on important issues since our mother's death. I found myself plunged head long onto this merry-go-round, of "please do not be direct" dialogues that I had forgotten. I finally asked Louise for the telephone number of Virginia's son. I hoped to get some straight answers from him.

"What do you want his number for? Tell me first and I'll see if I should give it to you," Louise asked suspiciously.

"I just want to talk to him about what he is going to do for his mother."

"You can't have it. We don't want you to talk to him. You always blurt out what's on your mind and this is not the time for straight talk," she said unyieldingly.

I said nothing more and hung up.

In the past, this would be the button my sisters pushed if they were angry with me. I would come crawling back to them, ask what I had done wrong and beg to be included again. I saw it clearly now and was not willing to play their game. I was sad. After our experience with Mother in the hospital, I had hoped they would treat me with consideration but years had passed and nothing had changed.

I tried Virginia next.

"Louise wouldn't give me your son's phone number. I'd like to talk to him about what he's going to do for you," I spat out, unwilling to take the time to beat around the bush.

"We don't want you to talk to him. You speak from your heart. You are too straight and don't know how to turn corners," she said flatly. I couldn't believe she had used the same term my mother had used forty years before.

"I thought speaking from one's heart is good. You prefer me to be manipulative?" I asked, annoyed.

"You are just too honest. People don't like that." She sounded so Chinese to me.

"I don't like to be treated like a child either," I said firmly, surprised that I spoke up for myself.

A few days after my talk with Louise, I was on the phone with Teresa.

"Her son is a bastard. He makes good money and he should take care of his mother. He's waiting for us to make the first move," she said angrily.

"Somebody has to. Virginia needs help when she gets out of the hospital. Honestly, I don't think I can handle it. It's like Mom all over again," I said with a shudder.

"What's wrong with you? Don't you have any compassion?" She raised her voice, "This is family!"

"I took care of Mom for years. I still haven't recovered from it," I shouted.

"What's the matter with you? If something happens to me, you won't take care of me?" she screamed at me like a child.

My mouth became dry. My heart pounded. I couldn't tell her yes, even if I didn't mean it. The thought of taking care of any of my sisters on a long-term basis terrified me.

"Don't talk to me that way!" I yelled back. Tears rolled down my face.

"How can you be so selfish?" she barked.

"I don't want to talk to you ever again." I hung up. Every muscle in my body was taut. I found myself standing erect like a steel rod. My head started to throb.

That evening, I lay in bed waiting for David's call. I felt a heavy pressure on my chest and I couldn't breathe. I sat up. My heart was beating rapidly. The phone rang. I was so relieved to hear David's voice.

"Sweetheart, are you ok? You sound strained," David said, concerned.

"I guess I am ok," I hesitated. Then blurted out, "No, I feel terrible."

"Talk to me. Keep talking and you'll feel better."

"My heart is racing and I can't breathe." I was panting and sweating profusely. I felt dizzy and knew I needed to get up. I was afraid I would pass out. I walked out to the kitchen and started to pace around. My mouth was dry and I was shaking violently.

"Irene, talk to me. Are you ok?" I heard the alarm in his voice.

"I-i-its M-m-mo-mother all over again!" I had severe cramps in my stomach. I was confused. I gasped for air and was disoriented.

"You are not a child. You are a fifty-year-old woman. They can't do anything to you now. You are in control," he said firmly.

"I am not a child. I am in Ashland. I am in Ashland," I repeated, again and again. I walked into the bathroom and looked into the mirror. I saw the reflection of a woman with an ashen face. A woman, not a seven-year-old child.

"What can they do to you? Tell me the worst scenario," David said.

"They can get on the plane and come hit me. That's the worst they can do. But they are not going to waste their money on airfare. And besides, I can handle a few hits." I started to relax.

"Sweetheart, no matter what happens, I am here for you. Just know that I love you."

It was rare for us to spend uninterrupted time together. We usually saw each other between his work and busy family schedules, but today I was meeting David at Lake Shasta for a day. I ran to him as he got out of his car and planted a long, deep, wet kiss on his lips.

"Oh honey, so good to see you," I beamed. He slipped his hands under my shirt and said, " It's so good to see and feel you."

We laughed, because we couldn't help showing so much affection towards each other – even in public. We held each other close and as usual, it took us twenty minutes to walk a few paces because we couldn't keep our lips and hands off each other's bodies.

Within seconds of getting into our room, our clothes flew off. We both took a deep breath.

"I never have enough of you. I love you, honey. I missed you so much," I said. David pulled me closer and held me tight.

He kissed me tenderly. We made love for hours. Like marathon runners, when we reached our physical limits, we pushed on through spirit to euphoria.

We sat still, facing each other and took in the wonderment of our shared joy and gratitude.

"Wow! Look at our bodies!" David said in astonishment. The setting sun shone through the window directly onto our glistening bodies, covered with sweat. The light turned our bodies into glimmering gold, sprinkled with beads of silver. I turned and looked into the mirror directly across the bed, which was framed by an ornate golden frame. Within it, in the center, sat a pair of golden statues of lovers embraced on a soft white sheet in a timeless pose. We were mesmerized by the image of this living painting of us.

We decided to watch the sunset by the shore of the lake. As usual, it took us half an hour to get three feet from the bed to our clothes. It took willpower to concentrate on doing simple things like putting on our shirts.

We finally walked down to the shore at dusk, just in time to catch the last light of the sun. We sat on a boulder above the water's edge. The sun was setting behind the mountain across the lake. The water was calm. The reflection of the sunlight was like a vast sheet of gold laid across the lake. Lavender and pink clouds faded into the gray-blue sky. We sat in silence. David held me closer and said, "For many years, I've been in an inner struggle between living a life of little to no expressed intimacy and sensuality, and holding back the passion and joy that comes from deep within me. I can no longer not be my complete self. I must step out from my marriage."

I reached up and kissed him and put my head closer to his chest. He held me tight. I breathed in his breath. All of my life, I had walked against violent storms, braving fierce winds and rain. I'd felt I must go on and keep going on. Now I could relax in the warmth and magic of being in David's arms.

David was torn between his need to freely express himself and his reluctance to inflict pain on his wife and eleven-year-old son if he decided to dissolve his marriage. He talked about his immense fear of stepping out into the unknown. He was an established man. His whole life would turn upside down — especially economically. He might have to start all over again. To rebuild his life at fifty-three was frightening but he was so hungry to live a life of passion and to step into his full power. I, too, was wrought with fear of the unknown before I dissolved my marriage. The only thing I could do now was to be under-standing and supportive.

I told him numerous times that one day when he walked outside from his house, he would see the nose of a silver car sticking out from the corner of the street. That would be the

Silver Lady, coming to whisk him away, to take him out of his misery.

A few days after I came home from seeing David, I heard a very different tone in his voice when he called.

"My wife asked me if I am having a relationship. I told her yes. I have decided not to live my life in the shadows any longer," David said calmly.

I was speechless, not expecting the sudden change. I knew too well what would follow. All hell would break loose in his household. Now, more than ever I needed to be supportive, help him to stay in the center of the storm, and not get swept away.

"Honey, I am glad that you have decided to move on. Actually, you only have two choices. Stay in your current situation to wither and die or break out and face everyone with courage and start living. I am very proud of you," I told him.

Within a month, he moved out of his house and rented a much smaller one. He started going through the process of divorce.

We stayed strong and kept our sights on the tasks ahead. We both knew so well that we could do anything together. We became even closer as we went through the strenuous undertaking of David facing his family and their outrage.

"I don't have to come whisk you away anymore. You have extricated yourself from your shackles," I teased David on the phone the day before I went down to meet him at his new house.

"What kind of car were you referring to when you told me about the silver nose sticking out from the corner of my street?" David asked curiously.

"Remember the time I came down and rented a convertible? I loved it. I was thinking of buying a silver Mercedes SLK convertible as the Silver Lady. I have spent all of my life being practical. It's time for me to have some fun," I said half seriously.

"Sweetheart, it's about time! By the way, I saw one just the other day in a dealership and it caught my eye. It screams 'Irene.' When you come down, we have to go test-drive it," he said excitedly.

"Really? We have to! Let's do that."

I went down to San Francisco and stayed with David in his new house. He didn't have to leave to go back to his family at night. For once, I felt that I truly belonged in his life.

We went to test drive the convertible the day I was to leave for Ashland. The car was silver with a red and black leather interior. David was right. It had my name written all over it. I wrote the salesman a check and had them ship the car up to my house.

"Honey, guess what is going to happen when you come down to visit me next week?" David said in his usual soothing voice.

He couldn't wait for me to answer and blurted out, "It's going to be a full moon and we are going to the top of the mountain. I will blow the conch shell for us!"

"That will be amazing! You are a genius. You surely know how to melt a girl's heart. I am driving down in my new car."

"Yeah, the Silver Lady has manifested... In the sound of the conch shell."

After dinner under the full moon, David and I got into the little silver car with its top down, and headed into the mountains to blow on the conch shell. David drove, we had Janis Joplin blasting "Move Over." I felt such joy — the wind blowing through my hair and against my face, the soulful voice of Janis, and David next to me.

When I looked up at the beautiful full moon, I noticed the towers of the Golden Gate Bridge passing by. I glanced down at the water. I saw the fifteen-year-old girl from Hong Kong looking up from under the bridge at the fifty-year-old woman, driving in her convertible with her lover.

I am the embodiment of her hopes and dreams. I am American, a citizen of this great land of the free.

———

GOING HOME

I woke up happy. I loved our southern bed. We had purchased it together. It was cozy with a fluffy down comforter. Defused morning light streamed through the striped curtains, casting shadows across the walls and floor.

"Honey, do you remember the recurring dream that I told you about?" I pulled myself closer, putting my head on David's shoulder, so I could snuggle against his chin and feel the stubble of his beard against my forehead.

"The one on the roof in Hong Kong?" David asked dreamily, stroking my hair with his hand.

"Yes, the one that I've had for thirty-five years. Every time I have that dream, I'm approaching the entrance to the roof of the building in Hong Kong. It is always dark and foreboding outside and I'm afraid to go out. Then I suddenly remember that I've forgotten to feed the pigeons and chickens for months or years. I am so afraid that they are dead because of my irresponsibility. I start to panic and wake up in a cold sweat." I felt uneasy just recalling the dream. I was grateful that I was here with David. I leaned closer to his chest and closed my eyes.

"Oh, honey, did you have that dream again?" David kissed my head and stroked my back. I sat up and straddled his legs. I could barely contain my joy. "No. I had a wonderful dream last night. When I approached the entrance of the roof, it was bright and beautiful outside. I walked through the threshold and stepped out. I had never seen such a beautiful blue sky. I felt the warmth from the bright rays of the sun. Vines with gorgeous flowers draped down an enormous arbor, forming a shelter. I walked under it and felt so happy, so content."

Reaching up, he pulled me close and held me tight.

"About time, honey. You have been out there alone long enough. You are safe now."

Tears rolled down my face onto David's shoulder. I did not remember the last time I felt completely at ease in another person's presence. Maybe I never had.

David's birthday approached. It would be the first time I could celebrate with him. I wondered what I could do to make it special. Mae had graduated from college and was studying at a well-known university in England for her master's degree. Sam was now a junior in high school and preparing to apply to college. He was on the high school varsity wrestling team. When I looked at my children, I felt a strong sense of accomplishment. I was a woman now and not the lost little girl who had to navigate life alone. It was time to go back and see my great grandmother. I picked up the phone and called David.

"How would you like to spend your birthday in Hong Kong?"

"What? Hong Kong? I would love to. But where did this idea come from?" He knew that all of my life I had kept pushing on, leaving my past behind.

"I don't know... I just have such a strong desire to retrace the steps of my childhood. I am solid enough to face my past, and I want to visit Great-grandmother's grave with you and Sam. I am happy at last. This will make me feel my life has finally come full circle," I said tearfully. Great-grandmother didn't have to whisper in my ear any longer. After thirty-six years, I was going back to face her.

I made arrangements to visit Hong Kong during the Chinese New Year. We would stay at the five star hotel I had seen with my mother when she took me to the Tsimshastui District when I was six years old. This was where all the foreigners and wealthy people stayed. I remembered peeking into the lobby, dazzled by the grandeur of the sparkling crystal chandeliers and the enormous, beautifully decorated reception area. I had wondered what it took to stay in a place like this. Even the doormen looked well-to-do with their bright uniforms and white gloves. It would be a great celebration to return to my roots as an accomplished woman.

I was amazed by the modernity of everything in Hong Kong, from the sleek designs and glowing neon lights of the international name-brand shops, to the trendy hairstyles and clothes of the fashionable young. People everywhere walked around talking on their tiny cell phones. I remembered laughing when my aunt refused to touch the telephone because she was afraid that she would accidentally dial 999 and get the police. Now I saw people her age with cell phones the size of half a pack of cigarettes.

As we drove through the streets to get to the hotel, we passed by hundreds of high-rises packed close together on this small island. Entire buildings were lit up with changing color lights. Greetings for the year of the horse covered most of the façades facing the harbor. Hong Kong had changed so much that I did not recognize it. There was nothing remotely close to what I had remembered. I felt like a tourist.

"The coffee is so good," I murmured, sipping it with satisfaction. It was rich and foamy. I nodded to the waitress for a second cup. I squeezed David's hand and said, "How wonderful it is to be here with you and Sam." I looked past them through the glass wall and watched the sun peeking between the buildings across the harbor. We were having breakfast in a café on the twenty-first floor of the hotel.

"Mom, did you taste the melon? That was the best piece of honeydew I've ever had." Sam leaned back and took a deep breath.

I could see the contentment on his face. I smiled and nodded. The quality of the food and service was exquisite. Slices of cantaloupe, honeydew, pineapple and strawberry fanned out on silver platters. Behind the sliced fruits were crystal bowls filled with yogurt and mueslix with pitchers of freshly squeezed orange and grapefruit juice. There were stations of smoked fish and meat. I ordered an omelet with seasonal vegetables and was surprised to find it was made with egg whites only. The waitress mysteriously appeared when we wanted something but never when we were engrossed in conversation.

"Did your butler bring you hot tea last night?" I asked Sam, who had a separate room.

"Yeah... I was surprised that he brought tea and a plate of candied fruit. I ate them all. I could stay here forever. I found a white piece of cloth on the floor next to the bed. What's it for?" he asked, while scooping up the last bite of his smoked salmon.

"That's linen, so your feet don't have to touch the floor before you put on the slippers when you get out of bed. Most Chinese don't walk around barefoot. It is uncivilized. Did you find the new white terry cloth slippers they put out for you?" I remembered how I always had slippers on when I was a child. I got scolded for being barefoot. Only poor people walked without shoes, I was told. Little reminders were slowly seeping in.

In the evening, we decided to take a walk on Nathan Road, the main thoroughfare where all the shops were. At first, I was shocked by the throngs of people on the street. They pushed their way through each other in both directions under the glaring lights from the shops. Loud speakers hawked the stores' merchandise. We were pushed along by the crowd. If we wanted to stop, we had to jump to the side of the road before we got pulled into the rushing tide of moving bodies. As we walked, I held David's hand, periodically looking back at Sam to make sure he didn't get separated from us. We were dazed. The loud noise, bright lights and lack of space made us dizzy but after a while, magically, I started to relax. The noise and the crowds seemed to diminish, I began to hear conversations and to notice the things people were buying and selling. I was getting back into the rhythm of the Chinese beat of life. I had been away for thirty-six years and I thought I had forgotten the way I used to live but it had been lying dormant. I was on familiar ground.

I set a day aside to visit my old school and the gravesites of my family. We took the number six bus from Tsimshatsui to Tai Po Road where I used to live. We had to travel the entire length of Nathan Road. During the ride, we sat on the upper deck in the front seat looking out the very large windows. Sam gasped when the bus stopped about six inches away from the one ahead of us. Everything in the city was tightly packed. Six million people live on this tiny patch of land. I had forgotten how crowded Hong Kong was. I tried to find the building where the herbalist had lived after he moved out of his tiny box. I saw a few familiar banks and tea parlors, but no sight of his building. Hong Kong had changed so much that I wouldn't have recognized it even if I had the actual address.

To my amazement, as we got closer to the end of Nathan Road, I remembered which bus stop to get off. I signaled David and Sam to get off the bus. We walked toward number six Tai Po Road, where our building used to be. I knew it was gone, and

I was sad to see that the replacement was a run down building with a solid iron gate for the entrance. All the buildings in the neighborhood that had replaced the old ones were already dilapidated and grimy. I stepped back to the edge of the curb and surveyed the nearby stores.

"Oh my God! Look!" I screamed in disbelief. It was the drug store where I'd bought distilled water and syringes for my father. The gold characters on a black background displayed above the storefront were exactly the same.

"Do you want to go and have a look?" David held my hand and asked solemnly.

I wanted to go, but at the same time, I was nervous to retrace the little girl's steps. Then I walked toward the drug store. David and Sam followed behind me quietly, giving me space to take this in.

The store was renovated, but the layout was almost identical to the old one. Glass cases on the left side of the store were filled with western medications. The opposite side had cases stocked with Chinese herbs and other concoctions in glass jars. The wall behind the Chinese herbal cases, which used to be lined with over a hundred small wooden drawers containing different type of herbs, had been replaced by a sheet of white formica. The floor was covered with linoleum instead of the tiny one-inch hexagonal white tiles. The merchandise was up to date, but the atmosphere was the same. I could almost see the tall, thin clerk coming up to me and asking if I had come for distilled water. I looked down at the floor, which I used to do whenever someone asked me a question. As I stared down, I noticed my big black shoes. Here I was: fifty-one years old. I looked to David and Sam, their forms blurred by a thin mist of tears. I was with my lover and my sixteen-year-old son in the drug store that had been the only link to my father, who had given me his time in exchange for my services. At last, here in this pharmacy, I realized I no longer needed to feel guilty about exposing him to the world. I could finally put Father to rest.

We walked on the dirty cement sidewalk towards the church where my primary school was located. I wondered if I was walking on the same cement slabs I had walked on in second grade, while carrying a school bag that was half my weight. I was surprised at how short the walk was to the church. Every day had seemed an endless journey walking back and forth from school to home. I realized what was speeding my journey now. I was without burden.

Inside the church, I dipped my middle finger into the holy water at one side of the entrance, making a cross with the water. I dabbed my forehead first, then both sides of my shoulders and my solar plexus. I bent my knees to make a gesture of kneeling, then straightened myself and proceeded to walk down the isle still flanked by the wooden benches I'd sat on when I attended church in second grade. It was here that the bodies of my grandfather and my father had been displayed. I sat down in the first row and looked at the three stained glass windows. I used to stare so hard at them, trying to see God through the image of Jesus adorned with his crown made of thorns, looking down at me from his cross. He had seemed so alive. The windows had lost their luster. I no longer needed to hope for a miracle to set me free.

The paint on the ceiling was peeling off in large chunks like bark flaking off a dead tree. The altar, with its magnificent crucifix, was missing. Also gone were the five foot tall silver candelabras and vases of sword-like gladiolas that used to fill the room with their coral and ivory brilliance. Instead, there was a makeshift table covered with a cheap piece of cloth surrounded by plastic plants. The beautiful statues of Mary and Joseph were gone. There were just big empty spaces in the recesses of the walls, revealing emptiness and ghosts. The ornate confessional booths were also missing. I looked back to the area upstairs where the chairs for the choir used to be. During mass, we would sit on the dark, smooth, old chairs and sing hymns in

Latin to the music of the magnificent organ. I didn't understand Latin and thought it was the language of God. Now there were no chairs or towering organ. Everything was gone with the little girl. I sat in church meditating on my life. I had risen like a phoenix from the ashes of my childhood. I was the embodiment of the young girl's wishes.

I gestured to David and Sam to follow me outside through a side door. We walked downstairs to the play yard of the school. It seemed so small now. I sat down on a low ledge made of stone and cement and looked at Sam.

"This is where I used to sit during recess. I spent a lot of time on this ledge." I ran my hand along the smooth surface of the cement. I remembered sitting here squeezing a jelly ball candy, getting it ready to ooze into my mouth. I smiled and looked up and noticed the leaves of the mimosa tree.

"I played with the leaves of this tree almost every day," I said to Sam. I'd thought it was magical when they closed up tightly from the slightest touch like clamshells.

"Come on, Mom! You used to play with those leaves? What did you do — climb all the way up there in your dress and try to reach them? They are above my head," Sam said incredulously. He was six feet tall.

I put my hand on the tree, looked at him and said, "It was just a little bit bigger than a twig thirty-six years ago. The leaves were not too far from the ground."

"Oh," Sam said quietly.

"Honey, look how it has grown. Just like you. You have grown to become strong and wise." David put his arm around my shoulder and I smiled. I instantly lost the desire to see through the eyes of the seven-year-old girl.

It was late in the afternoon. We took a taxi to the cemetery. After we paid the driver, I got out of the car and looked around. I remembered green hills and trees with fragrant flowers surrounding the gravesites, but now the dead as well as the living were packed tightly together in this dense city. The hillsides of the cemetery were covered with graves, waves of white dots going on forever. The more recent headstones were all identical. That gave me a clue to where my family's gravesites were. I recognized a wide path leading to an older section. I followed it to my grandfather's grave. I spotted his headstone almost immediately.

"There he is! Grandfather is right there!" I walked a little faster, excited to show Sam his great-grandfather's grave.

"Mom, isn't this my grandfather?" Sam called out from a few rows behind. I turned and saw him bending down to examine the gravestone.

"Yes, that is your grandfather. Say hello." I walked closer and looked at my father's picture. It was customary to have a photograph of the deceased processed on porcelain and set in each stone. I stood very still and looked at both Father and Grandfather's graves. Much had changed since I left Hong Kong but being here with them made it seem like I had buried them just yesterday.

"I have to look for Great-grandmother. I am not sure where she is. I left before she was buried." She should be close by, I said to myself, searching among the gravesites, completely forgetting Sam and David. Before long, I came across a grave that was marked only with the husband's last name, "Leung," and her family's name, "Wong." There was no other given name. I looked up at the photograph and Great-grandmother greeted me with a smile. I suddenly saw my resemblance to her, the round nose, high cheekbones and wide jaw. She looked so happy and peaceful.

"Great-grandmother, I am finally here to see you," I said softly. "I am sorry I took so long." I reached up and touched her face.

"Mom, look at this snail shell at the foot of the grave. I haven't seen one like this anywhere in this cemetery," Sam whispered, touching my arm.

I turned to look at the shell. I was stunned.

With a hushed voice, I said, "This is from a mountain snail. It is the same kind of snail that I used to cook for Great-grandmother when she broke her shoulder." It was a sure sign that she acknowledged our presence and was happy to see us. I had come home to her with my son and my love — an accomplishment for all of the women in my family. It was a long journey home.